The Truth Behind Going Postal

Surviving the Torture in the United States Postal Service

GARLAND D. LEWIS SR.

© 2017 Garland D. Lewis Sr.
All rights reserved.

ISBN: 1546816569
ISBN 13: 9781546816560

FOREWORD

By Scott D. Morrow
President of the Denver Metro Retiree Chapter, chartered by the American Postal Workers Union

I had already survived over two years in the United States Postal Service Bull Shit (USPSBS) in Denver, Colorado during the hiring frenzy in the aftermath of the Great Postal Strike of 1970.

I missed the eight-day strike spawned in New York City by Morris "Moe" Biller, the President of the local postal union. Considered illegal, it was the first strike in the history of the nation's postal service and it virtually shut down the post office during President Richard Nixon's first term. Nixon called out the National Guard but they were unable to sort and deliver the mail. By the time Biller, the postal workers' hero, was sworn in as the third President of the American Postal Workers Union (APWU) his polar opposite, Ronald Reagan, was taking office as President of the United States of America.

Shortly after President Reagan took office, he fired the striking Professional Air Traffic Controllers Organization (PATCO), one of the few unions that supported him based on his empty promises to give them a raise. Our contract negotiations between the APWU and the United States Postal Service (USPS) were going to be tough. It was in this atmosphere, the first week of May in 1980, that a special group of rookies came wandering out after their on-boarding orientation to join us.

Every two weeks, a new batch of employees came out onto the workroom floor of the Denver Terminal Annex mail facility where the heat exceeded 90 degrees and the noise levels cracked industry standards regularly due to the sea of Multi-Purpose Letter Sorting Machines (MPLSM). Back then, the maximum permitted decibel range designated by the Occupational Safety and Health Administration (OSHA) was 98 degrees for an eight-hour exposure. Today, for the same eight hours the maximum standard is 90 degrees.

The group was special because there were two men among the group who would become lifelong friends of mine. One, a friendly Jewish man small in stature. The other was a quiet, humble appearing African American man of noticeable stature (the author of this book). These men were about to suffer dire management abuse as they negotiated the 90-day probation period. During this time, they could be described as dead meat with no access to the protection of the APWU negotiated Collective Bargaining Agreement (CBA).

Additionally, new employees had to pass a "scheme" for distributing mail in a pre-determined time limit and if not, they were dismissed. My scheme was labeled "City A&B." To pass, I had to memorize the boundaries of every zip code for Denver and sort 100 cards to the correct zip code in a minute at a 95 percent accuracy rate. Once the scheme was passed, new employees moved on to trying to pass the requirements of keying on an MPLSM, again in a pre-determined time limit. Keying in the zip code on a 20-key piano style keyboard at 60 letters a minute, with no more than a 5 percent error rate, was the negotiated qualification standard. If they passed this and if their boss liked them, they would pass probation and become a part-time flexible (PTF) employee.

PTFs were subject to working any hours at any time, night or day. They were the first to be selected for overtime up to 12 hours daily, seven days a week. PTFs were the first to be selected to work every holiday. They did have access to CBA rights though and through that process I got the chance to meet Garland Lewis. I had the opportunity to become a union steward during my shift, the vanguard for protecting worker rights in the industrial relations setting. Garland made it several months before the decades long harassment would start and he would need my services.

Garland was a man who was scary to the brainwashed. He was over six feet, very muscular, and African American. Systemic racism had permeated the United States Postal Service (USPS) even though the mission was to be a model employer regarding civil rights and equal treatment of all. Garland's work environment was constantly scripted by his physical appearance which required my constant services as the union representative and the Equal Employment Opportunity Commission (EEOC) representative.

I say that with great sarcasm as I got a front row seat to the systemic discrimination against a cool brother, loving husband and great dad. Garland was also a great worker for the postal customer. That is what should matter. This book may appear as fiction to anyone never employed by the USPSBS even though totally factual. I personally witnessed many of the experiences and participated first hand in numerous investigations detailed in this book in real time!

Experiences were different for employees depending on the postal facility they worked in and who the supervisor was at the time. We could choose different jobs at different facilities based on our seniority. As employees gained full time status and acquired seniority, they could bid for better positions under the CBA. Eventually, Garland moved on to a station known to the public as the "Local Post Office" where individuals could mail items, pick up packages and get a P.O. Box.

I moved on to become the full-time President of the local labor organization known as the Denver Metro Area Local of the APWU. All labor organizations are required to establish a constitution and bylaws under the Labor Management Reporting and Disclosure Act (LMRDA). A requirement of my presidential duties was to establish the constitution and represent members before arbiters in arbitrations.

My final services to Garland were in that vein. He had been terminated from his employment at the Denver Downtown Station without just cause. Most CBAs require just cause for any discipline but especially for what we call the "death penalty" in industrial relations which is termination. My job was to prove to the arbitrator, with evidence, that the USPS failed to have just cause to fire Garland. The USPS carries the burden of proof in discipline cases meaning they need to prove convincingly that the employee should have been terminated. Like a hearing in a court setting, without the rules of civil procedure or as in discipline cases the rules of a criminal procedure, we put witnesses under oath, examined and cross examined any personal knowledge they had that appeared to be relevant and reviewed any additional relevant material regarding the matter.

Without going into the gory details of an actual conspiracy at a post office to unlawfully discriminate against a man because of his race and the color of his skin, it turns out the arbiter agreed with our presentation and brought Garland back with full back pay. What is my point with all this litigation history?

The author has lived through industrial hell and survived. I highly recommend the book for anyone who wants to get a job at the USPS or for those who have relatives working there and wonder why that person seems on the verge of insanity when they get home from work. Others may want to find out why there is a common term called, "going postal." For the rest of you, I think the book will provide you awareness of dire conditions that still exist today in a government corporation that still stands as the most efficient postal service on the planet.

I am not sure how that is but I do know there are literally millions of postal workers, like the author, who show up every day to serve you to the best of their abilities despite the rampant hostile working environments. Then they either die or retire. Many employees die before they ever retire.

I was forced into retirement for my advocacy at age 50 after 26 years. Most postal workers retire at age 55 if they were part of the now extinct Civil Service Retirement System. A very small percentage of retirees do so past 30 years of service. In addition, less than one percent make it over the 40-year mark, not including any military service to the country.

ACKNOWLEDGEMENT

I dedicate this book to the memory of those who lost their lives while employed by the United States Postal Service, including my brother, who committed suicide; not forgetting those who took the lives of others.

Special thanks to my wife and daughter for their never-ending support, and to the two brave co-workers who fought through this experience with me.

TABLE OF CONTENTS

Introduction   xiii

PART ONE   1974-1979   1
Chapter 1   Military Bound   3

PART TWO   1980-1990   7
Chapter 2   Highest in the Class   9
Chapter 3   Short-Lived Manager   11
Chapter 4   My Friend, Like a Brother   13
Chapter 5   Working with a Disability   15
Chapter 6   Character Assassination   18
Chapter 7   The Invincible Alcoholic   22
Chapter 8   The Administrative Scheme   24
Chapter 9   Under a Microscope   27
Chapter 10   Slippery Slope   30
Chapter 11   Bigger Than Me   32

PART THREE   1991-1994   35
Chapter 12   Rehab   37
Chapter 13   The Overtime Blues   39
Chapter 14   Hands Up   43
Chapter 15   Return to Work   45
Chapter 16   A Letter to the Postmaster   51
Chapter 17   911   52
Chapter 18   Big Black Guys   58
Chapter 19   A Badge of Dishonor   63

PART FOUR   1995   67
Chapter 20   Extensions of Management   69
Chapter 21   Drowning in the Alphabet Soup of Equal Rights Agencies   71

Chapter 22	Trial	73
Chapter 23	Investigations	77
Chapter 24	Handcuffed and Paraded	81
Chapter 25	Unemployed, But Productive	87
Chapter 26	The Appeal	89
Chapter 27	3rd Letter to the Postmaster	90
Chapter 28	Dismissed, Acquitted or Pending	91
Chapter 29	Summary Judgment	93
PART FIVE	**1996**	**97**
Chapter 30	Outcast	99
Chapter 31	Technicalities	103
Chapter 32	Depositions	105
Chapter 33	Restraining Order	108
PART SIX	**1997-1999**	**113**
Chapter 34	Reinstated, Eventually	115
Chapter 35	A Good Day to Die	120
Chapter 36	Persistence	123
Chapter 37	Integrity at its Best	124
Chapter 38	Walking On Eggshells	127
Chapter 39	Documentation	132
PART SEVEN	**2000-2004**	**135**
Chapter 40	Ruthless	137
Chapter 41	Martyrs and Innocent Bystanders	140
Chapter 42	100 Percent Right	141
Chapter 43	A Book on Grievances	143
Chapter 44	People's Lives	152
Chapter 45	No Satisfaction	156
Chapter 46	Temper Temper	160

Chapter 47   Breach of Bona Fide Contract   164
Chapter 48   A 100K Defense   169

PART EIGHT   2005-2008   **171**
Chapter 49   Jokes Between Friends   173
Chapter 50   Episodes of Pressure   177
Chapter 51   Job Taken Away   178
Chapter 52   The Quiet Before the Storm   179
Chapter 53   Number One   183

PART NINE   2009   **185**
Chapter 54   Saving Jobs   187
Chapter 55   Tour of Duty   196
Chapter 56   Window Qualified   200
Chapter 57   The Blue Line   208
Chapter 58   The Petition?   213
Chapter 59   My Health   221

PART TEN   2010   **225**
Chapter 60   Forced to Tell the Truth   227
Chapter 61   Hired Help   234
Chapter 62   The Tarnishing of Union Standards   237

PART ELEVEN   2011   **245**
Chapter 63   13 Below Zero   247
Chapter 64   The Sticky Glue   257
Chapter 65   A Walk in the Park   258
Chapter 66   Trademark Excuses   264
Chapter 67   My Brother   268
Chapter 68   Writing   274
Chapter 69   The Meeting   278

Chapter 70	On Vacation	284
Chapter 71	Motive	286
Chapter 72	The "F" Word	289

PART TWELVE 2012 — 293
Chapter 73	98 Percent	295

POSTSCRIPT — 299
Q&A with the Author	301
Tips to Protect Yourself on the Job	308
In Memoriam	309

INTRODUCTION

The most notable postal mass shooting shocked the country on Aug. 20, 1986 when postman Patrick Henry Sherrill shot 20 employees at a U.S. Post Office in Edmond, Oklahoma, killing 14 of them before committing suicide with a shot to the forehead. The American phrase "going postal" was born.

Six years prior to this mass murder, I began what would become a 33-year-career with the U.S. Postal Service. Three years into my employment with the agency I began to learn firsthand what actions can lead to going postal.

The purpose of this book is to recognize the cries of people whose lives have been forever changed. I have witnessed the frustration and disappointment on the faces of many employees angry with pain and suffering, and the animosity that developed into feelings of depression and emotional stress because of inhumane treatment by management at the postal service. I experienced it too. Fear, intimidation, apprehension, anxiety attacks, along with pain and suffering, can make for a lethal combination, especially when you find no safe place to go.

I am convinced that current and former employees of the agency can relate to the constant pressures and undue stress in the postal environment fueled by management's undermining tactics. Their abuse of authority and their persistent lies, threats and deception have created adverse conditions and a hostile workplace. Going postal is not a myth. Those who have killed others and even themselves in a postal facility do not always have "their own issues" and "mental instability" as management and authorities would like the public to believe.

Behind the front counters of the U.S. Postal Service, employees were constantly under attack and tested by managers and supervisors. Rules and regulations that governed the agency were compromised. Those who employed this destructive behavior have become party to legal prosecution.

Though innocent bystanders have been killed, others have been wrongly described as "martyrs" in mass shootings, when in fact they merely became victim to the monster mentality they themselves created – going postal.

Mass shootings involving postal workers include, but are not limited to:

- Oct. 10, 1991, Wayne, New Jersey: Fired postal worker Joseph M. Harris kills his ex-supervisor and her boyfriend at their home, then kills two former colleagues as they arrive at the Ridgewood, New Jersey post office where they all previously worked together.
- Nov. 14, 1991, Royal Oak, Michigan: Fired postal worker Thomas McIlvane kills four, wounds five, and then kills self.
- Jan. 30, 2006, Goleta, California: Former mail processor Jennifer San Marco, 44, kills six employees. She then commits suicide at the sorting facility.

Details of these killings, along with more than 20 other postal service incidents from 1983 to 2006, were compiled in a 2009 book, "Beyond Going Postal" by Stephen Musacco, Ph.D. He worked with the USPS for more than 30 years as an Employee Assistance Program representative and as a workplace improvement analyst. Details of the killings pop up regularly in news reports whenever a workplace shooting happens.

In the midst of news reports, after such massacres, the public hears that the employee was recently fired or disciplined and had a history of problems throughout their career. The focus exploits negatives and puts great emphasis on the crime itself. Opinions are formed, judgment passed and rumors are spread.

I, at one point, had guns pointed directly at my head by a half dozen police officers when at the end of my rope trying to endure the wrath of management. I am a survivor of the torture in the U.S. Postal Service, and I'm here to tell my story. I believe that I am telling and sharing a part of their stories as well. So, to the reader, the material in this book is true. I wrote this book about incidents that took place in my 33 years of working for the postal service. The contents are supported by more than 12,000 pages, including legal documents that I have kept in my defense as I was repeatedly accused of "unbecoming behavior."

I defended myself through personnel grievances, arbitration, equal employment opportunity hearings and legal cases played out in a court of law. I was required to name names, locations and describe unlawful situations in detail. No gag orders were ever issued. In fact, Denver's two daily newspapers, The Denver Post and the now-defunct Rocky Mountain News, as well as the weekly Westword newspaper, covered some of the atrocities happening at the postal service.

My life at the postal service stood as an open book long before I started writing my own. I quickly learned that when you stand for the truth, confidentiality goes out the window. I have not written this exclusive firsthand account of experiences to point the finger at any one individual, but to shine the spotlight on the system, which allowed each individual to make decisions without accountability.

I am a disabled Vietnam War veteran. I served my country from 1974 to 1979 in the United States Navy and received two honorable discharges. I am very proud to have been a member of the armed forces. As a combat veteran, I can tell you that war is hell. Never in my wildest imagination could I have conjured up the kind of war I would face upon my return home just to make a decent life for my family and to maintain the dignity any U.S. citizen deserves.

PART ONE:

1974-1979

1

MILITARY BOUND

I was raised in Denver, Colorado in a single-parent home as the youngest of five siblings. My father walked out of our lives when I was the age of seven. I had no contact with him until 16 years later when my brother and I searched for him and found him. I was 23 years old when I reconnected with my father. I never understood why my father walked out of my life. I guess at that time it really did not matter. I was a kid just wanting to play.

As I got older I wanted a dad I could look up to as a leader and a role model to guide me through tough decisions and those crucial developmental years. But I had all of my brothers and I relied on them. Like many young men coming out of high school with hopes and dreams of becoming a professional at something, mainly athletics, my thoughts and dreams never seemed to be those of such reality.

My mother remarried when I was about the age of 14. I got along well with my step dad. But, I did not see him often because he worked quite a bit, and as a result influenced my strong work ethic. I spent a lot of time around older people including my siblings and their friends. Often, I would hear my older brother talk about his best friend who had joined the U.S. Army, and as much as he talked about it I began to wonder if maybe he would join himself. My family talked about the military a lot and how the armed forces would make a man out of you.

In fact, I had brothers who were already enlisted. One brother had served four years in the U.S. Navy aboard the USS Oriskany in 1969 in Vietnam. Two other brothers were serving in 1974, the year I graduated. Being mindful of the trouble that could find me out in the streets the decision to go into the military after high school was an easy one to make.

I joined the Navy in June of 1974. My boot camp training was in Great Lakes, Illinois. My first tour of duty was aboard an aircraft carrier the USS Midway (CVA 41) stationed in Yokosuka, Japan. In November 1974, the Midway received orders to proceed immediately to Vietnam. Our mission was to assist in the evacuation of Americans and diplomats from Saigon. We spent many days and nights at general quarters, manning our battle stations. After seeing so much death I wondered if I would make it home. Finally, in June 1976 I was released from active duty with an honorable discharge.

My fascination for aircraft inspired me to negotiate with the Navy for the schools I would be able to attend for reenlistment. August 1977, I was fortunate enough to attend "A" school, known for technology. As a 3rd class petty officer and aviation technician I was stationed at Naval Air Station Miramar in San Diego, California and attached to Attack Squadron VF 124. My responsibilities were maintaining the readiness of F-14 Tomcats Fighter Jets and Pratt & Whitney PF-30 jet engines. They were some of the Navy's most sophisticated machinery at a cost of $100 million per aircraft.

As a technician, I was required to attend special technical schools to receive certifications as a high and low-power operator on F-14 jet fighters. It was essential to understand the functions of all instruments gauges and their importance in the pilot seat just as well as the navigators of this aircraft. Just as important were the emergency procedures in the starting and shutting down of this sensitive but powerful machinery.

In August 1979, I completed my term of service with the U.S. Navy, accomplishing my second honorable discharge. After my release from active duty I returned home and worked a few odd jobs but was more interested in a career, something with stability that had a future. Because I specialized in aircrafts while serving in the military, this seemed to be the most logical thing to do. I applied with many of the major airline carriers at Stapleton International Airport in Denver Colorado. At that time, the airlines were in deep financial trouble and were in the process of laying off people with 20 years of seniority. A future in the aviation field did not look promising so I continued to search for employment.

PART TWO:

1980-1990

2

HIGHEST IN THE CLASS

Still unemployed, times were getting hard and boredom began to creep in.

One warm spring day with the sun shining bright, I was sitting on the front porch at my mom's house as free as a bird with nothing to do when I saw the mailman making his deliveries. Once he got closer to me I asked him if the post office was hiring. I informed him that I was recently released from active duty and was in desperate need of employment. He didn't know if they were hiring at the time but he said that the postal service allowed veterans recently released from active duty to apply within a certain time of their release and test for employment. He then directed me to where I could go to apply. I applied that same day.

One week later I received a letter from the agency informing me of the time, date and location of the testing. On the day of the test I was very nervous knowing that this was a great opportunity for me to earn my independence in a job which I believed held a future for me. My test score was the highest in the class, giving me the number one spot on the seniority list for that group.

I was hired on May 3, 1980 with the U.S. Postal Service and assigned to the Terminal Annex building located in lower downtown Denver at 16th and Wynkoop. I was scheduled to work the first shift of the day which was graveyard and known as Tour One. My operation was in 030. I sat on a stool like a barstool for eight hours of the night, most times 10 hours with mandatory overtime. My duties included casing letters to the prospective slot by their zip code. The holding cases were four by four feet. They were box-shaped structures lined in rows of 20, sometimes 30 depending on the size of the operation. The aisles were narrow so everyone worked near one another. There were four, maybe five supervisors in charge of a single operation. Throughout the evening they walked up and down the aisles barking out commands such as, "face your case," "turn on the overhead light above you," "both feet on the floor," "throw more mail" and "do less talking."

You even needed permission from a supervisor to be excused from your case to take a restroom break, and you would be timed on how long you were away from your seat. It was a large facility with a boot camp atmosphere which had me questioning my decision to work for the U.S. Postal Service.

In late 1980 I was given a detail assignment and was transferred to the AMF (Air Mail Facility) at Stapleton International Airport in Denver Colorado. I worked foreign mail and parcel post packaging. I began setting goals for myself by exploring my options and looking into different jobs for advancement opportunities. I met a gentleman at this facility and we became good friends. We talked a lot about going into management, cliché as it may be, we both had much of the same ideals that we could make a difference in the way management treated employees. Together we went to the station manager and inquired about the supervisor position. Some time had passed before we were both given the opportunity to act in a supervisor's capacity on the workroom floor. It was short-lived for me. I did not care to be a part of management's expectations and their criteria for being a well-balanced and productive supervisor.

3

SHORT-LIVED MANAGER

Their autocratic and abusive management style was offensive and threatening to employees. Many times, it reached levels of criminal behavior, with management personnel stalking individuals and denying many of their civil rights, including speaking without hindrance of reprisal. Intimidation was a method used to control the employees and pressure was the key component in delivering this method to keep fear at the highest level. For example, an employee that followed protocol aligning with the American Postal Workers Union (APWU) grievance process for any dispute regarding a manager or supervisor, in many cases, would bring on a negative reaction by management.

Reprisal came in many forms including loss of overtime and accusations that employees were not doing their job. At the opposite end of the spectrum, management would reward others by providing more time for their breaks, use of sick leave hours without being written up for excessive sick leave usage, and long periods to sit and converse with their favorite supervisor or manager, neglecting duties that others would have to complete.

Once fear was established, control was easily achieved. It gave way to unconditional power, and brought life to the adage, "absolute power corrupts absolutely." People were afraid of management in this agency and I wanted no part of being looked at or perceived in that manner nor did I ever want to invoke these types of feelings, so I made the decision to leave management and go back to craft. My personality did not fit the criteria. I was not submissive to perform their will because I did not approve of their tactics. Soon after I made this decision to go back to craft, I was released from my detail assignment at the AMF and transferred back to the Terminal Annex. I had no regrets after leaving management. I felt relief and welcomed a restoration of my pride and a sense of calmness.

4

MY FRIEND, LIKE A BROTHER

Though my friend continued to supervise at the AMF our friendship remained strong. We would see each other now and then but we would mainly talk over the telephone. Ninety five percent of the time our conversations were about the post office and how he disliked his job. He would tell me how he would need to discipline employees for trivial matters and at times for no reasons at all, but many times because a manager or supervisor had a beef with a person.

I knew this person well. He was not only a friend but a brother to me. He was going through a tremendous amount of pressure in his position. His marriage began to suffer and eventually ended in divorce, which was one of the last things he told me about along with losing his job at the postal service. A week after our last conversation he died at the age of 46 in a manner that I still can't address to this day. He was never the same person while in management or any time after. Those many conversations that we had over several years, I realized later, were cries for help.

The postal service employed more than half a million people nationwide when I first started there. Facilities that I have seen are quite large with a variety of jobs and an equal amount of people who man these positions. Controversy seemed to always dominate conversations about management. Friends, who served as managers or supervisors, often described in detail the unrealistic expectations and demands that were made of them. Their positions would be threatened if they did not carry out ordered retaliatory acts.

I'm not the only one to have walked away from management positions with anguish and disappointment. But not everyone walked away. Some, who I thought I knew, stayed in management, experienced the power of authority, and it in fact changed their personality. Managers and supervisors in this agency will never agree or admit to that. They were forced and trained to defend their position and purpose. They were groomed into this destructive behavior.

5

WORKING WITH A DISABILITY

Mandatory overtime was consistent with day-to-day operations after I returned to the Terminal Annex to work on the (LSM) letter sorter machines. The long hours began to aggravate an injury that I suffered to my left knee while serving in the armed forces. Federal policies and procedures under the Americans with Disabilities Act prohibited discrimination against anyone who fell under disabilities defined in this act. It came to a point where I had no choice but to submit a 3971 – the postal service's leave request form – for an eight and 40, also known as an eight-hour work day, 40 hours per week. Medical documentation was required before approval.

The injury I suffered while in the military was exacerbated due to the long hours, two sometimes four hours extra work in a day—mandatory. From 1983 to 1985, I submitted more than a dozen different requests with medical documentation provided. All requests were denied except for one that was granted for one week. I was forced to continue working long hours if I wished to keep my job at the postal service. I suffered excruciating pain daily, and my body was pushed to its limit. One night the pain became so severe that I could not complete my workday. I requested to go home and use sick leave, which was granted.

However, medical documentation was required upon my return to work. I provided the necessary documentation, yet I was given a letter of warning for "failure to follow instructions." I did not sign this letter as requested by my supervisor as this would be an admission of agreement. Management had no justification for taking this action. I filed a grievance with the APWU. Filing this grievance was unpopular and was taken as questioning the supervisor's authority – a personal challenge. This was not the case at all. I could feel the tension that had developed between the supervisor and me, especially after I won the grievance. The letter was removed from my file, but soon after he began having discussions with me about my productivity. I perceived this as retaliation because it simply was not true. His reaction to fraudulently make up a vicious lie made me nervous and concerned of what was to come.

Working under these uncomfortable conditions and having this type of relationship with my supervisor was the last thing I wanted. I believed I had an obligation to at least explain my circumstances to the supervisor in hopes that it would be taken more as an apology for going home sick that night. I began scheduling numerous visits for therapy sessions that consisted of strengthening exercises for my condition while also taking prescription pain medication. I wanted to be prompt in attendance and make every effort to alleviate all tension that had built up between the two of us. The situation had the potential to escalate and get out of hand. In time, the therapy did bring comfort and eventually I no longer had to rely on an eight and 40.

Years passed before I requested another one. In spite of my effort it was not good enough. It appeared it had become personal with this supervisor by his ongoing actions. I continued to be criticized for not doing my job, not working enough mail, not dispatching enough mail in a timely manner or missing cut off points in the dispatch of mail. By his standards I never seemed to meet his expectations which created resentment in me, and I knew it was time to look for another position at the agency.

To change jobs, employees were required to bid on available positions listed on the (DPM) personnel management forms. The positions would be rewarded by seniority so I bid from the LSM machines into the registry unit. A change was very much needed. I realized I was on a collision course with management, something I desperately wanted to avoid at all costs.

The registry unit was a new beginning for me and I approached it as such, keeping the past in perspective and being very careful not to bring any attention to myself. I was extremely careful in ways that I would interact with the supervisors in the unit while not forgetting my reasons for leaving the LSMs. I had heard gossip about how the supervisors in this agency passed on negative remarks to the next, especially of those employees who they did not particularly care for or get along with for one reason or another.

My objective was to do my job which could only give a good impression, leaving the rhetoric and storytelling to the people who had nothing better to do. So, I figured that maybe if I had to be judged they would judge the person in front of them and not what they may have heard about me. I was optimistic in what I considered a new beginning and I tried to do what was needed to stay under the radar.

6

CHARACTER ASSASSINATION

One day I submitted a request for a day off. The request was timely and what I believed to be a reasonable request. It was denied by my supervisor, Richard T. Sandoval. When I asked for a reason, he said, "No," and that it was just a decision that he made. Many of my co-workers were at the time allowed to take time off and I believed that he was being unreasonable and unfair. Out of frustration, I called in sick for the day that I wanted off. Upon my return to work the next day I was given an AWOL (Absent Without Leave).

I had not violated any rules by calling in sick, yet disciplinary action was taken against me that was improper and not justifiable. Once again, I was forced to make an unpopular decision which was to file a grievance that resulted in another unfortunate situation with management. It had progressed to the point where I had to keep the APWU on speed dial due to the disciplinary action that I continued to face. Sandoval was outraged because of the grievance. It was a typical reaction that seemed to be a pattern of management.

He learned that I prevailed in this case through the grievance process and it brought on retaliation that created a chain reaction of events. I was treated differently from other employees. I was written up for frivolous infractions. Lies and rumors had begun to spread about me saying that

I was harassing and intimidating co-workers, not doing my job, creating a hostile work environment and planning to cause injury to U.S Postal Service employees. It was an assault and an all-out attack on my character.

Between March and July 1988, I was forced to file seven different grievances against management after being written up and disciplined for alleged infractions. In each of the grievances I prevailed. The true perpetrators were management themselves and those co-workers who aided them, better known to managers and supervisors as "team players." Exercising my rights and standing up for myself caused me an enormous amount of pain and grief. It became obvious to me that I was being set up and was now a target in this agency. Management now had my undivided attention.

The tension was so high that I did not want to go to work. People in the unit were very much aware of what was going on but were afraid of getting involved and speaking the truth about management's aggression towards me. They feared retaliation and being treated the same. Then there were those who took advantage of management's dislike for me. They were the ones always in the office talking with a supervisor and keeping their distance from me, showing their loyalty to management. The unit was being divided and had developed into a cliquish atmosphere.

Sandoval was out of control. His obnoxious behavior intimidated most people and his predatory nature kept the registry unit in disarray. His acts of aggression and abuse of authority were unlawful and sinful, to say the least. His desk was positioned in a location where he had a view of all employees in the unit. He would glare from his desk for long periods of time at whatever employee he selected as his target for the day. Not long after, he would walk directly behind that individual and stand a foot or two away over their shoulders for very long periods of time. I eventually became his favorite target.

Very seldom was there a time when Sandoval was around that there was not chaos. Many in the unit were afraid and some even terrified of him. His intimidation of others had reached a point where employees somehow found the courage to band together and report his behavior in written statements to his superiors. Seventeen individual statements were given to the APWU and upper management expressing their concerns about him. My name was mentioned in several of the statements that talked about how I continued to be harassed by him. Though his behavior was reported to the union and upper management by a variety of people who showed a genuine concern, nothing changed.

I knew that this harassment of me, especially stalking me, was to create an adverse reaction and it was working. It began taking a toll on me, knowing that upper management showed no concern and did absolutely nothing to rectify the situation. I was a recipient of this abusive managerial style and was a witness to the agency's involvement. They not only condoned the aggressive behavior of this supervisor but encouraged it as well. They did absolutely nothing to deter his aggression after it was reported by many. I was not the only one in the unit who expressed their true concerns about this supervisor, yet he could remain in a position of authority.

Pressure continued to mount throughout the unit. Everyone could see that there was absolutely nothing being done about this supervisor's erratic behavior. He remained in the unit even after many, who were afraid, stuck their necks out to expose him by writing letters to the APWU and upper management. I became very discouraged and unhappy, but most of all angry. I had come to the realization that there was no one and no entity within the agency that I could turn to or even trust to challenge the wrongs of management and to put them on notice. It was obvious that the APWU was limited when it came to disciplining management for violating the zero tolerance policy in the U.S. Postal Service.

While few in the unit expressed their concerns, most workers would not acknowledge the erratic behavior of this individual. Management catered to those individuals who remained silent. I took offense to those who covered up the truth and had absolutely no desire to communicate or have any sort of involvement with them. I was afraid of not knowing what their motives or intentions were, and mainly how far they might go to maintain the status of a team player. Most of all, I believed that they were a danger and a threat to my existence in the agency because I wasn't like them. I wasn't afraid of management. I trusted no one.

Intimidation had gotten to those employees who at one time stood up for what was right. I personally believed that management could go only as far as you allowed them and I saw it to be more of a cowardly act, seeing how one could be frightened into submission. But it was also greed because submission was rewarded. They felt it was a dignified way to work. I rejected each one of those in the unit who carried themselves in this manner and would converse as little as possible unless it was absolutely necessary and only when it pertained to the job.

I found out quickly how I felt about those employees; and my decision to stay away from them only enhanced the gossip, the chatter, the lies and rumors that were being spread about me. The buzz was that I was a trouble maker, threatening to others, insubordinate, intimidating, a bully, anything negative that management or those co-workers could label me. I had no idea of how to handle this sort of pressure. It affected me to the point where I began making a lot of bad moves and some terrible decisions.

7

THE INVINCIBLE ALCOHOLIC

One of the worst decisions that I made was to self-medicate through the excessive use of alcohol. At the time, it felt good. I did not realize that I was under the illusion that all my problems did not exist, and the daily stress and tension was a figment of my imagination. The amount I was consuming daily was destructive but at the time I believed that it enhanced my awareness and built a defense that made me believe I was invincible. I would challenge anyone that I felt was infringing on my space or disrespecting me for any reason whatsoever. For my actions, there were reactions.

Management and the people that I had considered my enemies took advantage of what they labeled as aggressive behavior and used it against me. I continued to react to anything that was said about me from any comment to lies or what I believe to be provocative gestures. It gave management the opening they desired to increase their intensity by using the disciplinary process against me.

October 1988 through May 1989, seven different letters of discipline were entered into my files, ranging from "unbecoming conduct" to "insubordination." These actions taken against me by management had no validity but were made worse because of me losing control of my temper. I had displayed irrational behavior by making provocative comments and at times used profanity in defense of myself against my attackers. I had fallen victim to their game.

Management took full advantage and used me as an example. I was in a strenuous situation in an antagonistic environment where I was constantly under a microscope and my every move was scrutinized. My anger was exacerbated due to the maltreatment where I continued to be singled out. My employment with the U.S. Postal Service was being threatened by the continuous disciplinary actions taken against me for minor infractions as tedious as being a half minute late to work. Sometimes I simply did not move fast enough for the manager or a supervisor's expectation, and they would declare it "insubordination" or "failure to follow instructions."

Management's arrogance and bullying tactics were the tip of the iceberg. They kept me angry, aggressive and at times arrogant and obnoxious. Being in this state of mind resulted in consequences that did not concern me. I didn't give a damn about much. The anger and aggression was hard to fight back. It had taken control of all rationality which presented a very serious problem. I reacted to the rumors of me being threatening and intimidating in a destructive manner. I verbally confronted those who I felt were talking about me behind my back. I was constantly being disciplined by management and that alone supported and brought life to a negative image of me that was being portrayed by people in my unit.

To a degree I had become the image management had painted for my co-workers and other management. My attitude was being molded into just that, but it was necessary to defend myself in the workplace against management and those team players. The team players or puppets were rewarded with overtime opportunities, job selection, time off and reputable detail assignments, to name a few.

8

THE ADMINISTRATIVE SCHEME

Before reading further, it's important to understand the "administrative scheme."

I believe it exists to systematically weed out people of their choosing. It incriminates and eliminates employees procedurally through the disciplinary process by utilizing the zero-tolerance policy. Management could use their discretion to direct strict policy with severe consequences including removal of anyone accused of or in violation of this policy. Threats, intimidation, harassment and sexual harassment are a few things that are considered unbecoming behavior of a U.S. postal employee.

To avoid becoming a target of managers and supervisors in the U.S. Postal Service from day one, employees must meet certain criteria that goes far beyond work ethics and job performance. First and foremost, they must be subservient to the subordinates, gaining the label of team player. They will hold this status for as long as they kiss their supervisors' asses. I have seen what fear can do and what it has done to far too many people in this agency, stripping them of their dignity. At one time, I also feared management's aggression because of the many ways that they could alter my lifestyle.

Emergency placement from the building was protocol for those in violation of the policy. This meant that the person accused of violating the policy could be removed from the facility until an investigation was conducted, which could take months to be completed. Management used its own discretion when determining which employees would be governed under this policy.

Favoritism played a major role when determining who was exempt and who was not. Disparity of treatment created division and animosity among the workers, resulting in workplace violence. Dissension occurred among those who were subjected and unfairly held accountable to these rules. These rules were in place for everyone. Its purpose was to govern the entire agency. This maltreatment of certain employees bred hostility and anger among the workers which compromised morale and the safety of the unit. That made for a volatile work environment.

Fear was only a part of why people were submissive and subservient. One's dignity and self-esteem played a very significant role. Managers and supervisors sought out and took advantage of people who were also suffering from low self-esteem. They abused their authority when they let their tempers flare and violated an employee's space by getting very close to their face.

This was where they depended on team players and those that feared them to protect their best interests by ignoring the situation or to say they did not see or hear anything. Most would flat out lie and say that it never happened or report that employee as the aggressor. This was the sort of loyalty that was expected of team players. These were very dangerous individuals whose commitment superseded rationality and who conformed to those dictators in this agency.

Assertiveness was taken as a threat to management. Standing up for your rights labeled you as a troublemaker, singled you out and eventually made you a target and a victim to harassment. It violated one's civil rights as an American citizen. Zero tolerance in the postal service did not mean absolute zero. The policy was nothing more than a formality to post on bulletin boards throughout mail facilities. Pure propaganda.

Being recognized as a team player promoted favoritism and favoritism was one of the deadliest games played in the postal service. Accolades were specifically for team players and non-recognition was punishment for those who were not. Management's refusal to fair treatment for all its employees had caused dissension among workers that continued to create hostile work conditions, fueling division and breeding violence. Management thrived on it. They accomplished complete dominance and total control when workers were at each other's throats.

Without unity, much was lost and little was accomplished. For management, it presented many opportunities to weed out those of their choosing. Discipline was carried out on those that were not team players. Extra attention was given to those employees. Management could refer an employee to Employees Assistance Program (EAP), an entity within the agency to help resolve employee's issues – personal or private. The EAP process, though structured differently, functioned like the Equal Employment Opportunity (EEO) agency where management oversaw both departments and where the counselors were postal supervisors.

An employee could seek the help of this agency by request but could also be referred to the program by a manager or a supervisor for corrective action. The EAP was designed to assist employees through difficult times but could also function as protection of employees against discrimination.

Every facility that I have been in or have had some sort of affiliation with had a group of workers that had personal connections with management. They were those that were always talking with a manager or supervisor for excessive amounts of time in their offices. In addition to being labeled as team players they were also known as pets, informants and snitches. A lot of fellow employees looked up to them for this role. Subsequently, cliques were formed in the postal service where obedience beyond the job was rewarded.

9

UNDER A MICROSCOPE

On May 5, 1989, I was written up with a recommendation for my removal from the U.S. Postal Service. The charges were, "Failure to Follow a Direct Order," "Away Work Assignment," and "Belligerent Apparent Intoxication."

I had been drinking for a good part of the day before I had reported on duty. It was my way of preparing to deal with the stressful environment that I faced each day in the unit. At that time, I believed that alcohol was my best friend. It provided an illusion by removing any and all obstacles before me. I feared nothing and no one.

From the time I arrived to work, I was under a microscope consistently being watched by Sandoval, who was a thorn in the side of most people in the unit. His arrogance was annoying and uncomfortable to the point that made me feel threatened by his actions. It pushed me to a breaking point where I felt compelled to confront the situation by letting Sandoval know that I did not appreciate him standing over me and that it was annoying, which led to a verbal altercation between the two of us. Each day I was micromanaged in that unit. I was challenged, ridiculed and provoked. On many of those days I struggled to resist the temptation to become violent.

An enormous number of disciplinary actions had piled up against me. For that reason, I transferred out of the registry unit. Because of this altercation, he responded by proposing to the postal service that I be removed from the agency.

I was disappointed in myself for giving management the control they so desperately wanted. I came to work while intoxicated. That alone played into management's hands and opened me up to further scrutiny. This supervisor had a history of complaints over several years for harassment and had taken unwarranted disciplinary action against employees. After grieving this proposed removal, I was punished for the part that I played in the altercation and was given a "NO-TOL #3," which was entered into my personnel file for a period of two years. "NO-TOL" was a disciplinary process or series of steps to correct employee behavior. "NO-TOL #3" represented the last step before removal.

I felt the severity of the punishment was unjust because of upper management's awareness of Sandoval's history and this unit's dysfunction. This was the so-called zero-tolerance policy that all postal employees were supposed to be governed under including managers. If there was any sort of investigation to those allegations of this supervisor history, their findings were ignored. The postal service never addressed the issues or showed any concern about the obnoxious behavior displayed daily by this individual. That would come back to bite them.

I had to go through many disciplinary hearings with him just to listen to the lies that poured out of his mouth about me. That angered me to the point where it brought on rebellion. The dishonesty of certain co-workers, those team players and those who were afraid had me at odds with many of them who would not tell the truth about this supervisor. I was disgusted each day that I walked into my unit to see this supervisor who had the authority to harass me while my co-workers fully supported his actions and behavior by remaining silent. I had a full understanding that if I defended myself there would be severe consequences to my actions. That infuriated me. Rage and anger controlled me and the drinking got worse.

I consumed an overwhelming amount of alcohol daily while contemplating revenge in hopes of being inebriated to the point that I could find the courage to carry out my thoughts of causing bodily harm, preferably killing him. The more I drank, the more I wanted to act out my frustrations. Getting my hands on a gun would be no problem. Flashes of me pulling the trigger poked at me constantly. The target could have been him. It could have been me. It didn't matter.

My marriage was also in trouble. The drinking and the stress at work had a lot to do with it. The thought of killing anyone that was not in self-defense was completely out of character for me. It was a very low point in my life.

10

SLIPPERY SLOPE

On Aug. 29, 1989, I was emergency placed from the building for apparent intoxication. I continued a path of self-destruction. My weakness had been discovered and their philosophy was simply, "feed me enough rope to hang myself." Disciplinary action in my personnel file was active and the paper trail was extensive. This led to a "last chance" and next would be termination. I had no concept of how to protect myself especially now that I knew there was no place in or outside of the agency that would provide any sort of protection for me. Alcohol was my only answer and now I was dependent on it.

I did not like the dark person I had become. I had little faith in people and no trust for the system. My years in the U.S Postal Service brought back memories of survival while in Vietnam. I came across people in the agency that were wounded just like me. Some had fallen and others were falling, looking for a soft place to land just to survive. Many were using alcohol and drugs just to cope with the pressure and difficulties. I found myself in their company. I wanted to be heard. I was tired of being ignored, pushed around, singled out and portrayed as a bad example in front of my co-workers.

I began associating with people who I believed could relate to my pain because they knew of the struggle and what it was like to be a target in this agency, experiencing unjust consequences. There were many stories like my own. Some were fighting and had fought to get their jobs back, others awaited possible disciplinary actions from suspension to removal from the agency. I was too familiar with this confused and chaotic environment after hearing and seeing the pain of everyday people suffering, trying to decipher the injustice in a place where one's character was constantly challenged and scrutinized.

I was on a slippery slope. I would not conform and I voiced my concerns about the torture and ridicule of me. Management responded by referring me to EAP.

Throughout the many referrals by management to the program I found the counselors were often biased. Professional help in my case was never rendered and a solution was never explored. The EAP convinced employees that they were the problem. For instance, management believed they had the right to mismanage. This could mean various infractions and a host of infringements of one's rights. Every EAP counselor that had interviewed me suggested at one time or another that I should accept what happens in the unit, right or wrong, to get alone with my superiors.

The EAP was nothing more than an agency that produced a trail of paperwork that eventually ended up being used to prosecute employees instead of assisting them. When the program was first established it was introduced as a program of confidentiality. This description was a myth. Management used the specifics from those meetings to enhance their case against me when charging me with a violation and putting me in for disciplinary action. It was a strategy to remove me from the U.S. Postal Service. Unfortunately, I was my own worst enemy by engaging in arguments with co-workers, and being intoxicated while on the job.

I got so wrapped up in my emotions that I lost perspective of my surroundings by allowing management along with co-workers to dictate who I was. I had become a product of my environment, confrontational with no remorse. The retaliation I sought controlled the erratic behavior that I displayed over the years, which led to constant disciplinary actions and now a "last chance" that void any rights to challenge or appeal. In other words, one more write-up and I would be automatically terminated. Management had me where they wanted me and I knew it was time for me to go.

11

BIGGER THAN ME

On Dec. 30, 1989, I transferred away from the Terminal Annex to the main office located in the heart of downtown Denver at 951 20th Street. I was there on a "last chance," never forgetting that I was carrying baggage. It was hard not to speculate or assume anything working under cruel circumstances and terrible conditions. I now had close to 10 years with the agency. To many, I was a seasoned veteran in the agency. For the change to work, I first had to understand that changing the location and the people who were around me wasn't the only change that was needed. I was a very troubled individual with a chip on my shoulder.

If I did not change my ways, the loss of my job was imminent. Alcohol was my menace. But, it was not like a light switch that could be turned on and off. It was extremely difficult for me to be optimistic about this new environment after going through the horrific adventures and unlawful practices of this agency. Over the years I had realized the potential danger ahead of me. While this was a different facility it was still the United States Postal Service.

My use of alcohol reached a point of intolerance. The negative affect it had on me and my obsession to get revenge on the people that had caused me an enormous amount of pain and grief wasn't going away. I was an angry person with an extremely unhealthy attitude. The impurities of the alcohol that streamed toxin throughout my body had control of me physically and mentally, and became a significant factor not only at work but in my private life. October 1990, my wife and I separated.

I was on an emotional roller coaster and I didn't care. After the separation, I had no one there for me. During this time, I developed a routine each day that consisted of a strenuous workout for hours while consuming alcohol. Dangerous, but true. I would then go to work and after work I would go straight home and self medicate with alcohol and marijuana. Together, the two drugs enhanced my appetite where I would consume an excessive amount of protein and carbohydrates that would increase my performance in the gym. But then I would reach a point of fatigue that induced a sleep-like coma allowing me to fall asleep and stay asleep until the next day.

I very much liked that because in that state I had no problems. I would repeat this cycle each day. This transformed my body into hard rock muscles with five percent body fat which was also dangerous. My weight increased from 225 to 255 pounds, every ounce of it full of anger. Before I began self-medicating, I suffered from insomnia. This was a big part of the anxiety attacks that plagued me daily as a result of a stressful work life.

I was fed up with people and not concerned with my health or fitness. I was preparing myself physically for battle with anyone that stood in my way. I could not and would not let go of the inhumane ways I had been treated in this agency. The thought of letting it go was inconceivable. I was a sleeping giant waiting for anyone to wake me and all hell was going to break loose.

At the same time, I gave no provocation to promote any situation because I kept to myself and respected the distance of others as they did with me. I believe that it helped to keep the facility quiet for the first three months that I was there. I truly did enjoy the tranquility and knew that if I would ever allow my guard to come down it would have been an awfully big mistake.

Time brought on curiosity that surfaced over the months and people began to gossip. Rumors began to spread throughout the facility. People wanted to know the last facility where I worked and the name of my supervisors. Many stories were being told.

But there were those who did show a genuine interest in getting to know me. They were more interested in me as an individual and not overly concerned of where I came from or my personal life. Still, that did not restore my confidence in people and I was very careful, selecting those I would converse with every now and then. This wall I had up was draining me. I was tired of being so tightly wound, making each day intense. I wanted to have friends, people who I could enjoy talking with and be around.

For seven years I had defended myself in the U.S Postal Service just to keep a job with the agency. I missed interactions with people. I was tired of living my life in fear and suspicion of everything and everyone, looking over my shoulder, hating everyone. I wanted very much once again to be a part of society, to live with some trust and to avoid everything always being a battle. It was an overwhelming concept that eventually broke me down.

I missed my family and I truly wanting my life back, but I knew that the possibility of this happening would take a sincere effort on my part because I desperately needed to be fixed. Alcohol was the root of my problems and I had allowed the system to take control of how I rationalized things. What was even more troublesome was that I had acquired a taste for it and I loved the illusion that it provided and how it made me feel. It was a problem that was bigger than me and that only the "most high"– God – could rectify.

PART THREE:

1991-1994

12

REHAB

In September 1991, I checked into an outpatient alcohol rehab clinic, which allowed me to work and earn a living while in treatment. I remained in the program for two years going through extensive treatment plans with professional therapists while attending evening group sessions. When I was not there I attended Alcoholics Anonymous meetings. Though the treatments were extensive and at times very personal they were also amazing.

I was blessed to have some very smart doctors and psychologists there that showed the utmost sincere and genuine concern for my future. My wife showed her support by attending group sessions and by participating in private conferences with staff members and doctors to better understand my behavior and upcoming challenges of living with a recovering alcoholic.

The next three years I dedicated my life to that road of recovery in hopes to erase a dependency that took control of me for many years. It was a difficult process but an adjustment that had to happen. The happiness I long yearned for would have been forever lost and the road that I was on would only lead to dying at a young age. I knew many people in the agency that were alcoholics who were also recovering. The postal service was cancerous with a very contagious environment that had driven people into self-destructive behavior.

Fortunately, some had the opportunity for a second chance as I did. Unfortunately, there were those who did not, like my friend, who was like a brother. I had a great deal of animosity because of his death and cursed the people in power of this agency. Without a doubt, they contributed to his death and to many other innocent lives that had been jeopardized and forsaken because of the control and dictatorship of a dysfunctional agency. The time was right now for me to take my life back.

Rehab had a distinct purpose to get me better. Going through the program made a difference each day in my life. My perspective had changed in respect to how I carried myself and the ways in which I would approach and look at situations. I dealt with issues and problems in a positive and a nondestructive sense. By no means did the thought of letting my guard down ever occur, knowing I was amongst egotistical human beings that would stop at nothing to enforce their will or to prove a point. Survival was the focus of my attention.

I continued to keep a low profile. Nothing had changed as far as that was concerned. I was familiar with the cliquish atmosphere in the agency and my past experiences with these groups of people gave me all the precautionary measures to avoid contact. The years I spent in treatment changed me. I remained observant but I had the presence of reason to keep things in perspective, but not in judgment.

I could see clearly now, no longer was my mind obstructed and distorted by any type of controlled substances. Keeping my distance was nothing more than survival. My goal was to stay alive and finish what I started with respect to my career. That would take a sincere commitment on my part by not ever forgetting those atrocities and to never put myself able to where I could fall victim to management's assaults.

13

THE OVERTIME BLUES

The U.S. Postal Service and the APWU had a contract in place called the collective bargaining agreement (CBA.) It addressed many procedures and detailed fair practices concerning overtime. The agency paid out hundreds of thousands of dollars a year because these procedures and rules were constantly manipulated and violated by managers and supervisors. The management at the downtown station had absolutely no problems violating the contract on a regular basis. Overtime was controlled and distributed through a sign-up sheet for those employees who desired to work more than an average eight-hour day and more than 40 hours per week.

Overtime reigned supreme in the U.S. Postal Service. A vast amount of people occupied the overtime list because many depended on it as a supplement to their regular pay. To tamper with it could greatly impact a family's income. Management was aware of this and used overtime opportunities as a tool for discipline, retaliation or reward.

When overtime was needed, it operated by following a rotation system that was regulated by seniority and specific qualifications for a job. Full tours were eight-hour days an employee worked his or her day off to take advantage of those hours. The distribution of overtime hours could be easily manipulated and was done so on a constant basis by the management staff at the Downtown Station.

When an eight-hour overtime shift came up, the senior person was first in line to receive those eight hours. Managers and supervisors made up the work schedule and knew the day before if an eight-hour shift was needed for the next day. If there was a need for an eight-hour overtime shift on that day and if the employee who was next in line was one who management did not particularly care for, they would offer that employee two hours the day before to push that individual out of the next person in line for overtime. Therefore, the rotation was followed and there was no contract violation.

An employee could reject or turn down any overtime offered to them. If this was the case, that eight-hour shift would follow rotation where the next person would receive that full tour of overtime for the next day. This was one of many ways they manipulated the system, which prevented those unpopular or assertive employees from receiving eight hours full overtime tours.

This action rewarded those who were submissive and subservient, pushing those away who stood up for their rights. By the time the grievance process would take affect the overtime rotation was back to the employee that was violated from the beginning.

Overtime was the beginning of many issues that had directly impacted me. I was bypassed and denied overtime daily and it was done in many manipulative ways. Filing grievances was the only way I could retrieve some of the overtime opportunities and at times receive pay after being ignored and bypassed. By doing so, I began to attract attention from management. New facility. Same U.S. Postal Service.

My low-profile days were over. I was now in the forefront of management's tangled web. And I didn't back down. I was never one to retract grievances. I saw them to the end. Management began testing my resilience in measures of intimidation, and once again harassment reared its ugly head.

On Aug. 14, 1993, I was emergency placed and removed from the building because I voiced my concerns to my supervisor, Reginald Chapman, about the unfair overtime opportunities given to co-workers. It was specifically defined as "verbal assaults or threats." I explained that I was not given these opportunities and I would have loved to earn a larger paycheck. His immediate reaction was spontaneous and irrational. Co-workers stood and watched as he aggressively displayed his anger by having me escorted out of the building. I was stunned by this instant uncontrollable reaction. There was no doubt the action taken was predetermined and I knew much more was to come.

But no longer was I on that roller coaster of confusion with a short fuse and a quick temper. The time had come for me to be responsible and act in the upmost appropriate manner. It was time for me to lace up my boots. Being a person of interest in this agency was brutal and a constant battle. Management had a variety of ways to flex their muscles and impose their will. The astonishing proficiency of it all made it a standing practice in this agency.

The next day I was ordered to report back to work. In that 24-hour timespan rumors about me had surfaced and spread like wildfire. Unsolicited comments were made by management and their team players, saying that I was out of control, being loud and obnoxious while making threats.

This was an alibi made up to justify their actions against me. They enlisted dishonest people who they could rely on to back them up. This combination of control and vengeance instilled misery and hatred in those falsely accused. This is what the public does not see, what is behind the counters in the U.S. Postal Service stations and offices alike. This out-of-control supervisor should have been an embarrassment to the management staff in the agency, especially those that appointed him in charge, but they continued defending his obnoxious behavior and aggressive demeanor.

They had assassinated my character and made me a symbol of violence. It was done in numbers to make it believable, that the emergency placement was justifiable, and hopefully because of so many of those impressionable co-workers and their input would assure that disciplinary action would stick. Once again, I was forced to react through the grievance process.

Psychologically, I was tired of looking over my shoulders fighting a system that had been in existence before I was born. I was finally realizing that I was being victimized by this system. I thought that maybe it was time for me to accept the fact that there wasn't a place in this agency where I could be treated as a human being with dignity and respect. It was a disappointing concept. To believe that people would go to the degree that these people had gone was outrageous. I was filled with anger and frustration which made me realize it would not have been in my best interest to report to work for the next couple of days.

14

HANDS UP

The night before a possible third day of being absent was unbearably stressful and sleepless for me. I felt that I had no future in this agency because of the many uncertainties that I had already encountered during my young career there. The anxiety and pain were so intense that I once again felt I needed alcohol but that was out of the question. I was in trouble and in desperate need of help.

After having exhausted all avenues in the postal service, I called the hospital. I was vulnerable and needed emotional support from someone in a professional medical capacity. I needed someone to give me confidence and assurance that everything was going to be okay. I could speak with the nurse on duty when I began explaining the nature of my call.

I informed her of my desperation for help and that I was sick and tired of being humiliated, tired of being harassed, and singled out by the manager and supervisors including many of my co-workers in the U.S Postal Service where I worked. I explained that I had informed many agencies and the Equal Employment Opportunity office about this on-going problem, but to no avail. I expressed my concerns about reporting back to duty because of this uncomfortable and very hostile environment.

She sounded sincere, genuine and asked different questions that were comforting and encouraging. After about five to six minutes on the telephone with her, she asked me to go to the front door of my home and informed me that the paramedics were outside of the door and that they would like to talk with me.

As I opened the front door and looked out, to my surprise, the paramedics were standing in the street next to the ambulance vehicle. Help, finally. I then opened the screen door and as I did this I heard a voice that was a lot closer to me than the paramedics. The voice said, "come out with your hands up" and "do not make any sudden moves."

I was terrified. My life had become even more complex. My mind was racing a million cycles per second. For a split moment, I believed that I had lost the concept of reality. I did not know what to do. Out of nowhere I gathered my thoughts and walked out with my hands above my head.

It then became apparent that it was the police and conceivable that if I did not follow their commands that I could become a target of gunfire. There were six or seven police officers, with weapons drawn and pointed directly at me, coming from behind the trees in my yard and from vehicles that were parked on the street.

It hit me then that the call I made to the hospital was probably the emergency crisis line and at that moment I realized that the call was being treating as a hostage or a suicide situation. I was unaware if this was standard procedure.

My call was nothing more than a cry for help. I did not expect my life to be threatened with guns pointed at my head by Denver police officers. Once they saw that my intentions were non-threatening, the paramedics could approach me. They asked if they could take me to the hospital for some tests.

I was more than willing to go get help, which was my sole purpose for making the call. After five or more hours of going through a psychiatric exam I was diagnosed with depression and was put on rest from work for a week.

15

RETURN TO WORK

On Aug. 20, 1993, I returned to work and was skeptical about entering the building. It was a cold and unsettled atmosphere. To make it through a day without incident would be an accomplishment. Surprisingly I did. The next day between the hours of 8 and 9 a.m. I was ordered by the supervisor to distribute a large amount of outgoing mail to approximately 38 carriers.

For one person to meet those expectations and perform this in the allotted time was not conceivable. It was a setup. I had no intention of giving this supervisor a reason to discipline me for job performance by not getting the mail out in a timely manner, so I requested help. In doing so, I was emergency placed out of the building for "Failure to Follow Instructions."

Upon my return to work I filed a grievance and once again management's actions were found to be unjust. I was awarded pay for time lost and all letters in my files were to be removed. Chapman was furious. Days later I was called by the manager, Toby Rampa, to report to his office. The supervisor was also present. The three of us discussed many issues about ongoing problems on the work room floor. I voiced my concerns over my separation from other employees and of the favoritism I witnessed. I spoke comprehensively about the supervisor's spontaneous overreactions that were always aggressive and caused havoc in the workroom that lead to unpleasant situations where I was constantly under scrutiny.

The supervisor's concerns about me had nothing to do with my productivity or work habits. He could not recite one problem where my job or a completion of a job that I was told to do was an issue. My personality was his problem. My confidence and the assertive nature in which I carried myself. This came as no surprise since there had been other supervisors in the past that had expressed the same sentiment. I was not submissive.

I despised dictatorship and the controlling behavior, and I refused to be molded into another human being's desires and expectations. Because I stood up for myself, I was labeled intimidating and threatening. Throughout the meeting I felt as though the two of them were trying to lure me into some sort of admission of guilt. The meeting did not accomplish a single thing and at the end of the meeting the manager expressed his feelings by saying that I was not a team player.

At this point I had been emergency placed twice from the building and had missed several days of work. People in the building were aware of the APWU's frequent presence representing me for one reason or another, and my constant presence in the office of the manager or supervisor. It was entertaining to many, yet there were those that were disgusted with the leadership. The separation of me from everyone else in the building brought on controversy, opinions and rumors that caused division between those few workers that were not afraid to be heard and those who were intimidated by management.

Those who management favored would glare at me and make various innuendoes, stirring the animosity that would heighten the tension. They knew this was pleasing to management and that they would back them up which kept the facility in turmoil. Management was the true reason why people in the station did not get along. They made a difference in people that developed into hatred and hostility. Favoritism was the main ingredient for this dysfunctional facility.

On Aug. 30, 1993, after working for two, maybe three hours, I put in a "Request for or Notification of Absence," to leave early for the remainder of the day due to a high-tension level I sensed on that day. People were glaring and staring down on one another. Co-workers were calling me a bully and claiming that I was making threatening sounds. They were accusing each other of taking long breaks and not doing their jobs. I felt uneasy and very uncomfortable. I saw every reason to remove myself from a situation that undoubtedly would turn nasty and define me as the aggressor.

The supervisor was reluctant to grant my request but I explained my reasoning for wanting to remove myself from this uncomfortable situation and demanded to be released at that moment. I informed him that this will be well documented and all remarks will be noted on the request form for leave, 3971. He released me.

Shortly after I arrived home I received a phone call from Rampa. His message was short and to the point. He stated that I was being referred for a fitness for duty medical psychiatric examination. He instructed me not to report back to work until further notice. In conclusion, he informed me that I would be receiving a letter of instructions that would have the name of the doctor, also when and where the examination will take place. I was not given a reason or an explanation as to why I was being sent for this examination. I did not know if this referral was ordered by upper management or if this was a self-serving and unwarranted act by the manager.

Not long after I received this information from the station manager, another call came in from the U.S. postal inspector. He voiced concerns about a threat that I allegedly made while talking with another supervisor earlier that morning before I left the building. She said that I said I was coming into the building to shoot and kill people. This lie and others were trumped up between the time I removed myself from the situation until I received this call. The very same day.

Their distortion of the truth was done in retaliation and was the result of me beating them to the punch by removing myself from a poorly thought out setup. The purpose for the psychiatric examination was to place the burden on my shoulders because the station was out of order and management had lost control behind the favoritism and the separation of people to different treatment. It was a diversion to imply that I was the bad seed and the reason why the troubled existed in the station.

Failure to pass this examination would result in my termination. This would solidify their attack and conclude their mission to remove me from the agency and give the perfect alibi as to why the station was dysfunctional. This would leave me with full ownership while management received praise and recognition for a job well done. The inadequate supervision would go uncontested and forgotten. Problem solved.

I received the letter, dated Sept. 8, 1993, through U.S. mail. The instructions and the manager's worksheet were attached. It referenced the reason he believed the referral was warranted. The worksheet painted me as a psychopath. He described my behavior as that of a mad man and a deranged out-of-control individual capable of doing anything. His imagination was vivid. He embellished stories that were completely inaccurate to accentuate the severity of my behavior which justified the referral. In addition, he expressed management's deepest concerns regarding my unwarranted intentions of coming into the building shooting people. The exam was scheduled for Sept. 23, 1993 at 8 a.m.

I had no intention of attending that meeting without an APWU steward. On that day, the union representative and I were punctual. I had known him for 11 maybe 12 years out of the 13 years that I had been with the agency. He was articulate, assertive and believed in justice, not only for the employees but for management as well. I felt a sense of relief at the opportunity to reveal the truth about what was actually going on in that station to someone other than management. Yet, I was nervous and uncomfortable about the postal service referring me to a doctor of their choosing to determine my fate with the agency. The thought of telling the truth outweighed my fear.

The psychologist was an elderly gentleman with a professional demeanor. We exchanged greetings and the examination began. Through the entire interview I spoke from my heart, being as truthful as I could. I expressed my sincere concerns about what was going on with management. But I mainly focused on the separation of me from all other employees and that I had always been under scrutiny. I gave examples in detail.

I presented a true and honest assessment of the Denver Downtown Station to the doctor, including my belief that this referral was a callous and evil intent to have me removed from the U.S. Postal Service. In my conclusion, I assured the doctor that I was not inferior to management and that I would continue to express the unfair treatment I endure daily to anyone I am referred to. The lack of fear for management was the reason among many why I was before him today. I asked only of him to judge me in all fairness. The exam took about two and a half hours. The doctor expressed his appreciation for the participation of me and my union representative and he wished me the best.

Several days had passed then I received the doctor's report. His diagnosis: personality disorder. He based his findings on my sensitivity in nature and what was being said about me at work. He gave no scientific analysis in support of his findings. He stated that he saw no signs of thought disorder or cognitive impairment. I was found fit for duty and returned to work. Management had lost another round in their quest to eliminate me from the agency. But it scraped the surface of more things to come.

The doctor's psychoanalysis did not address or fix the issues at hand or the stress and tension that I was under each day. Returning me to work was unfavorable for management but it was a victory for me in a sense, at least for the time being. I knew that I would never be left alone because of hard-core people in the postal service who lived by the sword.

It had been more than a month since I last was in the facility and nothing had changed. Animosity and tension remained at a high level in the station during my absence—a very important statement as far as I was concerned. The attention had shifted back to the downtown office. News travels fast, especially bad news. Many in other mail facilities had heard about the trouble in the downtown station and that I had been sent for psychiatric evaluation. They heard about the APWU's repeat visits to the downtown station because of contract agreement violations by management, overtime issues and favoritism that created verbal confrontations between employees. The word spread throughout the city.

The day of my return many of my co-workers were curious about why I was sent for a fitness-for-duty psychiatric examination, which was supposed to be confidential. The privacy act had been violated.

This ploy by management failed to remove me from the station. Not only did they lose that battle but they lost the confidence of employees who had bought into their story that I was the sole cause of this hostile environment. They saw that nothing had changed in the station during my absence. The animosity and hatred was more intense than ever. I heard many stories about something unpleasant happening from one day to the next.

This response from many of the employees forced management to create a diversion to try and regain the people's trust. Notices, memorandums and directives were being distributed and placed on bulletin boards in the facility. Their messages conveyed the deepest of regrets for an undesirable workplace and that they were doing everything conceivable to rectify the situation.

Stand-up talks were being held weekly for all employees. Handouts were being given pertaining to postal rules and regulations. Violence in the workplace was the theme, but deception was the ruthless game that was being played. Those who were handing out this literature and giving the stand-up talks were the true perpetrators.

This was a diversion to separate management from any wrongdoing and to impose a false sense of concern and security. The literature and stand-up talks captivated the emotions of people that were desperately in need of calmness and tranquility. The talks were deceitful and the literature was propaganda. The rules did not apply to everyone and were subject to compromise, and enforced only at the discretion of management. After hearing the charade and watching the masquerade of events, there was no doubt a storm was brewing.

I had learned my lessons on how to survive in the U.S. Postal Service the hard way. Awareness of your surroundings along with a strong sense of skepticism are essential for survival in any agency ripe with criminal mischief.

16

A LETTER TO THE POSTMASTER

I had made a sincere effort to find common ground to the madness in this facility by following the chain of command – a requirement before you contact the postmaster's office. I had contacted many officials in different agencies within the postal service either in person, by telephone, or certified letter, until I reached the postmaster's office. My letter to him expressed my concern and my disappointment surrounding the lack of attention to this intense and ongoing situation at the Denver downtown station. Management in this station had made a mockery out of the U.S. Postal Service's zero tolerance policy.

I informed him of how management removed me by emergency placement from the building twice without provocation, which in both cases was proven unjustifiable through the grievance process. In closing, I reiterated the importance of this matter and that it demanded his immediate attention. He replied that he was aware of the situation and that they were working with management to rectify it.

17

911

On May 16, 1994, the Denver Police Department was called to the station by a co-worker after allegedly being assaulted by Chapman. The altercation was reported to have started on the workroom floor and ended up in the office of the supervisor. It apparently got out of hand and escalated into a physical altercation while in the office. I was at my workstation when I heard loud voices coming from the supervisor's office. As I turned and looked in that direction I could see the office.

I saw Chapman walking out of the office moving at a very fast pace. He was being followed by a co-worker in close pursuit of him, step for step, as he was screaming, "Why did you hit me?" He repeated himself several times. Chapman did not reply. He appeared more interested in keeping an arms-length distance between the two of them.

The distraction attracted much attention on the workroom floor. People stopped what they were doing to see what the commotion was all about. Eventually the two of them separated when the supervisor briskly walked in one direction and my co-worker walked toward my workstation, which happened to be the opposite direction. He was hysterical as he approached me, screaming in a high-pitched voice that the supervisor had assaulted him by slapping his face. As he got closer to me I could see that the left side of his face was flushed and his left eye was red and teary.

He had been assaulted. Together, we both decided that this should be reported to the police so he called 911.

Ten minutes later the Denver police arrived. I allowed the police officers access into the building which was permitted if a postal employee escorts any visitors while in the building to the office, which I did. As I escorted them to the office I gave the officers my name and a summary of why they were called and what I had seen. Shortly after the two uniformed police officers' arrival, a plain-clothes detective and the postal inspector, Larry Christenson, came on the scene. Ironically their initial reaction wasn't to identify the person that made the call. Instead, they first interviewed – for almost two hours – the supervisor who was accused of assaulting an employee.

During that time not even as much as a word had been exchanged between the police and my co-worker, who had made the call. Team players that the supervisor had identified as witnesses were interviewed before interviewing the employee who was assaulted. Several hours had gone by before the police made their first attempt to have any sort of contact with the victim. His interview with this detective lasted all of 10 minutes.

Upon his return to the workroom floor he showed me a summons that he received from the detective to appear in court for making a false report and giving false information to a police officer. In his interview with this detective he also gave the names of people, including mine, that he called witnesses that could add information. About 15 minutes had gone by since my co-worker had returned to the floor and there was no sign that I would be called into the office.

This was strange because I distinctly brought to the attention of the police officers what I had witnessed and I gave them my name. I gave them a physical description of what I saw pertaining to my co-worker's injuries. I continued to wait patiently in anticipation of being called to the office. Not a moment later after the thought of not being called into the office, the detective and the remaining officials walked out of the office heading toward the exit doors.

Instinctively I immediately intercepted them before they had reached the exit doors. Once again, I introduced myself for those who were not there when the police first arrived and I gave my reason for stopping them. I expressed my concerns by asking why I was not called to be interviewed. The detective's reaction was cold and callous. He turned his head away from me and ignored me. I found this to be very peculiar for a law enforcement officer to react this way.

I especially was surprised by his lack of effort to collect as much information as possible for his investigation in achieving proficiency. It was apparent that my name had been mentioned, where I would have bet that it had even been discussed, and dragged through the mud because of his negative reaction towards me, especially not knowing me. The information that I had to give was pertinent to the investigation. It would have gone against any reasoning for him to issue a criminal summons for my coworker to appear in court for giving false information. It would have also challenged the detective's so-called investigation about why he claimed that he saw no visual injuries to the victim's face in his report.

He took the time out to interview each one of the supervisor's witnesses. Why was I not interviewed? It was a one-sided investigation to protect management. I would not allow them to leave, and continued to express my concerns in what I believed to be an administrative scheme because I was disregarded and did not matter to the Denver Police Department or by the United States Postal Service. The detective saw that I was not going to go away. He told me to put it in a statement as he walked out of the double doors. The uniformed officers remained there at the station until I completed my written statement. I made copies and released it to them.

I felt deprived of my rights as an American citizen. I was dehumanized by those whose job it was to protect and serve. Once again, I was judged in the lowest form.

What had transpired that morning came as a complete shock to many who were in the facility at the time and for those who learned the details later. It was talked about throughout much of the day and for many weeks thereafter. The assault of an employee by a supervisor was pretty much unheard of and was probably the reason that it was so shocking to many and taken very seriously. Even more shocking and serious was the way it was handled by both the Denver Police Department and the U.S. Postal Service.

The mishandling of this situation, in my mind, classified it as both alarming and frightening. My co-worker expressed he felt like he had been interrogated. I was insulted. We were so involved and stressed to the point that neither one of us was thinking rationally about what had just taken place. We needed desperately to take a moment and gather our thoughts to contemplate our next move and what was needed in order to protect ourselves and how to bring out the truth. His face continued to swell and his eye remained teary and that was what gave me the idea for him to leave work immediately and go to the hospital to be examined by a qualified physician. Not only would his injury be confirmed but it would be documented by medical doctors. It would provide proof to any dispute or doubt.

He agreed that it was an excellent idea. Without hesitation, he went to the office and requested a 3971 and left the building.

The radiology reports from the hospital showed soft tissue and swelling over the left side of his face and contusion of the left jaw, something the detective claimed to have not seen. This vital information was left out of his report. He lied about it and ignored it. If this information had been put in the investigators report, he would not have had justification for issuing a criminal summons to my co-worker for giving false information to a police officer.

The next day my co-worker went to the Denver Police Department with this report he received from the hospital. He was directed to go to the Crimes Against People unit where Det. Pennington from the assault division handled his complaint. The detective went over his allegations and reviewed the hospital report and found substantial evidence to validate his complaint. He telephoned Chapman the next morning to inform him of a criminal summons to appear in court on assault charges. Later that evening my co-worker received a telephone call from this detective informing him that somehow the detective who initially investigated the case at the Downtown mail facility intervened and somehow intercepted the summons for the supervisor to appear in court. The supervisor never made an appearance and was never charged for assaulting my co-worker.

Three days after the assault on May 19, 1994, I was called over the intercom to report to the supervisor's office. As I entered the office there sat the detective along with the postal inspector who was with him on the day of the assault and accompanied him through the investigation. The detective invited me to have a seat as I entered the office. From that very moment, I could not take my eyes off the two of them seeing the grim look that was on their faces.

The detective, who did not officially introduce himself to me, confronted me about a threat that I had allegedly made against another coworker. This presented a problem and nothing but absolute trouble. It was then that I requested that a union steward be present, only to be denied by the detective by saying that if the union steward is not an attorney then they could not be present in this interview. The postal inspector was a veteran of the postal service.

The agency held a strong pride in its inspection service for being among the elite personnel that were highly qualified and trained with superb knowledge of the rules and regulations of the agency. Christenson, a highly trained inspector should have known that any time an employee who is accused of a crime where a postal inspector is present that the employee has the right to union representation. The inspector never recited or acknowledged this right.

I brought this to the attention of the detective and reminded the inspector of those rights which irritated the detective immensely. His face turned flushed as frustration took over the little amount of control he was so desperately trying to maintain. It was then he blurted out in an uncontrollable and robust tone saying that either I could talk to him here meaning the mail facility or we could go down to the jail which was nothing more than a threat. Observing his body language throughout what was an interrogation and hearing the hostility in his voice was more than a police officer investigating.

This had become personal to him and I believed that it would have been to my advantage and in my best interests to keep the interview there at the station. I agreed to talk with him to avoid any additional pressure and stress that could only lead to a nasty situation considering his state of mind. The truth was that I was forced to participate in what he referred to as an interview without being protected by representation where my civil rights were violated by threats and intimidation of my freedom.

18

BIG BLACK GUYS

Detective James Rock conducted the entire interview. He talked to me as if I was a hardened criminal. He would ask and answer questions that were directed to me, and he would then follow those questions with accusations. He was rude and aggressive given those characteristics. I would best describe him as someone looking for trouble. He was at the point of being deranged. Whenever I was given the opportunity to respond to a question that he asked he would cut me off in the middle of my response by answering or challenging any uncompleted answer or statement. Refuting anything he said was futile. If I lashed out, he would intensify his obnoxious behavior to try to provoke me to do something crazy.

After about 30 to 45 minutes of this unlawful interrogation he realized that his desperate attempt to lead me into a hostile confrontation was unsuccessful. He made one last attempt to hit below the belt when he expressed his dislikes for big black guys like me. He said that he believed I could be an asshole and he also believed everything that he had heard about me. My perception of this detective as a mean racist bigot was 100 percent correct. I had been acquainted with him for not even a week and I hated his guts. He was the real asshole who judged me and that made everything personal from the time we met.

I refused to give in to his bigotry throughout the entire interview. He accused me of being intimidating and said that I approached a co-worker saying to him that he was the president of the "wacka doo club." He revealed this co-worker's name, and added that I had called other names too, but he never revealed these other employees. The result was that, with zero evidence and witnesses, I was given a criminal summons to appear in court for "Disturbing the Peace" and "Threats to Injure a Person or Damage of Property." I knew his intentions while in the office. After leaving I clearly understood his motives.

He had an uncontrollable temper with an obsession for me that compromised and impaired his judgment to be fair. He was a discredit to the Denver Police Department. No matter what I said throughout the entire interview, it was irrelevant. The detective was racist by his own admission and it was evident to me that he was trying to make me out to be what he was – a criminal.

At 9 a.m. on Tuesday, May 27, 1994, eight days after I had received a criminal summons to appear in court, I received a telephone call while at work from the detective asking me if I would come to the postal inspector's office for a moment to clear up some matters that he did not quite understand in our last "conversation." This would be three blocks away from the station.

Something about this just did not seem to be right. After eight days he needed clarity? He also informed me that it had already been cleared by my supervisor for me to come to the inspector's office. On the telephone he sounded pleasant, yet I remained skeptical of interactions with a person I knew hated me for various reasons one being the color of my skin. His cantankerous behavior seemed to be unleashed anytime I was in his presence. I was weary.

I called the APWU to notify them of what was taking place at the moment and that I was instructed to report to the inspector's office by this detective. The union's office was a good 25 miles away from the station, which was a factor that had a significant role for the lack of their immediate presence in the station which the detective knew.

Yet it really did not make a difference if the union was in the building or not, knowing that the detective would violate postal service procedure and not allow me to be represented by a union steward. I felt that my whereabouts should be well documented and that someone should know where I was at all times. I was continuously pursued and hunted down by this deranged individual. There was one thing for sure I knew and that was I needed to report to the inspector's office. Failing to do so without a doubt would have landed me in jail.

Around 9:30 a.m. I arrived at the inspector's office where I could easily see into two adjacent offices because the walls were glass. As I glanced in one room I could see the detective sitting in one of the offices as he waved for me to come inside. In the other office sat another man at a desk. He was motioned by the detective to come into the office where the both of us were waiting. The detective introduced him as Postal Inspector Mike Cronke as he closed the door behind him. Trouble.

He was not the same inspector that accompanied him in his first visits to the station but it seemed that he had some sort of knowledge as to what was going on because of the material in his hands. He was prepared to take my fingerprints.

What was said was contrary to what he had stated over the telephone. This detective was the worst thing that could have happened to me and I had a premonition that something bad was about to happen. First and foremost, I wondered why would a postal inspector need to be involved in what was portrayed as clarity issue. Why couldn't this have been easily handled over the telephone?

The conversation began with the detective accusing me of harassing a female co-worker by making derogatory remark about her anatomy, specifically calling her a "roly-poly ass." It was outrageous and ridiculously insane for a detective with the Denver Police Department to pursue this outlandish rhetoric that was nothing more than downright juvenile allegations.

This type of illustration could do nothing more than show embarrassment on behalf of the Denver Police Department. He went on to say that this incident occurred on May 5, 1994. I informed him at that moment that

I was not scheduled to work on that date, so I was not even there on that day and that I would be glad to provide proof of my time card.

I was being set up. Not only was I not at work on that day but this supposedly had taken place two weeks before my co-worker was assaulted which was two weeks before the detective ever came to the downtown station and the first time that it was ever heard of.

I remained calm and asked the detective why is it that the people who have claimed to be witnesses to the assault case are the exact same people that are now making allegations against me. I asked him why he continued to give me and my co-worker these frivolous citations. He refused to answer the questions and he also rejected the invitation to look at my time card.

The results were the same as the first time. I was called asshole by him numerous times and was given a second criminal summons to appear in court on charges of harassment. I was taken to another office by this inspector where I was photographed and fingerprinted. The trail of events and the people involved confirmed that it was a joint effort from a group of individuals imposing their will to break me down into submission.

This signed criminal summons, based on false allegations and documents as well as unlawful interrogations, was a relentless attack of my character to slip a criminal jacket on me. It supported my claim that the United States Postal Service were dictators, ruling by fear and intimidation.

The detective had an obsession to break me as did the managers in the U.S. Postal Service and their team players at the downtown station. The facts supported the evidence and the evidence could not be refuted. It was a heavy burden on me each day. A challenge not just for me to go to work but to make it out of there not knowing what the end results might be on any given day.

The pressure was unbelievable that kept me guessing if today was the day that I would be jailed or even killed in what was shaping up to be a witch hunt. The pieces were in place for management to execute an all-out assault with life changing consequences.

They now had a source in the Denver Police Department who had proven to be my adversary and continued to show that he was through his aggression by giving me and two of my co-workers unwarranted criminal summons to appear in court. Management and their team players saw that he was a dirty cop as we all did. They continued to call this detective knowing that it would lead to us appearing in court.

19

A BADGE OF DISHONOR

Defending yourself in a court of law can take a financial toll. They took every opportunity to use Det. Rock to their advantage to impose their will. The detective, in abusing his authority and position, demonstrated that he had no regard for the law. He felt entitled to exploit the judicial system. No man should be justified in using a badge to satisfy his personal hatred.

Four months had gone by since I had received my second summons to appear in court. The station was in turmoil, people were full of hatred and animosity. The game had gotten a lot more serious and the stakes a lot higher now that this detective had come into the picture and that led to a surmountable amount of bitter feelings throughout the station.

On the morning of Oct. 17, 1994, production was at a steady pace and moving right along issue free. On that day once again, Det. Rock made his appearance at the downtown station along with what I now refer to as his accomplice, the initial postal inspector. My heart skipped a beat the moment I saw the two of them knowing that anytime they came around it spelled trouble. Everyone who was a part of that station also knew that it spelled trouble and many knew they were coming for me.

People watched and glared at the two of them, and to see the expression on many of their faces was in anticipation that something was about to happen as they walked into the supervisor's office. I believe at that moment I was the only one that had a true sense of what was about to take place. Moments later my co-worker, who had already received a summons from the detective to appear in court, was called over the intercom to report to the supervisor's office. He was terrified to go into the office as I was. He ignored the page.

Five maybe six minutes had gone by when the detective came storming out of the office. He was walking at a very rapid pace towards the work area where my co-worker and I were performing our duties. It was obvious that he was angry. His face was flush and his body language was excessively aggressive. He was still six to seven feet away when he began shouting in a loud and obnoxious voice telling my co-worker that if he did not come to the office to talk with him that he was going to take him to jail.

He chose to go to the office. No more than five maybe 10 minutes later he came out of the office with another criminal summons he received from the detective to appear in court on two counts of "Disturbing the Peace."

Again, two of the same people continued to make calls to this detective, one of whom had made a complaint against me a few months ago claiming that I had harassed her on a day that I was not at work.

Because of interactions between this detective and the postal inspector, they encouraged and supported those who willfully and knowingly continued to break those laws. They were those who constantly made frivolous complaints on those few who did not and would not go along with management's illegal action in breaking the law and undermining postal policy. The detective provided his personal telephone number to those that made these complaints against me and my two co-workers. They were the same witnesses for the supervisor on the day he assaulted my co-worker.

When he did receive calls from those select individuals that had this private number he would not hesitate to respond and issue criminal summons against the accused and those who management had personal vendettas against.

My co-workers nor I was ever given his private telephone number. This detective was a public servant that continued to commit serious crimes such as, obstruction of justice, malicious prosecution, and false imprisonment of me and my co-workers. Not long after my co-worker received this second summons another co-worker was paged to the supervisor's office.

She was given a criminal summons to appear in court for "Disturbance of the Peace" because she had made a comment on the workroom floor pertaining to one of the supervisor's witnesses. She reportedly said the witness could not tie the strings together on the apron that she was wearing. From May 1994 to October 1994, Det. Rock had issued five different criminal summons to me and my co-worker. Now another co-worker had been added, totaling six different summons.

The detective seemed to be inspired when he received a call. None of them ever hesitated to dial his number and the response time was always immediate, where he would make his appearance to the station and issue criminal summons to the same three people. It presented him the opportunity to express and carry out his hatred for black men while hiding behind his police shield and the law.

I was spending hours in courtrooms sitting and listening to cases of others, while waiting for my case to be called by a judge. Often, I waited only to hear the judge say that the case had been postponed and would be rescheduled for a later date which could sometimes take up to months. My out-of-pocket defense expense over an eight-month period had reached an access of $7,935.32 between the hearings, pleas, motion hearings, trial settings and attorney fees. And it was rising.

This was at no cost to the detective, management or the people that were making calls to the police because they all were being represented by the U.S. Postal Service and the state of Colorado. It was tearing me and my co-workers apart financially not to speak of the emotional distress. I tried using every resource available to me within the agency in hopes of getting my story out to alert and get the attention of someone, anyone of authority, who could and would possibly address these on-going issues and put a stop to this attack and brutality of a select few in the station.

Between March 1988 and August 1994, I filed six different EEO complaints with the Equal Employment Opportunity agency and 12 different grievances with the APWU in relation to the unfair practices and the many violations of management. The 12 grievances were either ruled in my favor or settled by management in avoidance of advancing to arbitration hearings. The six EEO complaints that were filed were denied.

This came as no surprise to me being well familiarized with the low percentage rate of complaints that are substantiated by those who file with the EEO agency in the U.S. Postal Service. I had filed complaints that I knew without a shred of doubt had validity and they were either dismissed or not accepted. But, U.S. Postal Service employees were not allowed to go outside of the agency to the Equal Employment Opportunity Commission – a separate entity outside of the U.S. Postal Service EEO agency. I discovered this when I went to the EEOC with my complaints and was turned away because I was a postal employee.

PART FOUR:
1995

20

EXTENSIONS OF MANAGEMENT

On Jan. 25, 1995, I was emergency placed from the building for "Disrupting Day to Day Operations." An altercation occurred on the workroom floor that day when I was struck by a worker who was pushing some mail gurney equipment through my work area. Yet I was emergency placed. Once again, I exercised my right by filing a grievance with the APWU. After following protocol and going through the process, the action was found to be improper and had no merit. I was made whole and paid for the time that I was not allowed to come to work. The emergency placement letter was removed from my files.

I had exhausted all avenues known to me through the chain of command by informing the APWU president, the Violence in the Workplace Team, the Inspection Service, Labor Relations and EEO about management's harassing behavior towards me. Except for the APWU, none of these agencies got directly involved and conducted a serious investigation.

Labor Relations, like the EEO agency, was an extension of management. Supervisors and managers were judged by their peers who head these agencies in any dispute or disruptive situations. I had direct contact with Char Ehrenshaft, the labor relations manager, through meetings on several occasions. The meetings turned out to be nothing more than formality where the managers and supervisors were given the benefit of every doubt.

The Violence in the Workplace Team consisted of managers and supervisors, and approached the situation in an entirely different manner. It was labeled as an investigation which was tedious and a non-factor that had no parley to a serious investigation. The process included selecting names in numerical order from the employee's roster to be interviewed about the situation in the downtown station.

Many of the employees that were selected to be interviewed were not in the station during much of the chaos. Some had only been in the station five maybe six months at best and did not know the history. It was a smokescreen to avoid talking with those who actually knew of the dysfunction in the station. It was a cover-up and solved nothing.

21

DROWNING IN THE ALPHABET SOUP OF EQUAL RIGHTS AGENCIES

My two co-workers and myself where the victims of this violence in the workplace. We were never contacted to be interviewed. If we had been interviewed, management's practices would have been exposed. At this point, I was fed up.

Four days later, on Jan. 29, 1995, once again I wrote to the postmaster. This time I was adamant in voicing my concerns about the attack of me and my co-workers by management and the Denver Police Department. I explained my efforts to alleviate the problem by following the chain of command to seeking solutions but to no avail. I listed the different agencies that I had contacted and provided him with the two citations that I received. I expressed sincere desperation for his help and undivided attention.

The postmaster didn't respond. I realized that this was a lot bigger than I first imagined. The torture I continued to face left no questions or doubts that management was on a mission not to only remove me from the agency but to ruin me professionally and personally. I had exhausted all avenues for solutions within the U.S. Postal Service. It was time to go outside of the postal service.

On Jan. 29, 1995, I wrote to David Skaggs, United States representative for Colorado's 2nd district. I followed that with a letter to the American Civil Liberties Union of Colorado (ACLU) and to the Civil Rights Commission (CRC), both dated Feb. 2, 1995. I wrote to the National Association for the Advancement of Colored People on Feb. 5, 1995. The representative did not respond to my letter. The NAACP wrote back and referred me to the different agencies within the postal system such as the EEO agency and Labor Relations – the same group of organizations I had already contacted. The ACLU wrote back informing me of their limited funds and resources necessary to take my case. The CRC informed me that they had no enforcement or authority in a matter such as mine.

I continued to be turned away from an American system of "liberty and justice for all." I put my life on the line in a war that left me disabled. Yet, my sacrifice appeared to have no value. I received no help, not even an inquiry. I realized that if I had to go down I was going down fighting.

On Jan. 25, 1995, just 24 days from when I experienced my first emergency placement out of the building by this supervisor, I was once again emergency placed from the building by him. On Feb. 18, 1995, the charges were "Failure to Follow a Direct Order" and "Disrupting Day-to-Day Operations." There was an expectation for me to do my job and the job of another employee, but I continued doing my job. This agitated him.

He abused his authority to satisfy his personal vendetta against me. I filed a grievance. The union's first proposal to management was that the emergency letter be purged from all files and to make me whole. In a later meeting with management the union took it upon themselves, without my consent, to agree that I would be made whole, but the emergency placement letter would remain in my files for six months. This was unacceptable.

22

TRIAL

A week before I was to go on trial for the harassment charge of May 5, 1994, I received a call from the detective informing me that he had added a second person to the charge. It was changed from one count to a second count of harassment. On March 23 and 24 of 1995, I went on trial for two counts of harassment. The prosecution brought in an entirely new face as a witness that had no prior involvement in this case whatsoever, and the judge allowed it. I was convicted on both counts of harassment and ordered to report back to the courts in two weeks for sentencing.

My attorney and I were appalled at the judge's acceptance of an additional charge from a completely new witness where there was no discovery process on that witness whatsoever. This new witness was part of the group that continued to call the detective to the station about me, but this person was not on record in the court case. We wasted no time appealing the conviction.

Arthur Fine, the judge in this case, did not appear to follow protocol or comply with the court's rules and regulations to set forth the motions under the municipal code according to my attorney, Richard Ott, who argued this point in the courtroom. This made it impossible for me to receive a fair and impartial trial. But the judge threatened to impose sanctions against him if he continued to argue the point. Lynch mob and witch hunt came to mind.

It was difficult to return to the workroom floor to face these false witnesses celebrating my conviction. I heard, "We got his ass," and "Taking care of business." The prosecution's special witness, who assaulted me with postal equipment, gave himself a pat on the back then bragged about how the jury bought his testimony on the stand. I envisioned choking the life right out of his body. I didn't realize my rage and anger could get to this level. Going postal made sense.

He continued to boast, making the sound of a baby crying, while rubbing and squinting his eyes and looking at me. Many saw it, but stayed clear. They didn't want to take on my role in management's eyes. I reported this behavior and nothing was done. I knew the smug display on the workroom floor was intended to provoke me, and management approved of it.

I refrained from acting out my thoughts, but did tell him that his ass should be in jail for perjury. I immediately reported my comment to the supervisor, Joyce Amos, who had very little response. Ironically, one of the truck drivers for the station approached me around midday. He was aware of the situation in the station and told me he had overheard the conversation.

He was a friend to both of us. He expressed his disbelief in hearing this person say that he lied. I was surprised and elated to know that someone had heard what I considered a confession to perjury. I was hesitant to ask him if he would repeat to management what he heard. We talked for a brief moment. I was very careful in selecting my words because I didn't want to scare him away. After a short time, I concluded that either he would or he would not. So, I asked him if he would repeat what he heard and surprisingly he had no problem with it.

The two of us went to management with this information.

A week had gone by and I heard nothing. Management completely ignored me and the witness. I refused to allow this to go uncontested so I filed a complaint with the EEO and brought this to my attorney's attention. My attorney believed this information would be strong in a court of law and very damaging to the prosecution, if a sworn affidavit was included in the appeal case. But he was the only person that came forward to let the truth be known. He showed that he was not afraid of management threats or retaliation.

The second week after the trial, I reported back to the court for sentencing as instructed by the judge. I was ordered to write two letters of apology to people that I honestly considered to be perjurers and law breakers. I was also ordered to transfer out of the station and to report to the probation department. Because the conviction was under appeal, by law I was not required to act on the sentencing order, including reporting to the probation department.

I followed the instructions that were given to me by the appeals court, yet the municipal court put out a warrant for my arrest that read "A Request for Warrant" and "Complaint to Revoke Probation." The warrant was not lifted until my attorney appeared in court to go over the rules in the order. I was at the end of my rope and fighting to keep my head above water to survive and stay alive. I hung on because I had something bigger to fight for: my innocence, my family and then my dignity.

Even if I were to find a job in a totally different industry, my innocence would still be hanging in the balance. The fact was that the U.S. Postal Service was one of the few places, if not the only one, where black people could earn a salary that allowed them to live a middle-class lifestyle.

The agency had shown that retaliation is a source used to justify the means. An article in the Postal News talked about a postmaster who had filed an EEO complaint of discrimination and was retaliated against by the U.S. Postal Service. This is one of many reasons why I considered this driver to be a person with morals and integrity who knew of the danger he was putting himself in by defending me. His courage was impressive.

It gave me the confidence in him to ask if he would sign an affidavit and testify in a court of law as to what he heard and saw on that day. He had no problem with it. A few days later after I had filed an EEO complaint, management received a call by an investigator from that office about my complaint.

The supervisor made a statement about that day. She stated on the morning of April 6, 1995 I came to the office and made a complaint to her about being harassed by a co-worker. She responded that she told him to stay away from me. This information conflicted with the testimony that she gave to the postal inspector when she called him later that day. On that day, the supervisor called the inspector at 2 p.m. and reported the incident.

This would be six hours after it originally had taken place. It further contradicted the supervisor's subsequent statement to the inspector's office she would make seven months later, where she stated something different. She said that she did not remember me informing her of anything that morning but did remember that the other person reported to her that day that I threatened him, and that she called the detective about the matter.

23

INVESTIGATIONS

In the EEO investigation, a reason was never given for the supervisor's contradictory statements and why she waited six hours to report an alleged threat. This was a key witness as to what took place on this day for this detective to later arrest me. But she never testified at any of the hearings and was never a witness to any trial including the arbitration hearing. The arbitrator questioned her absence at the arbitration hearing.

He saw the investigation was self-serving for the detective. It was a one-sided investigation. Neither I nor the witness were ever interviewed by management or the inspection service, only by the detective. He requested written statements on Denver Police Department forms only from the alleged victim. The purpose of him interviewing me was primarily to obtain an arrest warrant on criminal charges.

The detective claimed that he had found a person whom he presented as a witness to the April 6, 1995 incident other than the alleged victim. It was the only way that he could obtain an arrest warrant and have me arrested. This investigation included a statement that the detective wrote himself, detailing what was seen and heard on that day for this person that he claimed was a witness.

The statement incriminated me, imposing an admission of guilt, but the person who the detective said wrote this statement did not sign it. In fact, this person told management and other officials that he did not see or hear any conversation on the morning in question. He was never a witness at any court hearing or the arbitration to verify what he reportedly had said to the detective. Yet, this statement was in the arrest warrant unsigned and used to arrest me. Management used this opportunity to continue their process of removing me from the U.S. Postal Service.

After reporting the incident on the morning of April 6, 1995 to the supervisor I learned later that she informed the day supervisor of the incident the next day. This was Chapman, the notorious supervisor who previously perjured himself in the assault case. After he learned of the incident on that day he prepared a D-2 Form, a supervisor's worksheet for disciplinary action. He made no inquiries regarding the specific charges and made no independent investigation. He relied on the IM (inspector memorandum) and made an impetuous request for me to be discharged.

After relying on the IM that accused me of making threats, he waited 10 days later to execute an emergency placement.

When asked his reason for the placement, his answer was of concern for the safety of others. His answer made no sense as to why he waited for such a long period of time dealing with a safety concern. The issue was pursued further but he changed his reason for the emergency placement. It was now because of my arrest on April 17, 1995.

This was not unusual and was not out of the ordinary for management to change their stories. Playing make believe and embellishing lies appeared to be a passionate hobby for them. The alleged victim was given 12 additional days to revise his statement. This allowed him to write three different statements regarding that morning which authorities labeled as clarifying statements. By the time the investigation was complete, which took a maximum of 14 days, the supervisor changed his position once again. His request for my discharge was now because of my conviction.

On April 10, 1995, one day after the warrant was lifted for the sixth time, Det. Rock and inspector paid a visit to the station. Five minutes later I was called over the intercom to report to the supervisor's office. I was accused of "Threatening to Cause Injury to a Person." It was the same person that the prosecution brought in the trial at the last moment as their surprise witness, the same one who was involved in April 6 incident. The detective said that he knew I threatened this individual because I was an asshole. He then said, "when I find out that you did this I am going to throw your black ass in jail."

Surprisingly, I walked out of the office without a summons to appear in court which probably wasn't a good thing. But, I believed he was putting lies together in order to arrest me. This psychotic bastard was obsessed with me. For him to say that he was going to throw me in jail was in no way an idle threat. I knew that would be next to come and there was nothing that I could do about it. The trial in which I was convicted of harassment was under appeal. My attorney and I felt that we had an excellent chance of being granted a new trial or an acquittal.

Four days had gone by since the detective had threatened to incarcerate me. I was a bit surprised that this guy's obsession allowed him this long to arrest me. I thought by now his anxiety and uncontrollable desire to incarcerate black men would have killed him. He had the authority to arrest me at any time. What he was fighting was how to articulate the lies to make them believable to justify his actions for arresting me. On that fourth day, I went on trial for the second time in defense of the second summons that I received for "Disturbing the Peace."

On April 14, 1995, the detective represented the prosecution's main witness. My accuser along with the two women that I was convicted of harassing in March –where the verdict was guilty—were also there as the prosecution witnesses. Throughout the trial, the detective's testimony was as harsh as when I was being interrogated by him.

He talked about how intimidating I was to the people around me and how threatening I was to society. He also mentioned my body language and how aggressively I carried myself. He was happy to say that I was found guilty of harassment in the municipal courts in March of that same year.

The prosecution's witnesses pretty much spewed the same cold and callous lies. Staying composed drained me, but stay composed I did. It was a very unusual trial for the most part, where the judge kept his head down through much of the entire trial. At the end, he ruled in my favor. I was granted a motion for judgment of acquittal. It was a God-given victory.

The detective was furious. Rejection was written all over the prosecutor's face as well as his witnesses. This was the same prosecutor that tried me in the harassment case and was awarded a guilty verdict.

Three days after the trial on April 17, 1995 at 8:30 a.m., I had come back from lunch and as I was punching back on the time clock. Chapman, who was involved in everything from the beginning, approached me. He informed me that I was needed in the office. As I began walking towards the office I could feel him on my heels.

24

HANDCUFFED AND PARADED

As I got closer I could see many people standing around in the supervisor's office. The closer I got, the more people I saw. As I entered the office there stood two supervisors, three Denver police uniformed officers, the detective, along with the postal inspector. One of the officers approached me as I entered the office, and asked if my name was Garland Lewis. I replied, "yes." It was then that he instructed me to put my hands behind my back.

I was handcuffed and he informed me that I was under arrest. At that moment, I felt as though my heart jumped out of my chest. It was a devastating blow. I then asked the arresting officer in a very somber voice "on what charges?" The detective said it was for the intimidation of a witness.

I was paraded throughout the building before my peers from the back of the building to the front. This was an entirely different route in the building that the police had taken from the last nine to 10 times they had come to the station. Their entry and exit each time had been through the back entrance of the building.

This display of me throughout the building in the presence of all employees was the detective making a statement. Once I had reached the front of the building I was walked through the philatelic area, also known as the front counter area where customers mailed packages and purchased stamps. They wanted the public to see me.

Outside the building were three squad cars parked in the front of the post office. I was placed in one of the cars and taken to jail. I felt violated. It was humiliating and degrading. Once I reached the jail I was photographed and fingerprinted. The charges making it official were then read to me: "Intimidation of a Witness," a third-class felony. If convicted it was punishable by five years in the state penitentiary.

I spent the remainder of the day and part of that night in a small jail cell with nine maybe 10 other inmates. My self-esteem was torn apart while my imagination continued to run wild. I thought about the many uncertainties that were ahead of me. I also recalled my first time being arrested at around the age of 14. I was walking at 28th and Fairfax in Denver's Park Hill neighborhood. The police approached me and said they were looking for a suspect. I told them I didn't know anything. They started calling my mother names. I responded, "fuck you!" I was arrested when all I was doing was minding my own business, and when that didn't work, in the mind of a teenager, I was defending myself. The stakes were higher with this most recent arrest, but the principle was the same. Abuse of authority is a very wicked thing.

Later that night, my wife posted bail and I was released. Upon my return home that night there was an envelope from the U.S. Postal Service taped to my front door. The letter read, "As of now, you are on emergency placement in an off-duty status reason for placement 'unacceptable conduct' to be continued until advised."

From Dec. 19, 1985 to April 17, of 1995—for 10 years—management had targeted me in one way or another. They humiliated and belittled me in the most unprecedented demoralizing ways. I had been placed in an emergency status from the building four different times at that point. I had been written up and put in for discipline 12 other times and was up for removal from the postal service three times.

The police and postal inspectors hounded me on a constant basis by issuing me criminal court summons and conducting interrogation interviews that continued to challenge my sanity. I had been arrested and undergone two different psychiatric examinations. At that point, I was awaiting an appeal on a trial where I was wrongfully convicted and was facing a third trial and the possibility of a third-class felony to carry with me for the rest of my life.

If convicted, prison time and removal from the postal service was imminent.

Now that I was unemployed for an extended period, I took every advantage of the time to prepare for this upcoming trial. They wanted to remove me from the U.S. Postal Service, but because I served in the military I was entitled to continue receiving pay until a final decision was made. My attorney, my union steward and I spent many days and nights with countless hours reviewing case law and gathering evidence and information to put before the courts in my defense. We went over statements of people who possibly could be called to testify.

I received a letter from the U.S. Postal Service on May 1, 1995 with instructions to report to the Capitol Hill station at 1541 Marion Street on Tuesday, May 9, 1995 for a due process hearing. This process affords the accused the opportunity to tell their side of the story. The detective had zero witnesses to the allegation of which he falsely arrested me and no statements in support of the arrest.

This due process was procedure when removing an employee from the agency and the questions that were asked were just formality in my case. The arrest and removal of me from the agency was done illegally, so whatever I said in this meeting was irrelevant. After about 30 minutes everyone in the room could see that the hearing was going nowhere and time was being wasted. I refused to be broken.

I followed procedure and completed what was required of me in attendance of this hearing. I was released early that morning from the hearing. On that same day, I received a telephone call from my coworker who was working that morning at the station. He informed me that both the detective and inspector were in the building earlier and charged him with two additional counts of harassment of the same two people that he was charged with for "Disturbing the Peace" back in October 1994.

The witch hunt targeting two black men continued. My co-worker and I were constantly tracked down by two criminals with authority: a Denver police detective and a U.S postal inspector. The detective continued to issue illegal criminal summons to the two of us to appear in court. That tipped the scales to malicious prosecution, false imprisonment, and obstruction of justice, and the U.S. inspector ignored postal jurisdiction.

This detective had now issued 10 different criminal summonses for the three of us to appear in court. Six of which were given to two of my co-workers and four of the 10 were given to me on more serious charges. On May 11, 1995, my attorney and I appeared in court to make a plea to the felony charges in the intimidation of a witness.

While we were sitting in the courtroom waiting for my case to be called by the judge, to our surprise the detective entered the courtroom. At that time, we didn't believe that he saw us sitting there as he walked toward the bench where the judge was seated. We overheard a request that he made to the judge for his signature on an arrest warrant for my co-worker.

My attorney and I looked at each other in shock. I then told him about the humiliation and embarrassment of being arrested in the presence of your peers at your place of work. We agreed that I should call my co-worker to inform him that this detective had just received the judge's signature on a warrant for his arrest.

I called the station and informed him of what had just taken place and for him to get the hell out of there, not to run from the law, but to save him the embarrassment. I told him that he could turn himself in later without the humiliation. He decided that would be in his best interests, so that was what he did. This denied the detective pleasure and the satisfaction to put on another side show using another black man for the entertainment of management and their team players.

I received a second letter May 17, 1995 from the agency. This was a proposed removal from the U.S. Postal Service. The reason was "Unacceptable Conduct." The letter contained many lies that depicted me as uncivilized and a threat. The agency referred to the conviction as felony harassment instead of what it was, and that was a misdemeanor. Whatever this agency did or would say about me was a desperate attempt to mislead and to distort the truth, making me out to be vicious and evil.

This caused co-workers to form negative opinions of me. This downtown station was infested with many people of that caliber, as well as the U.S. Postal Service as a whole. The station now had a reputation of being the worst postal facility in Colorado. Their deficiency had come to the surface and was being talked about at different postal facilities throughout the city.

A local newspaper in Denver, Colorado received word of this dysfunctional facility and wrote an article about the Denver Police Department's involvement and those conditions of the facility. The story came out in the May 17-23, 1995 edition of Westword magazine. It was entitled, "Pushing the Envelope: Downtown Postal Workers Take a Licking – and Keep on Ticking."

Now that the conditions of this mail facility and the involvement of the Denver Police Department had been made public, both agencies went on the defense. They tried desperately to cover up the leading role they played in the mayhem in the station and to justify their actions. The detective was quoted as saying in the newspaper that "the facility was like elementary school" with the postal service in agreement. Both agencies abused the system and misused their authority to affect the lives of people who did not fit into their circle.

The detective brought the courts into the situation. The U.S. Postal Service used the courts to justify their disciplinary action against my co-workers and me. A pattern was set and followed by the two agencies to build cases that would eventually meet the criteria necessary to remove employees from the agency.

The Westword newspaper displayed the police mug shots of me and my co-worker for the arrests that identified us as perpetrators. Our reputations were dragged through the mud. Gossip spread like wildfire, and that forced the manager of the Downtown Station to release a bulletin in an effort to try and salvage the reputation for them as individuals, the station and the U.S. Postal Service. The bulletin, dated May 18, 1995, was placed in a front glass case for all employees to read, and addressed how a few employees reflected negatively on the downtown station and the postal service as a whole.

It went on to talk about how conflict on the workroom floor was reported to the Denver Police Department instead of supervisors.

What was not mentioned in this bulletin was the fact that upper management including the postmaster and many other agencies within the U.S. Postal Service, such as the EEO and Labor Relations, knew for years that a severe problem existed in this station.

It was brought to their attention on several occasions by certified letters that I had written to upper management and required a return receipt signature. The bulletins failed to mention that the supervisors themselves were calling and had called Detective Rock to the station.

The heat was on. The purpose for the bulletin was to separate management from the team players. It was also orchestrated to misdirect those who knew nothing of the station's history.

25

UNEMPLOYED, BUT PRODUCTIVE

My time outside of the postal service was very productive. I was optimistic about getting my job back and clearing my name. But the thought of returning to work and for that matter setting foot inside of a U.S. Postal facility was frightening. I used this time away from the agency to be as productive as possible and on May 30, 1995 I wrote five different letters. One was a second letter written to the postmaster. The other four were follow-up letters to Det. Rock's office, the NAACP in Baltimore, Maryland, to my Congresswoman, and the last one was to the NAACP in Denver, Colorado.

The letter to the postmaster addressed the false citations to appear in court and the malicious prosecution that I had faced. At that time, each one had been either dismissed or received judgment of acquittal. I demanded a full investigation by his office in this matter.

On June 6, 1995, my attorney filed a "Defendant's Amended Motion for New Trial by Colorado Rules of Criminal Procedures Rule 33" in the March 23 and 24 conviction earlier that year. I worked diligently putting together evidence and the statements of others to present to the EEO. I filed four different EEOs, the nickname employees gave the filings, because of management's participation in the wrongful termination of me.

Unfortunately, each complaint reached the formal stage of investigation and then was denied.

On June 7, 1995, I received correspondence from the postmaster pertaining to my second letter to him on May 30, 1995. The correspondence was vague. He informed me that he was well aware of the downtown station situation. He believed my criminal summons from the Denver Police Department was a civil matter that must be played out in court.

26

THE APPEAL

The appeal for the harassment conviction cost me a total of $8,539.07. Filing for this new trial made a lot of people nervous and desperate, especially those that were directly involved. Suddenly, new evidence began pouring in from each of the alleged victims who perjured themselves on the witness stand in this trial. One accuser wrote six new letters of harassment, accusing me of the intimidation of others in the station. I was acquitted on each of his charges.

The second accuser said that she had a detailed diary that she kept since all of this had been going on and that both the detective and the inspector knew about it. Neither the letters nor the diary was ever presented in either of the two trials. The attorney presented these things as part of their defense for denial in the motion for a new trial. This was a failure to comply with Rule 16 regarding discovery in a court of law. Due to this noncompliance of the law, on June 15, 1995, we filed a "Second Amended Motion for New Trial by Colorado Rules of Criminal Procedure Rule 33 and Request for Sanctions," which was granted.

27

3ᴿᴰ LETTER TO THE POSTMASTER

I continued my pursuit of attention from higher officials in the agency as well as outside of it. On June 23, 1995, for the third time I wrote to the postmaster. The letter was a plea for him to get involved. I informed him of the many false allegations against me by co-workers that had either been dismissed, acquitted or were pending. No response.

June 28, 1995, I wrote to the Mayor's Office for the City and County of Denver in filing a personal injury claim against the detective for malicious prosecution. On Sept. 21, 1995, I received a letter back from Mayor Wellington Webb's office. The letter conveyed that the facts that were revealed failed to support any improper conduct on behalf of the police officer therefore my claim was denied. I would not be deterred. Their response only strengthened my will.

I made an extreme effort to reach out to people of authority in hopes that they would acknowledge my rights as a citizen of the United States and a combat veteran of the Vietnam War, but first and foremost to respect me as a human being. Clearing my name was important but what was just as important was for the people that caused me this enormous amount of pain and suffering to not go unpunished for their part in these horrendous acts.

28

DISMISSED, ACQUITTED OR PENDING

In fall 1995, I hired a private investigator that costs me more than $911.10 by the time their investigation was done. The investigation went on for six months. All of management and their witnesses declined to be interviewed. The detective was interviewed and so were others in his department but at the time they were all suffering from amnesia. They reported that they could not remember what was asked of them. The tide was changing. Most of the charges that had been filed against me and my co-workers had either been dismissed, acquitted or were pending.

A hearing was set for Sept. 26, 1995 for my arrest on April 17, 1995 for the third-class felony, "Intimidating a Witness." The prosecution's witnesses once again were the same old players that were in both trials. They were the same ones who claimed to have witnessed everything that had gone on in the station and who also continued to perjure themselves.

But when questioned by my attorney, their memories seemed to have vacated. The detective was present in every trial that he manipulated through the courts. He had an idea of what the outcome would be because he had no evidence to substantiate any of the citations given to me. However, he continued to try and get me convicted on anything, wasting the courts time and costing me a substantial amount of money to defend myself.

On Oct. 27, 1995, I received a letter of decision for the proposal of removal. It was signed by Ted A. White, manager of customer service operations. Their decision was to remove me from the United States Postal Service on Oct. 28, 1995, disregarding the appeals, acquittals and dismissal to many of the charges this detective had filed in the courts. I was not surprised. I would have been had the decision been different.

If this was their goal from the beginning, it was poorly planned and executed. Now I had a job to do and that was to clear my name and to prove the true thugs were those in positions of trust.

The many trials and hearings were costly. My savings were about depleted. The lawyer fees had me to the point of bankruptcy, so financially I was in serious trouble. Now that the agency had made it a final decision I was no longer being paid from the U.S. Postal Service. The only income was that of my wife, and the bills superseded her income. On Oct. 31, 1995, I filed for unemployment benefits. On Nov. 27, 1995, the State of Colorado Department of Labor and Employment sent a letter of decision to me about that claim. The U.S. Postal Service rejected the claim.

The decision stated that I was, "discharged after threatening to assault another person while on the job." Furthermore, it stated, "the division finds you were responsible for the separation and a disqualification is being imposed." My benefits were deferred for more than two months, and "reduced by the maximum amount permitted by federal law on this claim as well as any future claim filed. The balance on your claim is $272.00."

29

SUMMARY JUDGMENT

This gigantic agency had all the resources to knock me down and keep me down. My co-worker, who was also removed from the agency, had the same up-hill battle to fight. On Nov. 7, 1995, I filed a complaint with the Internal Affairs Bureau of the Denver Police Department.

On Jan. 26, 1996, I received an investigative report from the bureau that stated my complaint had been investigated and that the investigation was thorough and complete. There were numerous witnesses involved in this matter who were interviewed and some misunderstandings were present but the department was unable to find any Denver Police Department procedural violations on the part of this detective. It further stated that if I was not satisfied with this investigation I may request a review by the PSRC (Public Safety Review Commission.)

The same day I requested that review in writing from the PSRC. I expressed my anger to this one-sided investigation. I spoke with nine different co-workers in the station who had concerns about not being interviewed by anyone with the PSRC.

Their report expressed that there were numerous witnesses interviewed. The entire station was involved. Everyone knew what was going on. A key point and a valid one was in the detective's arrest report. He named a person who he said was a witness to the alleged threat that justified my arrest. The person that was named in his report never wrote out a statement. He did not testify to anything and never appeared in any of the many court hearings.

I revealed this vital information with proof to the commission and gave nine different names of those people who were never interviewed in this so-called investigation. On April 9, 1996, I received a letter from the commission in concurrence and in determination with the PSRC of the Denver Police Department. They strongly emphasized that no further action would occur. The evidence was ignored and there was no explanation as to why these people were not interviewed as they said.

I continued to be turned away from agencies that supposedly exist to protect my rights as an American citizen. The evidence I presented was factual but not a factor and did not matter. The intangible demeanor of this government enhanced my fortitude that gave me the will to go on fighting.

My two co-workers and I filed a civil lawsuit against the United States Postal Service on Nov. 9, 1995 for harassment, conspiracy, malicious prosecution, discrimination and unlawful termination. The motions and hearings lasted for six years before going to trial. It involved interviews of witnesses, case law, depositions, and many other judicial procedures. Many motions were rendered throughout the course of these proceedings. Most of the motions were unfavorable for us.

The lawsuit named each individual that was involved on Feb. 23, 1996. These people never had to answer because the U.S. Postal Service included its name as "defendant" instead of the team players of management who were being sued individually. The courts dismissed each one of them and granted the dismissal to each of the claims pertaining to that person that weakened and negated the validity of our claims in the law suit. Anything we brought up to the courts was overruled and our motions to amend the acquittal and the dismissals of the many criminal summons were denied by the courts.

Throughout the trial we would not be permitted to talk about or even bring up issues pertaining to the individuals. It was as though we were on trial in defending the actions that we took for filing this law suit. The courts continued to remove pieces from the lawsuit that began with eight different claims and ended with two, and it got worse.

On Aug. 8, 1998, the detective was granted summary judgment by the court. I learned that this type of motion basically meant that the other side knew that what I alleged was true, but could still win based on the law. In the end, the summary judgment handicapped our entire case. We were not permitted during the trial to mention his name and we were reminded by the judge that if this happens he would declare a mistrial. The nucleus to this entire scheme was the detective who had orchestrated all involvement of the judicial system by abusing his authority.

The Achilles heel was management's inability to police its own agency to enforce the rules and regulations of its government in a fair and unbiased manner. Instead they relied on an outside source in the Denver Police Department and a court system that condoned his criminal action. They did so by approving the motion hearings that maliciously prosecuted innocent people that awarded him the status of judge, jury, and executioner.

The proceedings, the different court appearances, the incarceration and the loss of my job along with many other factors challenged me physically and mentally. My days and nights were filled with hopelessness due to the struggles and let-downs that had me climbing walls. My attorneys expressed their deepest concerns that I was falling into a depressed state and recommended that I have a consultation with a well-known doctor here in Colorado.

After visiting with this doctor, he determined that I should undergo a series of clinical and forensic psychological testing. He conveyed to me some of what he discovered and that it would be to my advantage to participate in a series of tests. I agreed.

I believed that it would provide insight in ways of keeping my feelings in perspective that would encourage a healing process that could possibly start the beginning of the closure of an awfully large wound. The testing consisted of 10 different segments that took an average of three months with two other doctors, including my own, to complete. The test concluded that I was suffering from PTSD (post-traumatic stress disorder) directly caused by my Vietnam War experiences and exacerbated by the events that took place in the United States Postal Service.

The cost of the visits totaled $2,388, an expense I had no idea of how I would pay. My bills continued to mount rapidly. On Nov. 30, 1995, I submitted an appeal for the unemployment division's decision. I had no income whatsoever and my debts went into default. At the time, I was paying child support, which also went into default. In December 1995, a "Notice of Termination of Wage Assignment" by the courts against me was invoked for that support. I needed to find a job before facing incarceration, this time for back child support.

PART FIVE:
1996

30

OUTCAST

The tribulations and pressures continued to mount and I wondered many times who would ever hire me after being fired from a government agency. I believed that any employer who had access to my past would never consider me for hire. My faith was my foundation in the heavens above. My faith gave me the understanding that in life sometimes we may fall but I had a strong belief that if I could look up, I could get up. My wife helped to keep things in order by shouldering the financial burden. During some occasions when I was emergency placed and ordered not to come to work, I would lead my wife to believe I was going to work. I didn't want her to be affected by this toxic environment. I tried hard to keep her out of the post office drama, but my family knew enough.

I began my job search, looking through the newspapers daily, submitting applications, asking around for work, doing odd jobs. I looked for anything to make some money. During those times, I began to sympathize and relate to those who at one time or another had gone through the judicial system. Your entire life was on display. In my case, I was guilty until proven innocent, an outcast to the world. The opportunities were slim to none with most employers if convicted of a crime.

I felt the walls were caving in on me with bills and those bill collectors calling. I was fortunate to have been called on a few job interviews but never lucky enough to land a job from those times. When the employers reviewed my history the one question that was always asked was, "Why did I leave the postal service?" The results were always the same: "Thanks for coming in" and "We will call you." The agency was having an impact on my entire life. I was unable to generate any type of money either through a job or unemployment benefits.

I continued waiting for my unemployment hearing. On Jan. 22, 1996 the hearing took place. Attorneys were called in from the regional office out of San Francisco, California. Again, the detective along with the main player, Chapman, were the U.S. Postal Service's main witnesses in the hearing. My employment attorney, Elizabeth McKendree, and I were present through the entire trial where witnesses were called in one at a time.

The postal service continued to paint me as a deranged bully. During the questioning of the supervisor, 95 percent of what was asked of him he could not and would not answer. He should know and be willing to answer any questions put before him in defense of his actions against me. He informed the hearing officer who was conducting the hearing that I was involved in three separate altercations where I harassed three different individuals.

When asked if he witnessed any of these altercations he replied, "no," but informed the judge that he did an independent investigation of these allegations where he interviewed the alleged victims. When asked did he get my story, his reply was, "no." Management's reaction was always the same anytime when I was accused of anything. "I did it," and there were no questions asked of me.

I was not afforded the opportunity to defend myself or face my accusers. It wasn't until two months after I was discharged in a due process meeting that I was able to give my side of any story. There were many important facts to this case one in particular which could not go unsaid.

The three people that I was accused of harassing, intimidating and even threatening never came in as a witness to testify in the unemployment hearing – the basis to their case to deny me unemployment benefits. After four to five hours of testimony where a few of my witnesses had testified, the judge gave instructions to both sides on when and how his decision will be rendered and if either side disagrees with his findings how an appeal could be asserted. He officially closed the hearing and the waiting game began.

Three days later on Jan. 25, 1996, the decision stated, "It is determined that the claimant is not responsible for the separation from this employment. A full award of benefits is granted...." A week later I received a letter from the courts informing me that I would not be receiving those benefits due to back child support.

On Jan. 30, 1996, the postal service filed an appeal to those awards of unemployment benefits. They must have been passionately obsessed with me. In return, I could be no less with them. I kept standing my ground. And the tide continued to change. That I could see as well as everyone else. The rulings were going in my favor.

The last three months my attorneys continued to answer all briefs of the postal service's appeal. My presence was mandatory in those hearings and very costly for me. I needed some sort of money so I went to an eight-hour agency that provides work daily for eight hours on a first-come first-serve basis. Some days I would work but there were days I wasn't so lucky. Every day was a struggle. I had many reasons to hold my head down but I had many others to keep it up because I had a very strong belief that the sun would shine again.

On April 5, 1996, that sun broke through. The harassment conviction was overturned. The appellant judge expressed his concerns as to why this second person was added to the initial harassment charge shortly before trial. He pointed out that the courts failed to give any limiting instructions and that defense counsel failed adequately to bring up issues required by law and failed entirely to seek a limiting instruction to the jury which undermined the fundamental fairness of the trial. In short, he said many errors were made in the trial.

I respected this decision, but these well-known politically correct phrases were used in a court of law to preserve the sanctity of the courts. I was there through every part of the trial. It was very unfair that I was even on trial from the beginning as well as the trial itself. In the trial, the judge overruled 95 percent of my attorney's objections when he sustained those of the prosecutor.

The U.S. Postal Service counted on the removal of me to hold validity so that a conviction of me through the court of law would justify the termination. The judgment of conviction was reversed and the case was remanded to the county court with instructions that it enter a judgment of acquittal on count two and that it hold a new trial on count one. The entire administrative scheme was taking a turn for the worse for management and the detective. The fabrication of lies that was pushed through the court system by this detective and postal inspector was losing its sting.

The agency had every opportunity to hold a new trial on count one but their credibility was in question. A new trial was never mentioned nor did it ever happen.

Management was so confident that I would never return to the U.S. Postal Service again that the job I once held was put up for bid. All postal personnel knew that anyone who worked for the agency that was put up for removal was considered an employee until they are permanently removed. I had yet to go before an arbitrator in order for the termination to be official.

At most, the job should have temporarily been filled.

31

TECHNICALITIES

Another story came out in the newspaper featuring me and my co-workers in the June 8-12, 1996 issue of Westword. It referred to the court dismissing charges against the two of us, and like the stories in the May issue, 95 percent of it was incorrect. Basically, the story insinuated that technicalities were the reasons for the dismissals. In the May issue they were quick to expose the conviction but at no time in this issue did they mention how the conviction was reversed and that I did go on trial for charges where I was acquitted of both through testimonies, not of technicalities. The slant of the articles planted a seed that ultimately had my reputation on life support.

In October 1996, the lawsuit that my co-workers and I had filed against the U.S. Postal Service began running its course in the U.S. District Court of Colorado. My case was "Garland D. Lewis, et al., v. Marvin Runyon, et al," otherwise known as Civil Action No. 95-N-2838. Depositions were being taken in preparation of the upcoming trial. I attended all of them. Det. Rock's deposition was the first taken on Oct. 14, 1996. His testimony was the same as in every trial, and every hearing that he was a part of including his reports filled with holes, lies and contradictions.

I was present during his deposition where once again he was suffering from a severe case of amnesia. He could not recall pretty much of anything. The inconsistency of his testimony was ridiculous and the lies were unbelievable. He denied ever referring to me as an "asshole." He denied saying how he hated big black men. He stated that the police took a statement from me 40 minutes after their arrival where I reportedly had said in my statement that I did not see a thing. The detective's 165-page deposition was full of inconsistencies, namely he said that I reported to the police officer at the scene that I didn't know or see anything.

Furthermore, the detective went out on a limb and concocted a story that had me making lewd and filthy remarks about a female co-worker's anatomy with another co-worker. It was about her "wet spot," basically where sweat settled at the seating area of her pants. She had allegedly become hysterical because of those comments that were written in his May 9, 1995 police report. In his deposition, the co-worker that I was allegedly talking to denied writing this in his deposition.

Reporters at Westword had read the detective's report and wrote an article about her in a June 6, 1996 edition. She had entered a big butt competition contest held by a local morning radio show. The article ran four months after she reportedly made those allegations against me. She seemed to have regained her composure after entering a contest and coming in third place in the competition, which consisted of a measurement of overhang while sitting on a toilet seat. In this competition, the heat that was generated in the crack of her buttocks was taken with a thermometer. Her apparent emotional recovery to what I supposedly had referred to as her wet spot, along with the lack of evidence, brought on many questions as to her credibility. She was dropped as a witness after the story ran.

32

DEPOSITIONS

There was a total of seven different depositions taken for the trial, including two women and two men for the prosecution's side that accused me of one thing or another. My April 17th arrest on the third-class felony had no relation to the two women. There were important factors in each one of the prosecution's witnesses that provided evidence that I was a target.

One of my accusers was quoted as saying, "I talked to the wrong people because they did not get along with Garland Lewis." Though she lied and went as far as to perjure herself on the witness stand, she was a victim herself caught into a web of a notorious scheme. She was a young lady that just wanted to fit in into a new place with a sense of belonging. She was someone that just wanted a job though it meant her choosing wrong over right.

Her weakness was exposed, abused and taken advantage of by the administration and their team players. Everything she accused me of was built on lies and second-hand information, just to fit in. She also accused me of directly confronting her on a day that I was not even there at the station and which the detective knew. Her deposition was 114 pages long.

The next accuser was an elderly female, who I believed was a devil worshipper with a controlling personality. Her deposition was taken on Oct. 23, 1996 and 133 pages long. For the many criminal acts that she accused me of there was no evidence, no witnesses, no dates or times. If any of these allegations were true and had evidence to back them up, I would have been in the penitentiary.

She talked about how threatening I was to her and others and the intimidating tactics I would use against them that she had witnessed for more than 25 different times in a year. She said I would put explicit sexual material on her desk at work and that I tried to kill her and her husband by running them off the road with my vehicle. She also claimed that I would call her home where she would hear automatic weapons going off in the background which had as much substance as the invisible man. There was no police report of a complaint made by either her or her husband. These were the stories that were told to the detective who submitted them to the prosecutor without any evidence. The prosecutor in turn acted upon this rhetoric about me and used it to prosecute me.

On Oct. 22, 1996 was deposition day for U.S. Postal Service supervisor Reggie Chapman. To say he lied is an understatement. He avoided answering questions to my defense attorneys by either saying, "I am not sure," "I can't remember," or "I don't recall." Altogether he said these three statements more than 150 times.

Before confessing to his bosses that he did in fact assault one of my co-workers, this supervisor had been committed to saying that he didn't in written statements, supervisor's incident report and through depositions. The reason for his lie was that he was afraid to lose his job.

A second deposition of Chapman was ordered and took place on Dec. 10, 1996, two months after his first one. It was more than 50 pages long. In this deposition, he admitted to lying about the assault under oath. At this point, the postal officials and the courts knew that he lied under oath and had perjured himself on the witness stand by giving false information to a police officer. He never faced perjury charges. The detective didn't charge this supervisor with giving false information to a police officer as he had charged my co-worker. He did not lose his job or go to jail.

This one lie that he held onto for years imprisoned two people under false pretenses. It cost me my job where I could not fulfill my obligations to my family. It portrayed me as a criminal and cost me close to $100,000 in court costs over an eight-year period. Why was this supervisor able to break the law and suffer no penalties under the law? He put me in for emergency placement four different times and was asked in detail in his deposition as to the many emergency placements and what constituted this drastic action.

There was no merit to his credibility. The grievance process had found him at fault in those emergency placements, and for each one I was paid for time missed. Still he continued to cost the U.S. Postal Service money where they continued to support his assault of me.

Had it not been for this lawsuit he would have taken this and many other lies that he had told to his grave. The depositions were a lengthy process that took quite a few months to complete. I was still unemployed at this time, fighting to right the wrongs that were done to me. It was a draining process, but I continued to walk in my faith.

On Dec. 30, 1996, I received a letter from the APWU notifying me of the upcoming arbitration trial in the removal of my job. It was scheduled for Jan. 16, 1997. The news was exciting for three reasons. First and foremost, I wanted my name cleared. I wanted my job back. I wanted the people that caused me so much pain and grief to feel the hurt that I had felt for years. They should not live their lives going unpunished for their participation in these criminal acts.

I had absolutely nothing to hide, and was relieved to face my accusers in a setting completely different from a court trial where we would be face-to-face. My union steward and I were optimistic about the arbitration hearing. We both were more than ready to present our case to the arbitrator. We had worked on it from the time I was removed up until now. We at this point had additional information such as the results of the court hearings, trials, the unemployment hearings and depositions. I hoped that the arbitrator would exonerate me and find me not at fault.

Almost everyone at the downtown station was aware of the upcoming arbitration hearing. Those who were involved were now feeling the pressure because they knew the truth and the reason why I had been cleared of everything else. An acquittal would mean the reinstatement of my job.

33

RESTRAINING ORDER

On Jan. 10, 1997, just six days before the arbitration hearing a restraining order was filed against me in the municipal courts by one of management's team players and a witness to everything. At that point, she had lost every case that she had filed against me and my co-workers. The restraining order addressed what I had been acquitted of in a court of law and exactly what was in her deposition where she had no witnesses, no proof or any type of evidence then or at this point of these series of allegations.

Even though I had been acquitted of everything, on Jan. 23, 1997 the case went before Lawrence Manzanares, the magistrate who granted the restraining order. This was not a coincidence. Anytime I was acquitted or found not guilty of one case, something else was filed against me, just like this restraining order. The intent of this order was to deny my presence at my arbitration hearing because she would be there as a witness for the U.S. Postal Service. If I entered the facility I would be in violation of a court order by being near her.

By law the arbitration hearing took precedence over the restraining order, and on Jan. 16, 1997, the arbitration went forward. The hearing started in February and went into May. On Feb. 7, 1997 my attorney and I filed for a new hearing in the restraining order case at a cost to me of $589.02.

I was constantly in court defending myself against lies.

After 16 months of unemployment, something good happened. I applied with a charter bus company that gave me a chance at a tour driver position. On the day that I applied for the position I asked the receptionist if I could speak with the manager about my background. She asked if I would have a seat and she would contact the operation officer. That day, I was given the opportunity to explain why I was fired from my job. I was candid and held absolutely nothing back.

That following week I was hired. I was grateful and happy to feel like a part of society once again. Not only for myself but to show my gratitude to the company for giving me a chance to reestablish myself and possibly a new beginning, but mainly for not passing judgment on me. The company was outstanding, and after five months on the job I received a letter of appreciation from the assistance operations manager commending me for a job well done. I was held in highest of standards with the company.

My job afforded me the financial latitude to attend the arbitration hearings. Final arguments were scheduled to end on May 16, 1997. The arbitrator's decision would be rendered by June 30, 1997. The summary award stated, "Grievant's emergency placement on off-duty status was not proper. Grievant's removal was not for just cause. Grievant shall be reinstated and made whole."

Through the entire arbitration, management pointed fingers as the factual evidence revealed the real stories of those that were never told. They were the nucleus to the many problems that were revealed in depositions, court hearings and through that confession of their supervisor. My accusers' stories, dates and times did not match up. Amnesia was working overtime.

The arbitrator took grave exception to the fact that management ignored the many complaints that I had brought to their attention. He wanted to know why I was arrested in the beginning.

Procedures should be followed for all terminations. It is a process through the chain of command, involving several people. In this case, the supervisors D-2 Form was signed by the district manager on May 9, 1995 and the area manager on May 21, 1995. By signing, they indicated that they had made a respectful review and concurred with the supervisor request.

The area manager did not testify in the arbitration hearing so there was no evidence of what he reviewed. The district manager's review was unclear and his testimony was vague and made no sense. He made no independent investigation and made his decision solely by relying on the D-2 and the inspector's memorandum report.

When asked about certain subjects pertaining to the D-2 Form he did not recall but "imagined" that he had read it at the time. After both managers signed the request the proposed removal went into effect.

After they signed, I was given 10 days to contact the district manager to set up a meeting where my side of the story would be heard, I was given from June 23, 1995 to July 3, 1995. During that time, the district manager was conveniently unavailable. This jeopardized the 10 days and a forfeiture of my rights. I was told by his office to wait for his return which was not acceptable as well as obstruction of justice. I immediately insisted on a meeting with someone of his equal in fear of the 10-day expiration date.

I was granted that meeting which was scheduled for June 29, 1995 with his replacement. As with the arbitration, this was my opportunity to not only disclose the incident on April 6, 1995, but also the important facts to prove my innocence and a show that I was a victim of management's abuse. I provided concrete evidence that the agency had targeted me, including my letters to the postmaster asking for his involvement that dated back as far as two years, all acquittals and dismissals, and even the unemployment hearing where I was found not at fault.

Despite my efforts, upon the district manager's return, he moved forward with my removal effective Oct. 28, 1995. His reason was that I did not respond to the 10-day letter and that I provided no evidence to convert the charges against me. He went on to say his decision was based on the IM and information obtained by his replacement who had met with me in his absence. He could not remember if his replacement gave him any documents.

The arbitrator's findings were like what my union steward and I discovered after researching and reading through an enormous amount of material such as personal statements, supervisor D-2 Forms, detective reports and the IM, etc.

The supervisor's concerns were not sufficient to act upon his suspicions and their actions are proven to be self-evident after the supervisor disclosed his reasoning for the emergency placement of me on April 17, 1995 after basing his decision upon relying on the IM when the IM wasn't transmitted until April 20, 1995. For these reasons, the arbitrator found and concluded that the emergency placement of me was both procedurally and substantially improper.

One of the most telling factors was when this alleged threat supposedly had taken place yet this person did not report this until an hour later and the supervisor did not report it until six hours later April 6, 1995. The investigation did not take place by this detective until four days later April 10, 1995. The arrest warrant wasn't obtained until two days later on April 12, 1995, and it was not served until five days later on April 17, 1995. Weighing the sequence of events, the arbitrator had to determine if there was imminent danger and if a real threat occurred.

The arbitrator noted that management did not have an obligation to conduct an independent investigation as required by the collective bargaining agreement where the arrest of me was not convincing evidence of guilt. The lack of an investigation and the lack of due process contributed to management's inability to prove the charges by even a preponderance of evidence let alone a higher standard.

The arbitrator expressed his sincere concerns with the supervisor's so-called due process of me that lacked any semblance or substance whatsoever and, was a denial of due process. Throughout this entire process I had expressed my concerns through a variety of requests to management and all officials to face my accusers. I was denied each time.

PART SIX:

1997-1999

34

REINSTATED, EVENTUALLY

The arbitrator strongly expressed that it was essential that I be informed in reasonable detail of what I was accused of and afforded an opportunity to confront my accuser. On June 30, 1997 judgment was granted in my favor. I was reinstated to my job. The ruling indicated that my emergency placement on off-duty status was not proper and the removal was not for just cause. I was also made whole with respect to wages, sick leave, annual leave, over time and time in service.

Management's all-out effort to sell their story of a deranged and dangerous individual and to place a criminal jacket on me did not prevail. What was revealed was an agency that violated rules and regulations that had broken many laws as far up as the postmaster's office.

I was overcome with relief of the arbitrator's decision. For years I carried that burden of uncertainty, unable to enjoy life pleasures because my life remained on hold, the effects were unnatural. This relentless attack of me over the years contributed to a declining of my health and exacerbated my pre-existing condition of PTSD. I witnessed the extreme depth that this agency and its people acted upon and the intensity of hatred from many that I didn't even know and the injustice of a judicial system that I put my life on the line for as a combat veteran in the United States Navy.

I faced a new challenge moving forward. I had to return to a place where I had been labeled an outcast, but planned to retire. I expected my employment there was going to be a bitch. I had no choice. I needed and wanted to provide for my family and it was the only career available to me at the time.

Weeks had gone by after the arbitrator's decision and I had yet to hear from the U.S. Postal Service informing me of the effective date to return to work. I could feel it. Something was wrong.

The arbitration ruling was issued on June 30, 1997 to return me to work. The agency waited more than three weeks on July 19, 1997 until the restraining order was imposed and went into effect on that date. The U.S. Postal Service had no intentions of honoring the arbitrator's decision until that order was imposed. This would be an unlawful order that prohibited me from entering the postal service building at the downtown station.

On July 25, 1997, the APWU president wrote the national president expressing his concerns about my return to work. He requested authorization to sue the United States Postal Service on July 31, 1997. The authorization was granted. The senior labor relations specialist for the U.S. Postal Service was notified of the lawsuit.

They used the restraining order as justification for why I had not yet been returned to duty. On Aug. 13, 1997, my attorney filed for a new hearing to modify or dissolve the restraining order. He argued the point repeatedly with the magistrate that grounds for this restraining order surrounded alleged behavior, and provided the magistrate with the arbitrator's ruling.

No surprise. No proof was necessary to convict me. I still had faith in the judicial system to a degree but evidence showed that there were people in the system that truly made a mockery out of the constitution and that racism has its place within its walls.

On Aug. 18, 1997, nearly two months after the reinstatement of my job, I had yet to return to work. I received a letter on that day from the union president informing me about the postal services' concerns about the restraining order and their reason for not bringing me back. He also reported that the union attorney had notified the postal service that since they were not a party to the restraining order they could not use it as a basis to deny offering me the opportunity to return to work. This denial showed motive and gave reason for the order all along.

After this discussion and after my attorneys recited what the law states, the postal service was willing to implement the arbitrator's award by allowing me to return to work at a duty station other than the downtown station. This did not follow the guidelines of the arbitrator's decision to make me whole as to alter my duty station. Their arrogance infuriated me. They did not want to follow the order and they wanted my experience with them to follow me to the end of my career.

I wrote to the union of my concerns that I believed it would put me in harm's way and would reestablish management's position but the union believed that if I would out right refuse to accept their offer it could eventually result in relieving the postal service of any further obligation for back pay. In other words, I had no choice in the matter. I accepted their offer and was returned to work at a different location in mid-September 1997.

The agreement between management and the union was that I would be placed in this temporary duty assignment for a period of 120 days and I would make a reasonable good-faith effort to obtain permanent duty assignment like my current permanent duty assignment in a work location other than the downtown station.

The agreement letter was dated Oct. 10, 1997. I had been acquitted, found not guilty and not at fault on all charges. Still I was forced out of my job and was required to work in a different facility to keep my employment in the United States Postal Service.

On Sept. 23, 1997, I was back in the municipal courts with a "Notice of Hearing on Defendant's Motion to Dissolve or Modify Permanent Restraining Order." Second to the conviction it was a very unfair and brutal hearing. It was a repeat of the lies and deceit everything that I had already been acquitted of. What was most important of this hearing was that this restraining order was not filed until a year and a half after I was fired from the U.S. Postal Service and weeks before the arbitration hearing.

My accuser's testimony in this hearing was so theatrical and bizarre. Her attorney's desperate attempt to convince the magistrate into making the restraining order permanent was just as theatrical. He informed the magistrate that because of the seriousness of the devastating effects of the alleged crimes to his client that the U.S. attorney for the postal service contacted him to talk about a monetary settlement of the case with his client.

The U.S. attorney was at the hearing and denied any settlement offer for her pain and suffering. Her attorney Joe Rogers said it was a decision about the procedures as engaged by the post office with respect to the firing of me. Part of this statement was true where management did violate my rights and did not follow rules or procedures, but what the attorney failed to tell the courts was that the arbitrator found his client not to be credible in her testimony and relative to the question of safety there was no credible evidence that I ever engaged in violent conduct such as might give rise to a reasonable concern of immediate danger.

This court failed to understand the arbitrator's reasons for his decision. Sadly, the magistrate refused to embrace the concept that the stories about me simply were not true. The restraining order was modified to 15 feet of contact distance.

By this time, I had now been in the U.S. Postal Service for 17 years. I was well seasoned and had gone through many trials and tribulations that would have challenged anyone's breaking point. I took absolutely nothing for granted and trusted few. I do not know to what degree other employees experienced maltreatment. I do know some killed themselves and others. Some were fired and never to been seen again on the premises, and there were those that were incarcerated.

Going postal is considered an alternative because there is no place to go for help.

Instead, I chose to fight for my rights. I chose to write about it.

I was at this point in a different facility. I was not comfortable. I understood that I was under a microscope and I could no longer have a positive attitude as I did going into the downtown station. Still the concept was the same, not to make myself vulnerable under any circumstances. I did what I was told and when I was told. I went to work every day on time. I just wanted to be left alone and finish my career in the agency.

On Dec.12, 1997, the union received a letter from management accusing me of not making a good-faith effort to obtain a permanent duty assignment. It was a sign of things to come, again. I had been under a microscope 14 of the 17 years in this agency at this point. I provided proof of three different jobs that I had bid on -- Oct. 7, 1997 and two other jobs on Dec. 30, 1997 and on Jan. 27, 1998. I also bid on two other jobs none of which I was the successful bidder.

35

A GOOD DAY TO DIE

I had read many different stories throughout the years of postal facilities across the country where this mentality and behavior exists.

A former employee in the mail processing plant in Portland, Oregon was awarded more than $1 million after being discriminated against and harassed. The supervisors were aware of the harassment which she complained and brought to the attention of the manager. There are thousands of cases like this in this agency where accountability, arrogance and the lack of leadership more than often is the reason why these things occur.

On Dec. 24, 1997, David Jackson, a mail handler, at the general mail facility in Denver, Colorado threatened the lives of seven postal workers when he took them hostage while gunning for two of his supervisors. Jackson stated that he needed help but could not trust anyone. He was fired after fighting with a supervisor. His intentions were serious and extremely dangerous targeting two supervisors, Tony Albert and Richard Sandoval. Reportedly he was armed with a 12-gauge shotgun, a 9mm tech, 9 pistols, a 38 caliber two shot Derringer, a large hunting knife, brass knuckles and body armor. The article also said he had 41 rounds of 38-caliber ammunition and 16 to 12-gauge shotgun shells. I personally knew this guy.

Jackson and I started our careers with the U.S. Postal Service around the same time. I found him to be a very quiet and well-mannered individual.

He lost hope and expressed his trust for no one. According to the article, he was driven to the point of using cocaine, liquor and marijuana in making his final decision to die. It ended when he surrendered with no one hurt. He told investigators that he could not live with the fact that he lost his job and he thought Christmas Eve would be a good day to die. He received a lengthy prison sentence.

I fought against being this kind of statistic for many years in this agency. My perseverance provided me with the fortitude but most of all my faith in "God," who blessed me to want to tell the most accurate and honest story possible of the truth behind going postal. Seeing his story on the news and reading more about it in the newspapers – the similarities to my own story were astonishing.

On Jan. 3, 1998 a story came out in the Rocky Mountain News about the hostage situation where postal workers requested that Jackson's boss be reassigned. More than 100 signatures were obtained at the time. They were expecting up to 250 maybe 300 signatures because employees were in fear of jeopardizing their safety. The president of the Local 321 of the mail handler's union said they've had a lot of problems with those two supervisors.

It shed some light on upper management's involvement and brought clarity to them about taking charge of a potentially hazardous situation. One of those supervisors whose history was very disturbing because of his erratic behavior was known by his superiors and well documented. He was the same person that I talked about earlier who caused plenty of pain and hardship in many lives in the registry unit for several years, mine.

Their behavior had gone on uncontested for many years. The U.S. Postal Service, through upper management, had allowed it to fester and reach a point where people were hunted like animals to be gunned down.

The next day, Sunday, Jan. 4, 1998, another story ran in the Rocky Mountain News. Thousands of grievances were filed yearly according to the article, "Postal Grievances are Filed One for Every Two Workers." The grievances spanned a wide range of complaints from working conditions to overtime to on-the-job injuries and suspensions. The article also reported that the president of the APWU said that employees believed the grievances procedure was the only way to be treated in a dignified manner by managers.

Questionable.

36

PERSISTENCE

In my experience with the agency, they have always needed persistent persuasion, through the grievance process and legal action, to do what was ethical and what was right.

37

INTEGRITY AT ITS BEST

Management checked on me quite frequently whether it was through the union or personal visits periodically at the station by upper management staff. Each time was a disappointment to those managers because I wasn't having any problems.

On Jan. 27, 1998, I received a letter from upper management ordering me to report back to the downtown station at 4a.m. on Feb. 7, 1998. I was accused of not conforming to the agreement. The proof that I had provided was ignored. I contacted the union the very next day where they talked with the area manager the same day expressing their concerns about having me return to the downtown station with a restraining order.

My union steward and I were convinced that management's intention was to set me up knowing that the order was filed for a specific reason in the first place, for preventing me from doing my job and for the arrest of me made easily accessible. I had no concept of how I would protect myself.

I decided to file a restraining order to prevent the staging of a violation to the 15-feet order if I was to return to the downtown station. I requested a special session with the magistrate to explain my reasoning for requesting this restraining order, which in his opinion was not valid, therefore he did not grant the order. The pressure and anxiety mounted as the time grew nearer for my return to the station. Flashbacks of those troubled times being paraded in handcuffs from one end of the building to the other had a serious effect on me. I had no choice. If I did not follow the order I would be terminated for failure to follow a direct order.

I told Ott, my criminal attorney. He was amazed by their actions and characterized them as unbelievable. I had never seen this reaction from him before. On Feb. 4, 1998, he entered his sworn affidavit into the courts about what he heard after the restraining order hearing to dissolve or modify the order. While in the hallway on Sept. 23, 1997, he heard a discussion by Michael Hegarty, the assistant U.S. attorney; Marsha Boyle, the labor relations specialists for the U.S. Postal Service; and Sharon Hill, manager of the downtown station.

The three were discussing the ruling in the hallway just outside the courtroom in the presence of my attorney. The labor specialist was speaking to the U.S. attorney when she said that she felt the ruling of the 15-feet restriction was beneficial to the U.S. Postal Service. She said it would allow them to fire me. She went on to explain to him how my job assignment would place me next to the person who filed the order and that I would necessarily be in violation of the restraining order.

She expected that this individual would immediately call the police to report a violation of the order and I would be removed from my station by the police and she could then fire me for not being at my workstation.

The U.S. attorney agreed that this was the way to fire me and noted that he could say that he tried to prevent this from happening by requesting the courts not to place a 15-feet distant requirement as part of the order. The labor specialist laughed at this and said that she was certain this was a perfect opportunity to fire me.

My attorney expressed his concerns and said to her that he thought she was being unreasonable and suggested that she consider alternatives such as reassigning me within the station but she refused. He then suggested that she allowed me time to bid out of the station to a different facility and work with the union to accomplish this. She refused that also. She and the U.S. attorney exclaimed with delight with the outcome.

She stated to him that her intention was to keep me in the station so I would be arrested and fired. Once again, my attorney asked her to reconsider and at the least allow me to bid out of the station and that I had already indicated that I would bid out. She refused while laughing. The U.S. attorney then advised her not to speak with my attorney any longer.

These were government officials who we the people put our trust and faith in to ensure that we are protected under the laws and the U.S. Constitution. To apply the laws with fairness and with the utmost dignity these were people with authority who abused it. My attorney, a prominent lawyer in the state of Colorado, whose dad was an attorney himself and a former judge, for him to sign his name on a sworn affidavit not only earn my highest respect but my sincere gratitude.

It is not every day that a person of his stature would put the family name on a public notice that could possibly jeopardize his career. As far as I was concerned it was integrity at its best.

He knew of this occurrence back in September 1997 at the recent restraining order modification but filed the affidavit five months later in February 1998. I could only imagine the empathy that he had for me in doing so after going to a series of hearings and trials in my defense. He knew in his heart that I was innocent and the U.S. Postal Service would stop at nothing.

The information in this affidavit was given to the courts and all agencies involved, and it was never disputed. I was not surprised by the content of this affidavit. I was intimidated, but knew that I could not give up looking for a solution. On Feb. 4, 1998, I wrote to the postmaster, Mike Flores, about this planned attack on me and efforts to have me arrested. I explained that it would be an injustice to return me to the downtown station, and by knowing this information that he would be a part of this plan as well.

I enclosed a copy of my attorney's sworn affidavit identifying him with the particulars. I received a letter, dated Feb. 5, 1998, in return from the postmaster giving me the permission to remain in my detail assignment for an extra 30 days. He suggested that I continue to bid for jobs outside of the downtown station where I would be returned on March 7, 1998.

He informed me that there were no guarantees that I would be extended any longer.

38

WALKING ON EGGSHELLS

The postmaster visited me at this temporary station just before I was to return to the downtown station. He reassured me that he would be more involved and he was well aware of labor's plan to have me arrested. Still this had no impact on my return. Some were not receptive to me coming back. Others embraced my return. There were many new faces that I had never seen before and most would have absolutely nothing to do with me. There were those who knew me that would now only talk with me if a supervisor wasn't present.

An unusual coincidence occurred upon my return. Ironically the person that filed the restraining order was no longer there at the station; she had been detailed days prior to my return. Much emphasis was put on leaving me on a detail assignment and by not doing that disrupted a perfect solution to a difficult situation but the motive was clear. The detailing of this individual did not occur until after the postmaster was informed and given a copy of this sworn affidavit that incriminated his colleagues and made it necessary to make an adjustment.

This drastic and sudden change of plan to remove this individual had to happen in order to protect those officials and not to reveal their obvious motive for placing me in the station. The agency's obsession with me proved to be top priority when the labor relations specialists and the US attorney's uncontrollable emotions gave reason to management plans being altered.

The two lost control at a crucial time compromising the agency position by complementing one another on their devious intentions and expressing their joy in the presence of my attorney to commit a crime by having me arrested. If the arrest of me had taken place the preponderance of evidence had now been established to suggest a conspiracy theory.

They removed me from the detail assignment that was working but where management portrayed it as such a problem to keep me there in order to put me in harm way. But the circumstances they now faced allowed them to overlook the detailing of assignments that was now given to my opposition.

My victories did not stop the U.S. Postal Service from attacking me and violating my human rights. They certainly did not apologize.

A Denver Post article was published on Dec. 22, 1998 about the hostage situation in December 1997 where a former employee took seven hostages. It reported that the seven hostages were suing the U.S. Postal Service for failing to protect them by ignoring threats and for breaches in the agencies security system. Other discrepancies were named but there was one that stood out. The suit stated that the U.S. Postal Service failed to heed complaints from two supervisors who were threatened by this co-worker who came after them because they were Hispanic. There was absolutely no truth of an act of racism whatsoever on the part of the hostage taker.

Though violence was not a justifiable means, human nature has its place when survival is at issue with no foreseeable recourse. His livelihood was taken away from him and his family at the hands of the two well-known troubled supervisors. It was standard practice of this agency to target African Americans. I saw it and experienced it.

I was harassed and targeted many times by one of these same supervisors, the very same individual the hostage taker went after to kill. To use racism as a motive on the part of this individual was absurd. The hostage situation and crisis in the U.S. Postal Service could have been prevented if accountability was part of the criteria in the agency.

With 18 years in the agency, I had no doubt the postal service was a dangerous place to work for people who stood up for their rights and walked with their heads held high. Not for one moment did I believe that I would ever be left alone. At the age of 42, I had 13 years to go before I would reach the retirement age of 55. In combination with my military service, I needed to give them just less than six years to retire with maximum benefits where I could collect 80 percent of my salary. The maximum benefit could only be achieved at 41 years and 11 months.

The station hadn't changed since my return. Hatred and confusion plagued the facility. I remained incognito with the few new supervisors and other new faces in the building that of course had formed their own opinion of me after hearing of the station history. I did the same as in each different facility that I had been shifted to over the years. I stayed to myself. I went to work on time and did my job.

Through the months there were many challenges. I relived the same discrepancies with some new players along with the old but the results were the same. By the 11th month, after close to three years away from the facility, history did repeat itself.

Management began calling me into the office giving me superfluous warnings and outrageous reasons claiming that they had been getting reports from my co-workers that I had been staring at them with intimidating looks or made threatening gestures.

These alleged violations went on for quite some time. I requested that management put them in writing every time I was called into the office and accused of something. Doing so would lead to me making a request for a face-to-face with my accusers to challenging their accusations. They also knew I had no problem filing the paperwork that would ensue. They did not put any in writing.

As I had in the past I continued to document everything in every sense of the word and I took full advantage of the postmaster's promise to me that he would be more involved. On Feb. 2, 1999, I wrote to the postmaster, in confidence, expressing my concerns of this chaotic environment and how I continued to be called into the supervisor's office on a weekly basis. I named names in the letter and asked for his immediate attention in the matter.

I received a letter, dated Feb. 11, 1999 from him –and copying Hill, manager of the downtown station – confirming receipt of my letter. It was revealed to the employees. I knew because my co-workers were making comments about the contents of the letters.

Comments were being made on the work room floor, stories embellished with lies and rumors regarding the letter, which was of no concern to me. It was documentation for my protection that management chose to release. The results also led to people confronting me where I had no problem in defending myself.

I had words with an employee on the work room one day and she wasted no time going into the supervisor's office. About five minutes after she had gone into the office, four different supervisors came out and approached me inquiring about the confrontation.

On April 2, 1999, I was referred to EAP to be evaluated for my participation in the matter. Confirmation from the grievance that I had filed show she was never referred for her participation. Libby Saracino, who referred me in retaliation, was the same supervisor named in my letter to the postmaster.

The EAP office provided a questionnaire for management to answer, specifically about measures, if any, that were taken to address these issues and identify the problem. Their response was that they had personal discussions with me over the last four months, which was not accurate. These discussions, which were accusations and allegations, were held on a weekly basis over a year and attacked my character. I, in fact, defended myself from the rhetoric every time.

Four years had gone by since I was put in for removal and it had been three and a half from when I was removed. Still, little to no involvement from the postmaster.

On May 6, 1999, I wrote to the postal inspector in charge after a lengthy conversation with him on April 26, 1999 about the conditions in the facility and of the postmaster's promise to be more actively involved with the station. It was important that I had the attention of someone or anyone that could possibly change the course of action and stop what was going on in the station.

Through the grueling years in this agency I had learned that documentation was invaluable. Though I had this proof, at no time did I ever believe that the information would have an impact or change the dynamics of the station. My situation was unique. It had one purpose and that was to remove me from the United States Postal Service.

39

DOCUMENTATION

The documentation that I had been collecting over the years served a very special purpose, to provide proof and show the necessary evidence to prove the facts in my story.

I never talked to or heard from the postal inspector after our conversation. That was okay because the letter that was written to him served its purpose to obtain a signature from his office that confirmed we had talked over the telephone and that the information was received and signed. I had no expectations of the agency and not hearing from his office was nothing short of the norm.

Documentation was necessary to offset the opposition because in every case I learned that it was what you could prove. I was always able to prove anything I would say when filing a complaint.

After about one month I still hadn't heard from this inspector or his office. I had given him a reasonable amount of time to respond by not making any hasty decision or reacting in a spontaneous manner by pursuing the matter with other entities or agencies. There were no signs that there was ever an investigation nor even an inclination that an inquiry was made of the situation at the station.

The station's history was not a mystery. It had been involved in the judicial system on many occasions and have been in the newspaper several times. Documentation was not lacking. The issue was that the administrative scheme was concealed within the confinement of the U.S. Postal Service were the information went no further than the inspector and the detective in the Denver Police Department. It was all about impeding justice. It was an issue that could not go unchallenged and at any costs I sincerely wanted to prevent what happened to me in the past when I was falsely imprisoned and terminated from my job.

The only thing that was left for me to do was to go outside of the agency by getting the attention of human rights organizations involving civil rights leaders and other agencies that had no affiliation with the U.S. Postal Service or the Denver Police Department. I began to write to different organizations during the time that I was waiting to hear from the postal inspector.

On June 1, 1999, I wrote and mailed letters to four different agencies including, the NAACP, Baltimore Maryland; the African American Male National Council, Columbus Ohio; the local NAACP in Denver Colorado; and the Colorado Civil Rights Commission. Each letter was by certified return receipt mail. After a week only two receipts were returned to me.

The only letter that I received about my own was on June 9, 1999 from the NAACP in Baltimore informing me that they were unable to offer any legal assistance in the matter and because of the scarcity of its resources maintains strict case acceptance guidelines. Along with the letter was a list of attorneys that maybe I could contact. The remaining agencies did not write back.

Their lack of response or decision to not be involved was not a deterrent. The letters with certified return receipts were documentation that people outside of the agency knew about this vicious cycle through detailed information in the letters that I had sent to them that revealed some of what was going on, not only in the station but throughout the agency and the names of those that contributed to my reasons for writing the letters.

I would continue to collect documentation until I was no longer hunted down by co-workers and managers or was no longer with the agency. Documentation was the key to beating all odds and for my protection.

Around this time something had triggered management to turn up the heat on me. More co-workers were accusing me of intimidating and threatening them. On Dec. 9, 1999, I again wrote Flores, the postmaster. It was eight months after my last letter to him. This letter was intended to get some rhyme or reason as to why he was not more involved. I also reminded him of his promise to be more actively involved.

It had been very coincidental that from the time I reported to the downtown station in December 1989 up until this present time, December 1999, the station experienced four different changes of managers. Each one had the same agenda and that was to get rid of me.

I took it that he looked at this entire situation to be a soap opera but it was my livelihood and sanity that was in jeopardy. I received the certified return receipt signed by his office confirming delivery of the letter. No response.

I knew that I had to continue to write to any and every source possible to proclaim my innocence and not allow anyone to slip a criminal jacket on me. On Dec.14, 1999, I wrote to Hill, the station manager, to verify the many one-on-one conversations that we have had regarding the ongoing situation in the station and to confirm their awareness. I asked for her immediate response, but it was the same as with the postmaster. No response.

I was the one that was seeking a resolution to the problems in the station. The managers in the station and upper management had no interests in any sort of solution because they were the perpetrators and the creators that continued to fuel this dysfunctional environment. Their obsession to get rid of me was passed from one manager to the next. The facts showed and the evidence was clear that every manager accused me of something and had taken disciplinary action against me at one point or another.

PART SEVEN:

2000-2004

40

RUTHLESS

By the year 2000, I had been back in the station after my termination from the agency for a little over two years. Looking back on everything that I had faced in the U.S. Postal Service, from the many legal proceedings, trials, the arbitration, and the false imprisonment, I was convinced it was a group effort. I sincerely believed that I would never be bothered again after proving my innocence in each case, but in all actuality, it was the beginning of my second phase of being tortured in the United States Postal Service.

I was stalked, hunted down and targeted. My cry for help was ignored by management in the station, those in upper management of the U.S. Postal Service, and now agencies outside. It was clear that the perpetrators were the same people in the agency who I was asking for help. This attack was ruthless and more so than before because vengeance was eating away at them.

They had failed to remove me and make it stick the first time. Their approach was identical to last time to discredit me so I would be perceived by new employees as this psychotic individual. They wanted to pressure me to a breaking point where I would commit myself by displaying anger and react in a violent manner.

My tolerance level was tested each day. I was accused of taking long breaks, not doing my job, not following directions, reporting late for work and leaving work early. My reporting time continued to change when others did not. They would do anything to inconvenience me and cause undue stress.

As a target in this agency I was exposed to and experienced life-changing situations that not only challenged my will but tested my better judgment and fortitude. I was not only watched by management daily but their team players as well. They were their eyes and ears, and would make up and embellish stories for a pat on the back. They were insecure people that depended on and needed each other's validation to function and management's approval to feel like they were somebody.

I ignored many things that were being said about me and turned my head away from potential conflicts. I was not going to be set up. My belief in "God Almighty" and the perseverance that he blessed me with took precedence over all matters and I refused to let management win. I was called a crybaby for the many times I went into my supervisor's office to report what was being said about me on the work room floor.

I was not intimidated and didn't have the slightest fear of the cowards that continued to challenge me. I knew I had to make these reports because there was a game that was being played and the traps were set.

On Jan. 7, 2000, I left work early. The stress was getting to me. It was a very uncomfortable situation where I was feeling skittish not knowing what I would face daily. I was mad all day, every day. I wanted it to have been well known and documented in its entirety that it was one of many reasons why I continued to report behavior towards me by management and co-workers. I had beaten management and their team players at their game in the past and I didn't believe I could go through that sort of torture again.

I was tired. Everyone has a limit and I felt that day that my limit had expired, so I removed myself from this toxic environment. The stress had reached a point that elevated my blood pressure where I could have easily gotten physical and the violence could have had turned deadly. I went to the hospital where I was treated for hypertension and upon my arrival my blood pressure was at a dangerous stage for a couple of hours where I could have easily suffered a stroke after spending three to four hours there. I was released later that day, and did not return to work until three and a half weeks later.

I filed a complaint with the EEO office after being forced to leave work because of management's refusal to leave me alone while encouraging my co-workers to do the same by provoking me into different situations so they would be justified in taking disciplinary action against me. It was one of the oldest tricks in the agency. While supervisors will swear that they have never encouraged or said to any employee to deliberately go out and harass another worker. Actions speak louder than words.

There are many ways – greed and materialistic desires – to encourage and condone the actions of workers that display this type of behavior.

But getting to why these things happen would take a sincere investigation. It would take honest people, those of integrity to dig deep into the heart of the matter and expose the truth. If there was something being done to correct and imprison those who violated the law, this behavior would not have continued to be as prevalent.

People have resorted to violence for a reason. They went gunning for not only supervisors, but those employees that aided management into making their lives miserable.

41

MARTYRS AND INNOCENT BYSTANDERS

I did not condone the killing of anyone. I sincerely believed that the public never got the real story or heard the true facts about why people who were gunned down were more than likely referred to as innocent bystanders. Not everyone gunned down was innocent. Not everyone was a martyr in a massacre.

True. Many people work in the large areas that are congested throughout the facilities where there could possibly be innocent bystanders. But when something unfortunate as a shooting happens these targets were planned and laid out for specific individuals. To block someone's pursuit of happiness could have deadly results.

So much could be avoided if accountability, essential in a civilized society, was the number one priority for the U.S. Postal Service. That should be the real concern instead of false advertisement of resources and the different entities within the agency that claim to protect the rights of employees. It was a myth that simply had no grounds to stand on, especially when less than one percent of EEOs filed in this agency were deemed in favor of the complainant.

42

100 PERCENT RIGHT

From 1983 to 2000 I had been forced to file more than 20 EEO complaints where not a single one had been deemed in my favor. As far as the agency was concerned the U.S. Postal Service was one 100 percent right in each of those complaints. There was not a single EEO filed by me that was a frivolous complaint.

I followed protocol in describing the occurrences and gave precise detail of those occurrences, showing that I was treated differently from all others and without a doubt was a victim of discrimination. I went beyond description by providing the proof of evidence and what I believed to be necessary documentation, some of which was legal documentation to prove my allegations.

That consisted of dates, times, court documents, health records, and personal statements that showed a preponderance of evidence that the complaints were not fictitious. This office's concerns were focused on technicalities that would prohibit the advancement of a complaint to move forward.

Many complaints that I had filed were dismissed after their investigators conversed with a manager or supervisor, and more than not their word alone was enough to dismiss my complaint. I would then receive a letter from the agency informing me that a thorough investigation had been completed and found no evidence to support the claim therefore the claim was dismissed.

There was never a mention of the overwhelming evidence of witness statements and proof of illegal transactions made that accompanied the complaint in support of my allegations. Though I knew that any EEO complaints I filed would receive the same attention, it was also a paper trail.

Both managers and supervisors welcome EEO complaints. There are even those managers that suggest and encourage employees to file with the EEO. Pure arrogance. Many have died due to these unsuitable conditions.

The agency gave me no choice but to file grievances and EEO complaints throughout what would be my 20 years of service at that point. I had been under 10 different managers, nine of them had put me in for disciplinary action for whatever reason. Their actions were found to be unjust after investigation through the grievance process.

43

A BOOK ON GRIEVANCES

In February 2000, Vince Fresquez was named acting manager for the downtown station. He was the sixth person assigned to the station in the last 10 years. Upon his arrival, he immediately changed the reporting time for my co-worker and myself. It had been only months before that I had filed a grievance and prevailed pertaining to these same issues with the last manager.

His successor picked up where he left off. His spontaneous actions led me to believe that he had been groomed and brought up to speed particularly concerning me. But I was intrigued as to why he would change my co-worker's hours. The co-worker was a co-complainant to the lawsuit that was pending against the U.S. Postal Service.

This would eliminate a discrimination complaint that I would have definitely filed with the EEO office about my hours being the only one that was changed. Changing one's reporting time 99 percent of the time was done out of personal vendettas or to send a message to anyone that does not conform to the will of management. Though these things may seem trivial, they are not when a person's lifestyle was continuously altered. It was a disciplinary action, a retaliation, under disguise.

I understood that the agency had needs for placing people in the right places at the right times. It was a necessity that goes hand-in-hand with day-to-day operations. But this authority was abused so much in this agency because in my case these changes were not beneficial to the agency.

When my hours were changed by the new manager I filed a grievance, not because I believed that my hours would be changed back to the original time, but for documentation and to receive management's reason in writing as to why my hours continued to change when certain others were never affected. This was another example of the many ways the agency could and would attack those of their choosing.

There were other employees who reported at the same time with less seniority and by contract agreement their times should have been affected before mine.

The manager's reason was because my original reporting time was 3 a.m., and there were no supervisors scheduled in the building at that time. He went on to say that he received a notice from his supervisor that I had requested for a supervisor to be in the building for my protection. This was false and absurd.

First, I never had that sort of trust in management to make such a ridiculous statement that I would be more comfortable or feel protected if there was a supervisor in the building. Second, the supervisors and manager were the predators that continued to violate my rights and jeopardize my protection whenever they were around.

Management remained frustrated with me because of my documentation. The manager's reason had no validity. The name of the supervisor who supposedly disclosed this information to him was never provided and I continued to be a victim of harassment. I made it a point to inform the union.

On Feb. 11, 2000, I met with the manager. I could not allow this to go unchallenged. They continued taking pot shots at me and I continued to answer the bell. Present were two of his supervisors and the union.

Introductions were unnecessary. We knew each other. The meeting started off with me requesting to know the supervisor that I reportedly made the request for a supervisor to be present anytime that I was in the building. Neither supervisor responded. The room remained silent for a moment. I then requested that my reporting time be changed back to its original time. The manager then asked for time to review the grievance.

On Feb. 24, 2000, I was informed by the union of the manager's decision not to change my reporting time back to its original time at 3 a.m. I was not allowed to be in the building before 4 a.m. when a supervisor would be present. There were more than 100 employees attached to that facility where I was the only employee who had restrictions to not enter the building until a certain time.

March 13, 2000, I wrote a letter to Fresquez expressing my concerns about his lack of fairness and blatant discrimination. I explained that upon his arrival he immediately changed my reporting time without just cause or actual knowledge of the operation itself. To suggest that time was needed to review the grievance instead of what should have been reviewed was the operation itself and understanding that this was not a one-man operation.

Copies of the letter were sent to the postmaster's office, my attorneys, office and to the EEO office. He never responded to the letter nor was it ever mentioned again. I wrote to him once again on April 13, 2000. This time I expressed my anger for his insensitivity, questioned his integrity and lack of professionalism in ignoring me as an employee with some very serious and legitimate concerns of the U.S. Postal Service policies in respect to the violation of my rights that I have undoubtedly earned as a combat veteran in the Vietnam War.

The year 2000 was a difficult and challenging year for me. Management continued to bypass me for overtime, denying my requests for schedule changes, and privileges that others had. For me to be recognized in having the same privileges I was forced to call in the union where 95 percent of the time I would have to file a grievance in order for management to acknowledge that I too was an employee of this agency and deserve equal treatment.

In April of 2000, alone, I was forced to file four different grievances. I use the word "forced" loosely because it was something that I took no pleasure in doing but circumstances along with the defiance and arrogance of management would always lead to that. I was exhausted, filing grievance after grievance for 17 years. I could have easily written a book on grievances alone. My reasons for filing any complaint was to right a wrong and nothing more.

It doesn't cost management a single dime to pay out a grievance or even the EEOs, the phrasing employees often used to refer to the act of filing a complaint. The managers and supervisors were paid their same wages. It was lost revenue for the U.S. Postal Service. Where was the accountability for actions that cost the U.S. Postal Service hundreds of thousands of dollars each year? Instead of addressing the matter, managers were disciplined by being moved from one facility to another?

My health had become a growing concern for me. I had developed many health issues especially hypertension that caused erratic changes in my blood pressure. There was an accumulation of days that I could not complete because of these elevated blood levels. I continued to write letters to the manager and supervisors and each time asked them why they were targeting me.

A letter dated July 13, 2000 was one example. I wrote a letter to my supervisor Sandy Ennis and gave her the names of the two employees that I compared myself with, whose reporting time and duties were the same as mine. One was senior to me and the other was junior to me. I understood why the senior person's reporting time did not change but I failed to comprehend as to why my time changed and the junior people remained the same. The certified return receipt came back with her signature but not a correspondence to the letter.

If management continued to harass me and treat me differently from all the other employees I knew that I had to continue expressing my concerns through documentation. If they don't recall something, they just flat out lie. Management showed frustration whenever these letters came across their desks, however, they weren't so flustered as to discontinue the harassment of me.

Changing a person's hours on a bid job defeats the purpose of bid assignment to that position, of course changes will occur and should be expected in such a large and unpredictable industry. To violate the national bargaining agreement, through vengeance by not following protocol and the structure in which this agreement was based, was not professional. It should have been considered a violation of the agreement.

They wanted me to bid out of the station, resign from the U.S. Postal Service or lose my temper and lose control. I was treated worse than a wounded animal left to die on a road.

There was one EEO complaint that I filed in April that caused me deep concerns. It was the complaint where I was out of work for three and a half weeks due to hypertension caused by stress on the job.

The redress hearing, also known as a mediation, took place on Aug. 29, 2000 and lasted a little over four hours. Management denied every single allegation and took no responsibility for a single issue that was presented during the hearing. My steward and I provided proof of the allegations from the many letters that were written by me to management in an effort to rectify the situations.

Judging body language in the room from members of management, it seemed obvious to me that everyone agreed that something was out of the ordinary and provided a reasonable doubt to management actually telling the truth. The material was damaging for management and forced them to save face by compromising and showing at the very least some sort of interest in a solution.

After four hours, an agreement was reached and signed by both parties including the mediator and the union steward. The manager agreed that he would adjust and reimburse me 49 hours of sick leave, part of the time that I was out. He also promised that management would make a commitment to immediately enforce equitable treatment to me. The agreement was broken in a matter of months.

On Oct. 16, 2000, I received a memo from my supervisor informing me that my reporting time was scheduled to be changed once again to even later hours, effective Oct. 23, 2000. My reporting time was now two hours later than my original bid of 3 a.m. The union could do absolutely nothing about it because, contractually, management was in no violation, but it was morally wrong.

It was done out of retaliation and discrimination, where the change proved to be unnecessary, that served no purpose and did not accomplish a thing except but to satisfy their egos. It was more to flex their muscles than anything and to show who was boss.

There were seven employees whose reporting time for work was subjected to change, five were Hispanic, one Caucasian, and I was the only Black employee. The manager and supervisor who were both of Hispanic descent made the changes. Basically, all seven employee jobs were similar and each worker was qualified to do the next person's job if necessary.

My reporting time was changed back to one hour later and my co-worker who was also a co-complainant, Caucasian, in the lawsuit against the postal service was changed back one hour later. Four out of the five Hispanics were left alone and had no change to their reporting time. The one Hispanic whose time was affected was changed by one half hour. There was a reason why he was the only Hispanic changed and just by a half hour which make the effects less strenuous but gave management a defense.

He was management's scapegoat and defense to an EEO complaint that they knew undoubtedly would follow. Two of the Hispanics that were not affected were junior to me and my co-worker. This was how management created hostility and dissension among the workers.

On Nov. 6, 2000, I filed an EEO complaint for retaliation and discrimination. There were three prior EEO complaints that I had filed against this manager and supervisor for similar infractions. This complaint went through a year-long process before it reached a formal investigation. Once again, the investigation came back negative.

The agency informed me that they found no signs or proof of retaliation or discrimination. In justification for changing the reporting times of two senior employees, my co-worker and me, the agency used in management's defense the one-half hour change to the one Hispanic to eliminate discrimination and retaliation was not a factor because two employee hours were changed along with mine. My co-worker also filed a complaint with the EEO office that came back with the same negative results.

On Dec. 4, 2000, it was my fourth time writing to the manager addressing the issue of the 49 hours of sick leave where he went back on his word and signed a false agreement that he would reimburse me and enforce equitable treatment of me. On Dec. 7, 2000, he did respond to a portion of the letter by addressing his reply on a routing slip, a form used by the agency for different requests and office-to-office communication. He stated that all start time changes will remain the same due to operational needs.

The 49 sick leave hours were not mentioned nor did I ever receive those hours. On Dec. 11, 2000, I filed a breach of settlement with the EEO office informing their agency of the violation of that settlement. I never heard a word back from the agency. The agreement was not honored and the settlement was never rectified and I received no compensation to right that wrong.

The year 2001 began like 2000 ended. Management continued to harass me. It seemed that my job was to file grievances and EEO complaints so I never quite understood their logic. But, I laced up my boots and continued the fight. On Jan. 11, 2001, because of continued harassment, I filed a grievance and an EEO complaint. It was past time that the EEO office did their job. I was well known to the personnel in their office because they would receive complaints from me every other month if not every month where the outcome was always the same — management did no wrong.

Filing grievances was tricky. I knew many co-workers who retracted their filings due to pressure and retaliation from managers and supervisors. Intimidation and fear of employees was a direct approach to most every issue including problem-solving in this agency. The Jan. 16, 2001 edition of The Federal Times reported a U.S. Postal Service clerk saying, "The Postal Service is characterized by autocratic abusive management style that is like boot camp in eight hours shift." This employee asked not to be named.

I had a very good understanding of my job that was explicit of my protection by doing the job that I was paid to do. Most importantly I did whatever assignment that was put before me and I did it well. I took pride in doing my job so the only way they could make any attempt to discipline me was to fabricate and try to provoke me into situations.

Employees lost their jobs in this agency because they gave management that stick to crack their heads with by reacting to the harassment and falling victim to exactly what it was intended to do – to control one's process to thinking clearly by frustrating a person to a point where they react more times than not in a negative manner. One example of the many ways they made lies believable involved a mail shipment.

At the time, the U.S. Postal Service was processing mail that was identified as Experian shipment. The product registration cards were mailed back to the company throughout the world where hundreds of thousands of pieces were shipped daily from all four corners of the world. The mail had to be prepped and sorted and had a cutoff time in order to reach its final destination at a precise and designated time as with all mail.

There were four different sections that worked this shipment in the station with one clerk for each section. That clerk was responsible for the preparation and dispatch of the amount of volume that was assigned to his or her section by the supervisors. Section four was my duty station.

This was how the supervisor distributed the amount of volume to each station. Section one had 19 direct shipments of Experian mail. Section two had 21 direct shipments, Section three had 18 shipments, and my Section had 56 shipments. I had three and a half times the size of every other section, which mathematically meant I was responsible for more than 40,000 more pieces than my co-workers. Trouble would ensue if I didn't meet my goals.

This was justification that discipline was for failure to follow instructions. I was fighting for survival, never losing sight of what I could prove, so I requested to see the manager and supervisor to discuss the issue. I took a co-worker along with me to the office as a witness. I expressed my concerns as to their expectations and the volume of mail that had been placed before me. I objected to this outrageous volume that was far beyond a single person's capability, and to perform this assignment on a daily basis that I would need help because the volume was absolutely too much for any one person to handle.

This was another EEO complaint that I filed with their office to prove discrimination and how I was treated differently from all other employees.

THE TRUTH BEHIND GOING POSTAL   151

To my surprise, the manager admitted to the volume of mail. He had no other choice because it was in black and white, and I proved the disparity. The EEO office refused to acknowledge the separation of me from other employees and did nothing to intervene.

However, the grievance process was much more effective and changed management's course of aggression by having them adjust the volume of mail to my section and distributing an even amount over each section.

The lawsuit against the United States Postal Service was in full swing and was to take place in one month. They terrorized me and I had an enormous amount of hatred for the individuals who wanted me fired and for the agency.

From April 16-19, 2001, the civil lawsuit trial was hailed against the United States Postal Service. The stage was set. Tension was high. It was uncomfortable, especially for the manager and his supervisor, who was not in charge now. Not even the postmaster had any control over these proceedings where he was summoned to appear in court for his role over the years.

This was the time to receive the courts instructions in anticipation of the truth to prevail and justice to ring out. But that never happened because of the judge's prejudicial instructions. The truth had no opportunity to present itself. The Denver police detective was granted summary judgment a week before the trial. That was the day that I understood the phrase that says, one "cannot fight city hall."

The detective was the nucleus of the entire scheme. He involved the judicial system from the beginning and the courts so gracefully accepted any summons he tossed their way. The detective issued between eight and 10 different summonses for my co-workers, requiring us to appear in court on 13 different charges altogether.

The summary judgment handicapped our case because his name or occupation could not be brought up in the trial. The judge was adamant when he announced that he will declare a mistrial if his name was mentioned during any of the proceedings. His disregard for the law, his dishonesty, and racial hatred for African Americans was rewarded. The summary judgment ruling was the epitome of injustice that carried on throughout the entire trial.

44

PEOPLE'S LIVES

The trial moved forward. As I walked into that courtroom on the very first day it seemed useless. Because of the summary judgment our attorneys possessed minimal material for the case. Our attorneys tried to be optimistic and cover up their emotions, but they could not.

Frustration filled their voices and tension covered their faces. The jury could not put it together because of what they did not hear. Summary judgment did exactly what it was intended to do, which was to confuse the jury, hide evidence and distort the facts. It put parameters on our testimonies and threatened a mistrial.

Judge Walker D. Miller made it no secret how he felt about the entire case. He never backed down from overruling our attorneys, whose tempers flared, and rightly so. He was unreasonable and his behavior was not becoming of a judge. Our attorneys questioned the judge repeatedly of the ruling that handicapped our case. They began to recite case law that disputed his rulings. This infuriated the judge and he began to threaten our attorneys with sanctions and once again of a mistrial.

I believe the judge should have been charged with obstruction of justice himself. The judge lost his temper when one of our attorneys pointed out specific case law that went completely against many of his unfair rulings. The language was explicit and clear to the point. I did not need to pass the bar to understand the lingo.

The judge had warned our attorneys for what he described as "demonstrations" in the courtroom for questioning and challenging his rulings. The judge scolded our attorney who brought this forward and for her "demonstration." He demoralized her with a speech that was degrading to her and our entire team. It was clearly an outburst by the judge who got caught up in the moment and lost control.

Not only was the judge ruling against us but his tongue lashing proved to be the breaking point of that attorney. In response, she packed up her belongings and walked out of the courtroom. My heart went out to her. She did not deserve to be treated in such a nasty and very unprofessional manner.

She was so upset to the point that she walked about four miles back to the law firm office, where she then took a taxi to the airport and caught an airplane back to Phoenix, Arizona – her home office. I never heard from her or saw her again. I remember her as a very compassionate person for the law and a very knowledgeable attorney, who believed in her profession and had the utmost respect for equality and justice for all.

The evidence that our team put together against the U.S. Postal Service would have been damaging to the agency had we been afforded the opportunity to present our case in its entirety. Many long hours and days were spent collecting and going over court transcripts, individual statements, depositions, EEO and grievance complaints – anything that the defendants swore to or signed their names to. We researched and extensively went over and compared each document statement to one another. We discovered many discrepancies, lies, incorrect dates, some with no dates, and there were some documents that had three or four different answers to the same question.

I learned that the boss's favorite people were very dangerous. They were the people with low self-esteem, who most likely existed in every company and corporation in America. There was no limit to what they would do to others to be recognized and validated by those in charge.

The summary judgment ruling was nothing more than obstruction of justice. We lost the case for that reason and no other. Our co-worker, who was assaulted by the supervisor received a small amount of monetary damages, no more than $10,000 for his pain and suffering and his attorney fees.

My other co-worker and I appealed the ruling, but later down the road realized that we could not finance another long drawn out process as this one, which took six years to complete. We saw no other choice but to settle the case with the U.S. Postal Service for $10,000 between the two of us.

Not one of the defendants had to answer to any part or the role they played.

For nine years, the postmaster, Flores, had the authority to take complete control of the entire situation in this downtown postal facility. He played a significant part, if not the leading role, in the animosity and hatred that had festered over the years due to his lack of leadership. He was never the solution, but the problem to the many unimaginable situations that could have easily cost the ultimate price – people's lives.

In June 2001, two months after the trial, it was announced in the Western Area Update newsletter that Flores received a promotion. He was named district manager of the Fort Worth, Texas performance cluster, where he would have executive management responsibilities overseeing 10,000 employees and 414 postal facilities. This was a prime example of a person with authority in the agency that made limited sacrifices for the safety of the employees and the production of a facility that had no more than 100 employees in the Colorado and Wyoming district. Accountability for management had no place in this agency.

He showed no interest in the trial other than the outcome. He did not show up at any time during the entire proceedings until the final day when the verdict was read and then was given an even greater responsibility.

The expectation that I would be left alone after the trial was fairytale thinking. I remained a target. I continued to be singled out and treated differently from other employees. At this time, there were five different EEOs that remained active. It made no difference. The outcome would be the same. In many of my EEOs I did not seek monetary damages.

Management could not and would not leave me alone and the EEOs continued to mount to the point where I received a letter, dated June 21, 2001, reporting the consolidation of my complaint. They combined every three to four complaints into one. No single infraction ever received the investigation it deserved.

At this point, I had been at the agency for 18 years, hurdling the traps set for me in hopes that I would fall victim to termination. My resistance was as strong as my perseverance. I had no intentions of allowing a group of people or management to remove me from a job or lifestyle that I had just as much right to as they did.

Mid-2001 a new manager had come to the station. My first instinct was to protect myself by keeping my distance. I did not want to meet or have any sort of interaction with this person.

45

NO SATISFACTION

Months after this manager was announced, a new supervisor was assigned to the station. Her name was Sharon Keeton, and upon her arrival she was taken around the facility by other supervisors and introduced to each employee individually. As with anyone in management I hesitated and honestly dreaded meeting her. I wasn't prejudging her. I was just so overwhelmed with exhaustion and fed up with receiving negative attention from management, old and new. I was skeptical, but we were introduced eventually.

She was a soft-spoken person who was new to the U.S. Postal Service with no more than five to six years to her credit. There were times when I had no choice but to talk with her, after all she was my immediate supervisor. She seemed to have a calm personality with a laid back disposition. But, she was still management.

The first meeting with someone was usually very pleasant. The truth in a person, however, was revealed in time. Several months had gone by and not one day had passed that I did not keep close observation of her and those she interacted with—especially my haters— as with all of management. She was new and she was vulnerable with an impressionable need to please her superiors. She needed to be watched.

It had been five months from the time she arrived at the station that I had yet to sense a change in her personality or in the way she treated me. Keeton was very respectful and treated me with the utmost courtesy. Gone were the days of a supervisor breathing down my back all day. I was impressed because this treatment was foreign to me in this agency. I was glad to have her as my immediate supervisor, still I was careful not to open myself up to vulnerability. At this point, I had shown and given her the respect that she had earned.

She seemed to be a very ambitious person with an inquisitive mind wanting to learn everything about the station and its operation. It opened dialogue between the two of us.

It had been six months to the day that I had yet to meet the manager of the station – Gina Salas. We had never been formally introduced and I had no intentions of introducing myself to any one in management. In fact, it was perfectly okay had I never met her. I did whatever possible to avoid her, not to have any sort of contact with her whatsoever, and apparently, she felt the same way.

My first encounter with her was November 2001, in passing. On the 22nd day of that month she took disciplinary action against me due to a verbal confrontation on the work room floor between me and another co-worker earlier that month. Understandably I knew better, because of the position that I was in, but he crossed that line when he began to use racial overtones referring to me as a "monkey boy."

It was a derogatory term used to insult enslaved African-Americans. It was the closest that I had gotten to getting physical with anyone in this agency in my career. He was one of management's pets, who took the altercation to an extreme level by using provocative names to provoke me.

I guess he wanted to take the credit for having me removed from the agency for fighting while on the job. It was an act that surely would have landed me in jail, not him. He was willing to sacrifice his health for that badge of honor. I could feel the anger raging throughout my body, so I pulled every fiber of my being to refrain from attacking this person. I walked away.

Management would get no satisfaction. Two witnesses were there at the time of the altercation. One person claimed to have not heard a thing while the other confirmed that there were racial slurs and derogatory comments made by the other person involved. Their statements were irrelevant. The manager's ultimate desire was to put me in for removal, but contractually she could not go beyond a No TOL #3 for any first infraction. But nevertheless, she did anyway. No TOLs were disciplinary actions in letter form. It was more corrective than punitive action. Therefore, it was numbered from 1 to 3 with a No TOL #3 being the most severe. The next infraction after this would automatically result in a last chance, then removal.

First and foremost, any disciplinary action should have been initiated through my immediate supervisor. I was never given the opportunity to tell my side of the story before the punishment was rendered. I filed a grievance in order for the case to follow protocol to go through the correct channels in hopes my side would be heard.

My union steward and I were given that opportunity to sit down and talk with my supervisor. I was very comfortable with Keeton. She had treated me with respect since the day she arrived. The three of us sat down and I expressed the true facts on that day. It was the perfect opportunity for me and my union steward, who knew as much as I did about the station.

I took ownership of my participation in the confrontation. I felt that she could relate so well to what I was up against on that particular day being an African-American herself. She did her job and she went by the rules and regulations of the United States Postal Service and charged me with unacceptable conduct where the No TOL #3 was reduced to a No TOL #1 and was to remain in my files for a period of one year.

I was at management's mercy where I faced an unusual dilemma. If I would react in defending myself the consequences would go against me. If I continued to turn my head I would be disrespected as a man, in a sense to be bullied on the playground. But the stakes were higher.

Those new to the station would have nothing to do with me because of my negative reputation at the postal service. But a few were brave enough to talk with me. I was assertive in standing up for my rights. I called out supervisors who confronted me for doing what others were also doing on the workroom floor, which was talking with co-workers. Their excuses would always be that they didn't see that person or for me to worry about myself and not others.

It wasn't a question of defiance on my part. It was disparity of treatment. I could and had always been one to follow any rules that the next person had to follow. To avoid a confrontation with me that could result in grievances and EEOs, when they saw me in a conversation with someone, they would call that person over the intercom to report to the office. It allowed them to control the situation at their discretion. There were no rules in place that employees could not converse with one another, but it was always an issue when anyone talked with me.

46

TEMPER TEMPER

I have seen many supervisors come and go out of this station. There was one supervisor in particular who was assigned to the station. Jackie Johnson had minimal control of her aggression and constantly barked out commands, challenging and questioning an employee's ability to perform his or her job.

Many employees complained about her aggressive nature and questioned her people skills. Her voice carried from one end of the building to the next. She was a very uncaring and obnoxious human being obsessed with control. Johnson insisted that employees acknowledge her as not just a supervisor but a VIP with authority. I did whatever it took to ignore and stay completely out of her way.

No surprise. The U.S. Postal Service welcomed and supported management personnel with behavior such as hers.

The longer that Johnson was in the station the worse it got, not just for me, but for most including her colleagues. They would argue among themselves, starting from the workroom floor, then moving to the supervisor's office where it would escalate. She was a danger to me because her aggression was out of control. And when it came to any of her attacks on me, management and select co-workers defended her. I surrounded myself with people who had no ill feelings toward me, watched over me and witnessed those attacks.

Johnson was a lot more aggressive than others assigned to the station. She was groomed to stay on target, and I was the target. I ignored much of what she would say to me. I knew my job much better than she did, if she knew anything at all about it. I continued to do my job and that was a problem for management because they had no reason to discipline me. And I did not treat her like a VIP. She was offended that I ignored her, and looked at it as a personal challenge.

The cat and mouse game went on for months between the two of us. There were a few times that I did go to my immediate supervisor with a few concerns and certain issues but she would say that Johnson also was a supervisor and I needed to follow any orders or directions she gave me. The problem was that she just could not leave me alone, though I knew the job that I had been doing for more than 14 years.

I was given commands repeatedly even though I was performing what was already assigned to me. She followed me and stood over me while I was performing my duties. She timed my breaks and made sure that I was following the lunch break schedules. I was constantly being micromanaged. I could not go to anyone in management in hopes of rectifying this situation. To involve the agency was completely out.

Documentation was my only source of protection.

June 3, 2003, I filed a complaint with the EEO office fully aware of my zero percent success rate, but this particular complaint had a chance because more people were inclined to get involved; so I thought. Others who had been affected by her actions told me they would provide written statements. As it turned out, they were only verbal promises. Most would not do so when the time came. People I knew who worked at the General Mail Facility, which was the main training facility for postal workers, were calling me on the telephone, expressing their concerns about her. While there, she had begun spreading negative rumors about me of a sexual nature.

No one in the agency ever needed a reason to harass me. I followed protocol and filed the complaint with the EEO office as usual, but I selected the redress program within the agency to settle this complaint. I even regularly reported situations to my immediate supervisor. I took my chances with the redress program.

This program provided the opportunity for management and the complainant to sit down together at a hearing and talk out their differences. The objective was to find common ground in hopes of some sort of solution. It was perfect for me. I wanted to know why she would not leave me alone. I wanted to know why she insisted on jeopardizing her safety. She sometimes positioned herself in my path when I was moving heavy equipment throughout the building. Each piece of equipment had a gross weight of 700 to 1,000 pounds. As usual, I reported and documented each occasion.

On Aug. 28, 2003 at 9:30 a.m., the redress hearing began and it was scheduled to last until completion. Present was my union steward, myself and Johnson, her representative Gina Salas (the station manager) and the mediator. The mediation hearing lasted for approximately four and a half to five hours. I presented the facts.

No surprise that my immediate supervisor was not present to confirm my many complaints about Johnson to her. Both management officials were very argumentative and denied whatever I said. Johnson was defensive and would not tell the truth. During the hearing, the conversation heated up where a few times the mediator had to make his presence known to both sides.

My request was not unreasonable. I was not seeking monetary damages or asking for any preferential treatment. I simply wanted to be left alone and to have no contact with her whatsoever. She was making my life miserable. I expressed myself sincerely with my deepest emotions that I was sick and tired of being trampled on and that I just wanted management to stop interfering with me doing my job.

After the hearing the mediator suggested that he have a private conversation with both sides. An agreement was reached and was written into a bona fide contract by the mediator. All participants signed the agreement that stipulated: "The supervisor and I will have no physical contact," "Management will follow all rules and regulations," and "No communication will occur between the parties unless absolutely necessary, each party will have a witness of their choosing for that communication to occur."

After 23 years with the U.S. Postal Service, I finally had a non-biased independent source to conduct a fair hearing. Through the process, I felt that I was heard and treated with some dignity and respect. My union representative and I were very satisfied. She said that she had never seen a contract written up in this form in any redress process where she had participated. Documentation and perseverance were key elements in getting this done. Timing also played a significant part because the aggression of both Salas and Johnson reflected their personalities, their arrogance and that sense of entitlement. This exercise revealed that neither one could control their temper.

47

BREACH OF BONA FIDE CONTRACT

After the mediation hearing a few months had passed and another manager, Don Stanley, was assigned to the station. This was the eighth person assigned to the manager position since I had been in the station. My position hadn't changed. The resentment that I had for all of management remained the same.

With these disturbing feelings swirling in my spirit, I felt that I could never relax. It reminded me of when I was in 5th grade during the 1960s. When I would go into a store, I felt I was always being followed and watched. I had a couple of white friends growing up. They were always so relaxed. That bothered me. At that time, I was too young to understand the history behind those feelings. Here it was again as an inferno inside me as an adult.

It restricted me from connecting with people, and took away my trust. The intensity was not something that happened overnight. It had festered over many years of abuse at the postal service. I wanted to do my job and finish my career.

The mediation agreement, where a supervisor could not have contact with an employee unless there were witnesses present, was unheard of in the agency. The contract fueled the fire. This supervisor lost the privilege to have any sort of contact or communicate with me. She could not give me a command without a witness present. She had to select a witness of her choosing and I had to select one of mine. Therefore, she was limited to a degree of retaliation against me.

I was surprised by my immediate supervisor's reaction to it all. She did not seem receptive at all to the agreement even though she knew of the problems that particular supervisor was causing, not only me, but others. Management's response was to isolate me from everyone else. No one could talk with me unless it pertained to the job. It did not matter to the supervisors if anyone else was in a conversation on the workroom floor.

That infuriated those who were harassed by management for talking to me. I obviously wasn't happy with it either. So, I asked each person, who management confronted about talking to me, if they would write a statement of the event. I explained in detail my intentions for using the statements in a retaliation complaint to the EEO office. I assured each person that I had nothing to hide and that I did not want anyone to go into this blind. I expressed my concerns of possible retaliation by management of any individual who provided a statement.

Two out of about 10 wrote a statement. I used what I had in support of the retaliation complaint that I filed on May 3, 2004 for a breach of a bona fide contract that management would follow all rules and regulations. It was just another complaint that filtered through the system of the EEO office just to be rejected and thrown out as the 25 complaints I had already filed.

The station was now under new management. Of course, each manager had their own identity and personality, but their demeanors were commonly the same. Grooming was an intricate part of a successor's inauguration in this agency. Newer supervisors were the most dangerous because they had something to prove. They were submissive to their superiors and had been known to carry out most any order regardless of the harm it may have caused to others.

At one time, I believed going into management changed people. I didn't believe that anymore. Being in management myself for a very short period and knowing many others before they had gone into management, opened my eyes. I believed it brought out your true nature.

The new manager, Stanley, made it known that the station needed a makeover. His idea of a makeover was to bring in Mike Silva, a former marine with a reputation of being a hard-ass. Silva had worked out of Motor Vehicle Service. He reported to the station around the end of August, maybe the beginning of September 2004. Employees in the building had an idea of who he was and why he was there based on the many stand up safety talks with the employees. It did not take long for him to live up to the reputation.

I was astonished that he did not single me out and attack me from the beginning as did most other management. He was obnoxious and nasty to everyone, some more than others. He was out of control. I had no intentions of challenging him. But, I eventually became his target. I knew how to protect myself, but most important I wasn't afraid of him. Again, documentation was my best ally and I was documenting his every move since the day of his arrival. It was about survival.

He repeated the same harassment tactics that I had faced for the last 24 years in this agency. Silva tampered with my overtime, stalked me, made accusations, falsely accused me of taking long breaks, among other things, and not doing my job. Anytime he accused me of anything I would get a witness and the dialogue would be documented. I was meticulous but more cautious than ever of this person because he was a confrontational and dangerous man, boiling over with anger.

Whatever he felt he needed to prove was none of my concern. My concern was to not allow him to prove it at my expense. He had the attention of most people in the station, even those of management's pets – the team players— who also had issues with him.

It was amazing to see them squirm and listen to their complaints to the manager about being harassed by this supervisor. Employees from his former job, the MVS, also vented their frustrations and hatred for him by writing graffiti inside many tractor-trailers. Silva's name was spray-painted with obscenities and phrases such as "butt plug" were commonly written in big, bold black letters. The station would receive seven to 10 deliveries a day by tractor-trailer with this type of graffiti.

It seemed to boost his ego. He displayed nothing but gratification at seeing his name smeared inside of those trailers. He swelled with pride to hear others talk about the many obscenities written about him. When I asked him about the graffiti in the trailers, he displayed nothing but delight and laughed.

And he continued his ways. He made a point to tighten the screws each day but he wasn't my only problem. The station manager, Don Stanley, was the real issue and the reason why Silva was in the station in the first place. I went to him with many concerns and issues about this supervisor as did many other employees. It was important that I followed the chain of command, I did not want any of my complaints to be thrown out due to a procedural technicality.

On Oct. 4, 2004, I filed an EEO complaint against Silva for harassment, abuse of authority and discrimination. The agency continued to receive many complaints from me, so many that they processed them immediately just to be rejected. Even going to a second redress was hurried.

It was scheduled for Oct. 21, 2004 at 8 a.m. Present was Silva, his representative, the mediator, my representative and myself. The facilitator went over the rules for redress. I already knew them. The meeting lasted about three hours, shorter than my first redress. Had the supervisor controlled his emotions and not demonstrated juvenile behavior, it could have easily wrapped up within an hour. On a lot of the questions, he would break out in a rage and storm out of the meeting. One of those times occurred when I brought up the many disputes he was involved in with other employees as well as his current litigation in a court of law.

My union steward said that I must have hit a nerve. The mediator did not appreciate this supervisor's disruptions. Finally, upon one of Silva's many returns to the redress, he completely let loose. In a rough, demanding, and angry voice he told the mediator that he better get control of the meeting. The mediator fired back by telling him to sit down and that he was running this mediation hearing. Silva rebelled and chose not to come to a settlement agreement.

The case moved forward through the EEO process where an investigation was said to have taken place by this agency, but the result was the same as every EEO complaint that I had filed. It was dismissed. I was then given the right to file civil action. This would have been my second civil action against the U.S. Postal Service had I chosen to move forward. I did not because of the potential expense and time.

48

A 100K DEFENSE

Many people who work for the U.S. Postal Service could not afford to engage in costly lawsuits of civil action that could take up to several years to complete with no guarantee that they would ever recover their loss.

My first case took six years to complete and cost more than $100,000 together for me and my two co-workers to defend ourselves against false accusations. In retrospect, I estimate that it would have cost me nearly $5 million in court costs over my entire career with the postal service if all my 39 EEO complaints had not been dismissed. Over my career, I didn't even make 20 percent of that.

Supervisors normally laughed when an employee threatened to file an EEO complaint. Employees then lost confidence and would not file. The mediation through redress did accomplish one thing. The supervisor stayed away from me and not long after the redress he left the station. I wasn't so vain to believe that it was because of what had transpired between the two of us. But combined with complaints from other people in the station as well as some of the team players, I do believe we all made a difference.

I was elated and celebrated his departure. It was short lived because there were many more just like him waiting and jockeying for a turn to prove themselves.

PART EIGHT:

2005-2008

49

JOKES BETWEEN FRIENDS

It had now been three years since my immediate supervisor, Sharon Keeton, came to the station and her personality had not changed. She continued to treat me with respect. For me it was an honor to have made her acquaintance. Other employees had talked badly about me to her and tried to change her perception of me, but she held her ground.

She shared that she had been ridiculed by her colleagues for her treatment of me where she had demonstrated leadership qualities. That included investigating any accusations, namely "intimidating gestures," and each turned out not to be valid. This was out of the norm at the station. I wasn't aware of anyone who did not get along with her or did not like her.

On Feb. 25, 2005, I was emergency placed from the building by Stanley, the station manager, for alleged threats against another employee – someone I considered a friend. On the morning of Feb. 24, 2005 between the hours of 4 and 5a.m., the two of us were engaged in a general conversation about a woman in the station. It was guy talk between two friends, nothing derogatory or out of place. When I made a remark about a specific young lady, specifically that she did not want him, he exploded.

He went into a rage and took the conversation to a different level. He became belligerent and began swearing at me. I laughed because it wasn't that serious to me. I never took it as a threat because I considered him to be a friend.

Had he not been someone who I thought of in that way I never would have felt comfortable making any sort of remarks, but most of all the conversation would have never taken place. My laughter could have inadvertently irritated him as well as the fact that other people were close by and may have heard the conversation. They probably witnessed his sense of rejection and embarrassment.

He walked out of the building and as he left he said to me that he would, "shoot the shit out of me." A co-worker, who heard the entire conversation, got involved by telling him that now he had just made a threat. I was concerned for my friend.

We were the early crew so there were no supervisors in the building at the time. My immediate supervisor, Keeton, wasn't scheduled to report for another hour. When she arrived, I saw her on the workroom floor and approached her, asking if she would come over to my desk because I had a matter I would like to discuss with her. At that time, she was making her rounds to secure the building. Around five to 10 minutes later she eventually made it to my desk. I proceeded to tell her about the incident that took place before she arrived to work.

I also saw him for a moment after the first time he had left the building. That was when I suggested that the two of us go outside off the workroom floor, that I just wanted to talk with him and that I didn't want or need the attention that was being generated on the floor in observation of his uncontrollable emotions. He used this gesture against me in a later statement.

I asked her if she had seen or talked with him since she had been in the building. She said that he came into the office just as she had arrived and said that he was going to take the rest of the day off and go home. She said he never mentioned that anything had occurred and that she wasn't aware of any problems. Hours later she called me into the office to tell me that she just received a call from my friend who explained why he took the rest of the day off. She said he apologized for leaving so abruptly.

He told her it was because I was "talking shit." She asked him what he meant. He did not respond to her question but he said," he has everyone scared of his big ass but I will shoot him. He is not going to threaten me". He made other false allegations about me surrounding intimidating threats, but did not elaborate. Keeton suggested that he talk with Stanley, the station manager. He was not there at the present time, but was told about the situation later that morning by her when he arrived.

Stanley instructed Keeton to call the employee at home and tell him not to report to work the next day until 8 a.m., when he would be there. She called and relayed the manager's message. While talking with him she informed him that the manager was in the office and was available if he would like to talk with him on the phone. My day had ended and I had gone for the rest of the day when all of this transpired so I wasn't able to give my side. The next day I came into work. On Feb. 25, 2005, I was immediately emergency placed from the building and charged with a "code of conduct unbecoming."

The next day while at home after being emergency placed, the true story began to unfold. Employees that were onsite the morning of the 24th were interviewed. No one had backed up his story that I had made any sort of threats. The only report the inspectors had of me making threats was from his statement. I was also interviewed by the postal inspectors. It was more of an interrogation than anything else. I was questioned about having weapons and if any, what type.

The entire interview was insulting and irrelevant because I was not the perpetrator. It was far beyond my comprehension why the person I thought to be a friend would try to lead me down a path of destruction. He compromised himself by losing his composure and giving management control of his destiny as far as disciplinary action was concerned.

I believed that after being home for a while he had time to think things out, realizing that he had made a mistake by threatening me in the presence of potential witnesses. He needed a way out or at least something that would take all the attention away from him so what would be better than to say that I threatened him. It would justify his actions at the least it would take me down with him. He was desperate so he tried selling this to the supervisor when he called that morning saying that I had threatened him. When he was asked to elaborate, he did not.

While I was emergency placed, he confessed over the telephone to Keeton that he did indeed threaten me but did not admit it in any other investigations.

He knew of the horrendous challenges that I had gone through with this agency. He had also shared with me his own stories filled with pain and grief of this bureaucracy where he was the subject and was targeted by people of authority. I came to realize during this entire ordeal that he really had no concept of what was going on around him. I knew that it would just be a matter of time before he would get lost and tangled in management's web due to his lack of attention to detail.

Two to three years later, after more than 20 years of service, he was given an ultimatum to resign or he would be fired from the U.S. Postal Service.

I was back at work the next week after the postal inspector investigation had given evidence to support my innocence to the APWU. They in turn presented it to management. I never heard of any discipline of my co-worker, my "friend," and it was a while before I saw him again. Disciplinary action remained in my file that was taken against me by Keeton on March 23, 2005 in the form of a No TOL#2 for "unacceptable conduct" and threats. Eventually it was removed and I recovered all lost wages and the file was expunged.

When I questioned why I was not given the opportunity to give my side of the story at the time that I was emergency placed, I was told by Stanley that I was emergency placed for my safety.

There were three sources throughout this investigation whose interests were only that of the truth and for justice to prevail which was the APWU, the witness and my immediate supervisor. Keeton's report was phenomenal. Supervisors in the U.S. Postal Service just do not do what she did for an employee, taking a stance in telling the truth. She stuck her neck out for me and was aware of the possible retaliation from her superiors. I had no doubt in some sort of way that she was reprimanded for her honesty.

50

EPISODES OF PRESSURE

On March 23, 2005, I was placed on sick leave for a week by my doctor after going through this latest drawn-out episode. My doctor wrote a letter to my supervisor and clearly identified the reason for my absence stating that, "stress level and anxiety was affecting my blood pressure." I had been diagnosed with it in1989 after being in the agency for nine years due to the hostile environment and the constant harassment.

My blood pressure had reached such a high level that the next step would have been hospitalization. This condition did not happen overnight. It was from years of abuse.

51

JOB TAKEN AWAY

During department restructuring my position and job responsibilities were realigned which resulted in my job being abolished. An agreement was then established between management and the APWU outlining how I would be reassigned to a job. It stated that I would have retreat rights to be the first in line to receive a job when a position was posted with the same hours of the position taken away from me.

On May 19, 2005, a new position was posted with the same reporting time that was taken away from me. Another employee, who was senior to me, bid for the position and was awarded the job. On June 1, 2005, I filed a grievance for the manager to even consider acknowledgment of the agreement that he had refused to honor. Specifically, I had retreat rights for the job that had been taken away from me.

It wasn't until the manager received a letter from the postmaster in Louisville, Colorado, that he finally acknowledged and honored the agreement. This postmaster was the manager in charge of the realignment and was also the negotiator in the agreement for the retreat rights. She reiterated that it was a certified agreement.

52

THE QUIET BEFORE THE STORM

For reasons beyond my explanation, 2006 was a quiet year. Of course, there were issues in the station that were never going to go away but they were minor issues that could not compare to the more than two decades of torture I had already experienced. My goal at the agency had not changed. I wanted to retire and not to become just a statistic. The year, 2006, turned out to be the calm before the storm.

On the morning of May 4, 2007, I was approached while on the workroom floor by Stanley, the manager and Johnson, the supervisor who I had entered the bonding contract settlement agreement with through redress. This was the one where witnesses needed to be around for us to have a conversation. It was a certified bonding contract that had been adhered to for close to four years up until this day.

At the time, I was alone doing my job with no one else within 10 feet. It was obvious that no one else was physically in the area when she and the manager approached me and she asked me a question. I looked away from her, and drew my attention to the manager. I informed him that they were in violation of the settlement agreement. He then stated that she could talk with me if she had a witness and that he was her witness. That statement alone confirmed the fact that he was aware of the agreement and its provisions, and the fact that I gave him a copy of the agreement four years ago.

I asked him if he had read the agreement in its entirety and if he understood the provisions that, I too, had that same privilege in having a witness of my choosing to be present. I also informed the manager that I would be filing a violation for breach of agreement.

It was a scandalous act with the intent of having the order revoked had I responded directly to Johnson. It also would have been a violation on my part that would have offset the agreement and terminated the contract. It was an inconvenience to management that one of their supervisors could not have any contact with an employee unless there were witnesses present. It sent a negative message that questioned the leadership in the station.

I believed that most of the employees in the building knew of the order and that it set a precedence for others. Many asked how I managed to get such an order and how could they get one.

On May 28, 2007, I filed an EEO complaint for breach of settlement agreement against the supervisor, Jacqueline Johnson. I received a determination letter, dated Aug. 27, 2007, from the Colorado and Wyoming District Human Resources. They determined that the breach was justified and found no fault in the supervisor's actions. Here's why:

> *A: Because she was under instructions of the manager.*
> *B: That I did not provide reason as to why it was necessary for witness to be present.*
> *C: That it did not cause me any measurable harm because the manager apologized.*

The EEO pre-complaint was not reinstated at this point, but was administratively closed. This agency gave management permission to violate a settlement agreement that was administered through their system and regulated by the agency that condoned and justified the breach. Their justifications for the breach were nothing but excuses. They excused management from being accountable because the manager apologized.

I could not threaten anyone in the agency because someone with authority instructed me to do so, and then apologize. Something would have been done. Hypocrisy.

They were careful in how they approached me because the contract remained active. In the past, I would have had several drinks and lost control of my emotions, but I had learned how to cope with adversity.

On Jan. 7, 2008, I submitted a request for reconsideration to the Colorado and Wyoming District Human Resources. I addressed those three reasons that were given in the determination of their humiliating and unfair decision. I expressed my disappointment that both agencies, EEO and DHR, had clearly missed the breach itself. Here were the reasons with my response.

> *A: Because she was under instructions of the manager.*
>
> *My Response: The supervisor revealed in her statement answering to the breach that she met with the manager and my immediate supervisor minutes before the incident took place where the manager was once again informed of the agreement and fully aware of the provisions. It was the supervisor's responsibility to follow this binding contract set forth in a settlement agreement that she herself agreed to. A commitment to follow in signing her name and because the manager instructed her to go back on her word speaks to their integrity the arrogance, and their disregard for rules and regulations.*
>
> *B: "That I did not provide reason as to why it was necessary for witness to be present before any communication could occur."*
>
> *My Response: It was not my position or responsibility to establish or give any sort of reason as to why the supervisor and I must have a witness of our choosing for communication to occur between the two of us. The facts were established and those reasons were given through testimony that was conducted by their own EEO agency in a redress mediation hearing. Testimonies concluded that it would be in the best interests of both parties and the U.S. Postal Service. That such agreement would be to the benefit of those involved for me to give reason as to why these provisions were constituted is irrelevant.*
>
> *C: That it did not cause me measurable harm because the manager apologized.*
>
> *My Response: The facts were that there was a willing consent between the manager and supervisor to violate a binding contract that was established through an entity and a service provided by the United*

> States Postal Service for the resolution of disputes and disagreements between management and employees. The point was that an order had been put in place for the protection of all parties involved a system to follow of protocol for people with such disputes.

The mediation hearing clearly stated how management and I were to proceed. If the decision was not adhered to by all parties it could and would cause distrust and unfair treatment within the organization. The primary issue was that I was not provided the opportunity to present a witness of my choosing as stated in the contract order. This could set precedence for ignoring future mediation decisions. These are people that hold positions of managers and supervisors in the United States Postal Service.

Their arrogance defines them.

In the end, the breach went unanswered but the contract remained in effect. My immediate supervisor, Keeton, experienced and got a firsthand look at how things were done at the Denver downtown station postal facility. She witnessed the dishonesty of her peers and the disregard that they both had for policy.

After this latest incident, I provided her with a copy of the mediation agreement out of nothing more than respect. I wanted her to be well-informed of the contract between me and this supervisor and for her not to fall victim too because I believed that her personality was nothing like her peers. It took me by surprise that she did not seem too receptive in receiving a copy of the contract.

Of course, retaliation followed this episode with management. My overtime immediately stopped and I immediately filed grievances. I refused to be bullied by their antics and reprisal. There were many times I had to file grievances and each time management was found to have violated the contract agreement. Either I was paid due to the infraction or received a makeup.

The negative energy intensified at work. My blood pressure elevated to migraine headaches. I often left work in fear of passing out or having a stroke. This environment took on characteristics of being at war, and having to be on alert all the time. Flashbacks to Vietnam came regularly. The aggression and humiliation was a constant reminder that I was a target and there was no getting around it. Twenty-five years later, I was still filing grievances.

53

NUMBER ONE

"Going Postal" had cost the U.S. Postal Service thousands of dollars in lost revenue and most importantly lives. During the 90s, the Denver downtown station was the number one station in the Colorado/Wyoming District. After that the numbers decreased dramatically, dropping the station to the lowest spot throughout the district, based on the memorandums that management placed on the bulletin board.

PART NINE:
2009

54

SAVING JOBS

In 2009, the U.S. Postal Service reported record-low mail volume where the economy took much of the blame. Nevertheless, the agency felt a need to adjust manpower and hours. Human Resources, again, implemented a plan to save jobs and money. At the time, the focus was strictly on the clerk craft. The reorganization was under the direction of each manager of his or her station. Their tasks entailed adjusting job positions, accessing and reposting jobs and the relocation of clerks to different postal facilities.

The process was to be determined and executed by seniority. As a result, the first position to be affected would be that of the junior person. The transition and the anticipation of these changes brought on more chaos and anxiety than what originally was in the station. Rumors began to circulate about whose job was going to be abolished and those employees who would be leaving the station. The manager didn't make things any easier, changing his mind from day to day. It depended on who was in his ear at any time. Favoritism played a big part.

It would have been an intelligent business move for management to take advantage of input from the clerks because we were familiar with the operation and effectiveness that each job entailed because we worked them. We had a good idea of the jobs that were possibly in jeopardy of being repositioned or abolished. No single person knew of every operation in the station. This made it impossible for anyone to accurately anticipate the amount of positions that could be accessed effectively without compromising the efficiency of the station.

Instead of focusing on these changes, they focused on removing me from the station. Yes. Me. It made no sense that an agency with such a huge responsibility in maintaining hundreds of thousands of employees would focus and give their undivided attention to a single individual. They went to extremes to jeopardize the productivity and the output of an entire station. I knew for a fact that I meant nothing to this agency, yet they continued drastic measures to remove me, at this point a 29-year veteran of the agency.

The manager and his staff put together the realignment of the station, which took several months to complete. The union was not involved in the process, but did see that the collective bargaining agreement was adhered to and there was no violation of the contract. Management was never in violation of the contract throughout the process but employees were sacrificed and productivity was forgotten to ensure that I would be leaving the station. It was a question of moral principle.

The U.S. Postal Service at that time had plans to save money in a weakened economy and a competitive industry that resulted in low volume of mail and lost revenue. It was precisely why human resources indoctrinated a plan to achieve savings. In order to remain competitive while delivering a good product and most importantly to provide good customer service, the realignment of any station would require precision and ingenuity.

Management had an idea of what some of the jobs in the station entailed, but mainly of the personnel that it took to complete anyone job. Productivity was how managers and supervisors received their bonuses. Employees were needed to produce. Sacrifices had to be made of everyone in the station to achieve the goal of the agency, so understandably an extra effort on everyone's part was needed.

Management sacrificed those extra efforts. They continued to lose revenue for months by ignoring the issue at hand, and that was to realign the station while maintaining its efficiency with fewer people. If done correctly, this would have resulted in less man-hours and an increase in revenue.

Employees that had worked in the station for years knew their jobs and what it took and meant to receive mail on time. These employees included: the clerks, who separated and distributed all mail; the carriers in the station; the drivers, who delivered mail to carriers whose routes were not in the building. It was a work of perfection when done accurately.

When employees voiced their concerns at the volume of clerk personnel being removed from the station, management did not listen. Most did not know what the exact number would be because it was only rumors that up to four or five clerks were going to be accessed. Yet all employees agreed that the most that could be removed from the station without jeopardizing operations would be three or four, at the most. It was a waiting game.

The anticipation was stressful to those with the least amount of seniority. Most believed that if you had at least 15 years of service you would be okay. I didn't.

I received a letter, dated March 11, 2009, from HR reporting that due to the needs of the section my job was being abolished. This was after 22 years in the facility and 29 years of service, and it would be effective March 28, 2009. My co-workers were dumbfounded. Nine different positions were accessed or abolished. Too many.

Employees voiced their concerns and opinions to management. The remaining employees would need to complete the job of two people. The station was in chaos. The manager and supervisors tried blaming HR. But it was up to the discretion of the station managers to the effectiveness in which the station could operate.

I don't believe it was management's intention to attract this type of attention but the realignment was the perfect opportunity to remove me from the downtown station. They had one hand to play, and they played it. Before management could abolish my position, contractually eight other junior employees would need to be removed. They were willing and ready to do this to remove me.

On March 16, 2009, I received a notification of a duty assignment abolishment effective March 28, 2009 where I would become an unassigned regular employee. I would retain my seniority and be eligible to bid, but if

I was not the successful bidder, or if I received a job where I failed to meet the qualifications, I could be assigned to any vacant duty assignment. This was notification that my job was officially abolished and that on March 28, 2009, my new job assignment would take me to a different location.

I was assigned to an entry-level position in automation for the new hire at the General Mail Facility. After 29 years of service my work schedule was from 10 p.m. to 6:30 a.m., with Tuesdays and Wednesdays as my days off. Now that the position I once held at the downtown station was officially abolished I began preparing myself as best I knew how for new and unknown horizons. The move to abolish so many positions was so bizarre. Everyone was asking, "Why?"

That answer came on March 26, 2009, two days before I was to report to my new position in automation at the General Mail Facility. On March 28, 2009, management postponed my new job assignment. Four other employees with less seniority were held over along with me. Our instructions were to remain in our job assignments at the downtown station until further notice. I saw this as confirmation that management knew their plans to remove that many personnel was wrong.

They sacrificed employees and lost revenue for the agency to nurture their hatred and to satisfy the obsession they had for me. This was not a reconsideration of my job because it was officially abolished and I was now an unassigned regular. Officially, I did not hold a position anywhere.

Once I understood the motive, the real question was what possessed them to do it in this fashion. Based on retreat rights, each person whose job was abolished was entitled to those rights through the national bargaining agreement. If a job was posted in the facility where an employee lost his or her job, then that employee had first rights to that job before any other employee city wide. Seniority should have been considered.

I was the senior person whose job was affected by the realignment. If a job or any jobs for that matter were posted, I would have been first in line to bid and receive the position. It appeared to be a plan meticulously thought out by management just to remove me from the Downtown Station. Their strategy was bad, costly.

Those employees whose jobs were abolished, were ordered to remain at the station until further notice. They were now receiving out of schedule pay. What this meant was employees who were performing the same job that was abolished were now getting paid extra money to perform it. Instead of their regular pay, it was now time and a half, pay. By contract, the postal service must have compensated an employee who filled in a position that was not a bid position of their own and who was out of their regular bid or assigned schedule.

For example, an employee whose pay was $26 per hour would now make $13 more an hour for a total of $39. Instead of regular pay at $208 a day, they would receive $312. That's an extra $104 a day. Instead of the weekly $1,040, it would be $1,560. Monthly, the regular pay of $4,160 would be $6,240. In short, the postal service was paying $2,080 more per employee per month to do the same job.

The reason, to remove me. At most, they would have been able to remove four employees to stay somewhat afloat. They removed nine. This meant four extra employees before me, to get to me, which made me number five and a total of nine employees.

This was a disservice to the agency. Some of those employees were held over for seven to eight months. No accountability for the loss of hundreds of thousands of dollars, no accountability for the grievances I filed. Craft employees were held accountable for performing at the highest standards of being a U.S. postal employee, so why was management not held at an even higher standard?

The station was mismanaged, performing criminal acts through the misuse of resources and authority. They did so to inflict unnecessary pain that promoted a hostile work environment. The manager and supervisors of the station were negligent in maintaining a productive level that would ensure all mail would make its cutoff point and be distributed in a timely manner to make its destination.

Months later the manager who oversaw this entire process was promoted for his incompetency to a higher level paying job at a different facility.

His successor had an awfully big mess to clean up. My immediate supervisor, Keeton, was temporarily appointed as acting station manager. Though she told me that she didn't want the responsibility, I believed that she wanted the position. I was happy for her personally to have been promoted, but a bit apprehensive in letting her know what other emotions where coming into play. I had sensed a change in her demeanor, something was not quite right. She had been actively involved from the beginning of this entire realignment process to the end. That could have taken a toll on her.

It was the manager's decision in the end as to how he would adjust the different jobs but he received a vital part of his information from his supervisors. They ran the floor and made up scheduling of job assignments for the employees, and knew what it took to process the mail in a timely and effective manner. To implement a plan to remove so many people would be self-destructive and would no doubt handicap the operation.

Now that my immediate supervisor had the duties of both supervision and acting manager, I wanted to believe that the station was in good hands because she was in control. Knowing her as I believed I did for more than three years, I honestly felt a sense of security and that she would do what was right. She knew a great deal about the operation and the station's history as well as my history within the station.

Still I did not put my full trust and faith into management. I did take into consideration that she was under the command of her superior, who was the person that left the station in this nonproductive predicament. She had every right to be given a fair chance and the benefit of any doubt.

I mainly did not want to sabotage a potentially good working relationship. There was a chance that this could, however, possibly happen now that she was no longer under the direction of her previous supervisor.

I believed the station could change but it would take a firm, but even hand. It would also take someone who believed in their job and who had compassion. The job required someone with integrity, someone's whose number one priority was to do what was right. I thought maybe she could be the one.

It had not been a month since the last manager had left and history repeated itself. On March 30, 2009, I was bypassed for overtime. What came to mind was the saying about a leopard not changing its spots. I contacted Keeton, who served as my immediate supervisor and station manager, to make her aware of the infraction. I explained to her that a non-volunteer and a nonqualified scheme person could work overtime, where I was a volunteer with more seniority and a qualified scheme person.

It was a violation of the national bargaining agreement.

Though she was aware of the situation she did absolutely nothing to resolve it and this was not like her. Something was happening with her, something that I dreaded to even think about. I thought maybe she was given too much responsibility too soon. Because she showed me that she had no intentions of rectifying the situation, I filed a grievance.

I regretted doing this. I did not want this single incident to become an issue that would interfere with what I considered to be a good rapport with her. The grievance was processed and filtered through the channels on April 24, 2009.

I was put on jobs that required two, at times three people, to complete in a timely manner. I received no help with the expectation of getting it done. I'd been here before. Textbook retaliation.

New supervisors were placed in the station to free up the manager from performing a supervisory role. Even though I had a new and permanent immediate supervisor, the acting manager continued to play a major role in the scheduling of employees. She spent 95 percent of her time on the workroom floor instructing employees. It was a confusing situation because employees did not know on a day-to-day basis the reporting order. One supervisor would give you one order. Another changed it.

Keeton loved telling people what to do. Never had I seen her demonstrate such dominance. She was a completely different person. The soft-spoken supervisor with a pleasant demeanor that I had initially met was gone. It was a gradual change that surfaced and became more noticeable during the realignment process. I clearly noticed the change after I filed my grievance. It irritated her after she lost the grievance. Management behavior was in full force. I knew it well.

I also knew the stress and pain that I would experience as a result. It exacerbated the knee injury I had suffered while in the military. Because of this injury, I received FMLA (Family and Medical Leave Act) certification back in 2006 and also the status of a disabled Vietnam combat veteran through Veterans Affairs. Furthermore, on March 20, 2009, doctors diagnosed the injury as a lifelong condition after an extended amount of examinations.

My survivor instinct developed during the war was even more sensitive and intense because I had no one looking out for me other than two of my co-workers. As with previous managers, I distanced myself from Keeton. My purpose was to survive, and so I continued to document everything.

On April 14, 2009, the union steward came into the facility for an investigative interview with management about bypassing me for overtime opportunities. The steward also informed the manager and supervisors of the contract agreement through the national bargaining. Management told the steward that this did not concern them and that they would repeat the process of violating the agreement, bypassing me for overtime. The next day, April 15, 2009, they did. A week later I filed another grievance and received the same results.

I also filed an EEO complaint about their defiance where I included the union step-two grievance appeal form. This form illustrated management's first violation of the national agreement and the union steward's statement where she quoted what was said in the investigative interview. Specifically, she noted where they said they would do it again.

This EEO complaint was investigated by the Washington, DC office, and was denied stating, "they found management's actions not to be discriminatory." But, the grievance was proven to be a violation of the bargaining agreement and I was awarded 16 hours of overtime makeup. The EEO decision was a manipulation of the system to justify an injustice that enabled employers to commit unfair treatment and practices of employees.

These types of rulings often came back with a vengeance where employees sought out justice themselves by gunning down their offenders and where, at times, innocent bystanders became victims. Keeton's action was deliberate to provoke me and, in my opinion, was with intent to cause an adverse reaction. Violence.

It was confirmed in a conversation that I had with my then immediate supervisor, Derrick Sharpe, on April 16, 2009, the day after the second violation that was approved by his supervisor, the acting manager. I asked, "Why?" He said he had to do what his boss told him to do. His boss was Keeton. It was now her way or no way policies. Procedures had no place under her supervision. It was beyond imagination to see the transformation in her.

This change had begun to hurt production, and that challenged and jeopardized the small amount of morale that had developed when she first took over as the acting manager.

55

TOUR OF DUTY

The U.S. Postal Service was a 24-hour, 365-day operation separated into three different shifts. It was identified by tours and numbers. Tour One hours were from 10 p.m. to 6:30 a.m.; Tour Two hours were from 4 a.m. to 2:30 p.m.; and Tour Three hours were from 3:30 p.m. to midnight. These were the operating hours at the General Mail Facility. However, station hours of operation could vary in time from 30 minutes up to two or three hours depending on the individual needs and the location. Mail was distributed from the plant to these different locations in a 24-hour period. My work schedule was from 2 a.m. to 10:30 a.m., so I was considered Tour One, along with two other employees.

The plant's dispatch of mail to the downtown station was at 1:15 a.m., 2:45 a.m., 4 a.m., 5:45 a.m. and 8 a.m. These were the scheduled times for the arrival of Motor Vehicle Service for delivery. The scheduling was in sequence with the dispatch times of the plant.

The mail from the 1:15 a.m. delivery would be there waiting at the station and ready to be processed and worked. The two of us worked it until the next delivery, which was one hour and 30 minutes later at 2:45 a.m. In most cases, we would have a higher volume of mail. One other clerk would arrive at 3 a.m., in time to help with that delivery. This mail was worked up until 4 a.m. when the station would receive the bulk of its mail and the rest of the working staff.

Eighty to 90 percent of this mail in most cases would be ready for the relay drivers who reported for work at 4:30 a.m. They distributed the mail that had been processed earlier to different buildings, in the downtown area where mail carriers received this mail in what was known as vim rooms. In those rooms, mail carriers made the final separation of the mail by addresses then made their daily deliveries.

I had been in the downtown station more than 20 years where the same system had been in existence and had been productively effective during that time. Reports were the acting manager had decided that a change was needed in scheduling and reporting times of clerks because mail volume was down and that the MVS had changed their delivery times. This was not true. MVS logs showed that dispatch was the same but the volume of mail was uncertain. No one could predict the volume of mail on a daily basis, but she tried. She tried to use that as leverage in justification to reporting time changes. I believe that change could be good, if for the better. It was not the case in this particular instance.

It was sad to see the change in Keeton. She had picked up were other managers had left off.

The motive for the time change was the discontinuance of Tour One. It was the only way that she could remove my two co-workers and me from our positions. The change was activated under false pretenses and she reported to her superiors that the MVS had changed their delivery schedule. It was not coincidental to me that this announcement was made soon after I had filed the two grievances against her.

The amazing part of it all was that human resource would take her word for it without double checking with the General Mail Facility. All they needed to do was request a copy of their dispatch schedule. It could have been faxed in a matter of seconds.

It held true for the downtown station that human resources could have requested a copy of the MVS log book that was signed each day by the driver showing time of arrival and departure. I could not say that human resource did not do this. Nor could I say the results would have been different had it been done.

The junior clerk, whose job was abolished, was relocated to the General Mail Facility. The two remaining clerks, another co-worker and me, were placed on Tour Two which was originally scheduled 4 a.m. to 12:30 p.m. My co-worker's hours of reporting were now from 4:30 a.m. to 1 p.m. My hours were scheduled at 5 a.m. to 1:30 p.m. Only one clerk kept the original schedule.

The MVS deliveries had not changed to what was reported by the acting manager. It remained the same where the mail continued to come in on the five different dispatch schedules. Because Tour One was discontinued, the mail would sit on the dock and pile-up for hours with no one to work it until 4:30 a.m.

It was the time my co-worker reported to work. It was a bad situation for everyone because when the four o'clock clerk reported to work he could not work the mail. His job was to open the doors, retrieve the mail from the dock and take each cage to its prospective staging area to be processed. This took time. By this time the relay drivers had reported at 4:30 a.m., the same time as the other co-worker.

Ninety eight percent of the time they had no mail at all to dispatch to the mail carriers in the vim rooms because it had not been worked. If there was any mail at all to be dispatched to the vim rooms, it was very little. They could do only one thing and that was sit around and wait until the mail was worked. Keeton used this reason as to why she discontinued Tour One: the clerks had no work to perform.

Many of the relay drivers had this bright idea that they could work and process the mail because they had nothing to do. The processing of mail was a clerk craft position and a violation of the national bargaining agreement. For those carriers to even touch that mail was crossing craft. Grievances were filed by clerks against the relay drivers and carriers, who were inappropriately doing clerk work. Relay drivers and carriers took those filings as personal attacks. Once again management had caused dissension among the workers. Keeton's decision cost man hours in overtime, and also lost revenue for the U.S. Postal Service.

Only one clerk reported in at 4 a.m. The relay drivers were in at 4:30 a.m., leaving 30 minutes in between where that one clerk had no time to process any mail. The relay drivers, in turn, were standing around doing nothing and the postal service eventually lost more money, paying for our grievances.

Management began bringing clerks in early for overtime at 4 a.m. and some were coming in out-of-schedule. In both cases, it cost the postal service extra money in lost revenue. Management could not bring anyone in for work before 4 a.m. That would be considered Tour One, which had been discontinued. Had they brought anyone in before 4 a.m., they would have had to reinstate the positions for me and my two co-workers.

Sharpe reported to me that Keeton had falsely reported to human resources that the volume of mail had decreased at the downtown station and that the delivery hours had changed. He had been at that meeting with her and was in line to receive a promotion to that manager's position at the station himself. It must have been an odd meeting because he, along with Keeton, the current acting manager were in line for that same job.

I went to Keeton and asked as humbly as I knew how for any reason why my job was taken away from me. With no hesitation, she pointed the finger at human resources. I quickly decided that she needed to know just what I knew and how I knew it, so I gave her direct information. I withheld nothing about my conversation with my immediate supervisor. She did not deny her report to human resources and only said, "What's done is done."

This was the turning point. My respect for her was no longer there.

It had now reached a point that whenever I would call in for sick leave request she would require that I provide documentation for my absence. At this point, I had never been on any type of sick leave restriction. She was violating the national bargaining agreement.

56

WINDOW QUALIFIED

On April 18, 2009, I called in requesting sick leave and was put in for LWOP (Leave Without Pay.) This meant that I would not get paid for this day until documentation was provided. She began watching the punch-in clock from the time I started work until the end. One tick before my reporting time would mean unauthorized overtime and unscheduled before the tour. One tick after my reporting time would mean I was late for work. One tick was the equivalent of one half minute which by human error would happen most every day with most every employee.

She would make some employees complete a 3971, otherwise known as a Leave Request Form. Too many of these forms could result in disciplinary action up to removal. I was required to fill out a 3971 when I was late. Certain team players were not required to do so when they were late. I documented dates, times and the names of those individuals who were not required to do so.

I couldn't recall a time when a week passed where I was not in contact with APWU. I was informing them by telephone, through grievances, statements, and at times, personal appearances of how I was being treated by management.

An independent investigation of this troubled facility would have been huge. Even as much as an inquiry to the leadership and the erratic behavior of those in this station would have been a start. I told them in letters I had written to them with certified return receipts mail.

It seemed that animosity and anger drove Keeton's spirit. She would not accept documentation when documentation was provided. Most everyone knew when an employee called in requesting sick leave that it would ignite her rage. She would walk up and down the workroom floor and aisles, glaring and barking out commands. I was cautious, but not intimidated by this juvenile behavior. I was a seasoned veteran of management's abuse. I wasn't impressed.

Many voiced their concerns, but only behind her back. They may have called her "bitch" behind her back, but they were careful not to draw attention to themselves by filing grievances. Most importantly, they remained in good standing with managers and supervisors by kissing their asses.

The most popular way that many managers used to harass employees was by accusing them of not doing their job, which was a sure way to disciplinary actions up to removal. Each employee had deadlines to meet in the production flow to meet daily goals recorded by managers.

On April 27, 2009, the union received a statement from one of my co-workers. She reported that she worked three feet away from me every day, all day and that management continued to accuse "Garland Lewis" of purposely slowing down the mail. She was explicit in saying that there was no truth to those allegations and that I would work steadily each day. She also reported that management would not give me any help. She noted that the slow-down was normal after so many jobs had been abolished.

The zero-tolerance policy was just a policy for me and very few others – not management. Everyone knew. The APWU could not give me any answers as to why management, who are employees of the U.S. Postal Service, was not under that same policy. I went to upper management for the answers. I had sent certified return receipt letters to the area manager, district manager, postmaster and other officials who would have this propaganda of the" zero-tolerance policy" placed on bulletin boards. That was strictly under the discretion of managers and enforced under certain circumstances.

It was perfectly okay for management to continue to lose grievances that would cost the postal service in lost revenue and redress hearings. That, in many cases, showed the negligence and arrogance of those managers and supervisors alike. They continued to demonstrate that the zero-tolerance policy did not apply to them. It was, in fact, the U.S. Postal Service revenue that paid for those perpetrators to continue violating policy.

On April 30, 2009, at approximately 10 a.m. I was at my workstation performing my duties when Keeton approached me and asked me if I would come to the manager's office so that she could talk with me. Trouble raced to the top of my mind. I could not imagine anything good coming from this. It had been quite a while since she and I talked without the end result being trouble. I was hesitant and uncomfortable, but there was no other supervisor with her when she approached me. At that point, the threat did not seem as intimidating.

Not even 10 seconds after I walked into the office, J.C. Jones, a floor supervisor, entered into the manager's office. My fear of trouble had become a reality. As he entered and before he could close the office door I asked Keeton, "What is this?" She then informed me that she was transferring me to the General Mail Facility. I immediately stood up and informed her that this meeting was over and if she needed to talk with me any further, especially about something of this magnitude, to follow procedure and have a union steward present. I told her that I would not talk with her or anyone else in management without one and I walked out.

Around 11:45 a.m., my name was called over the intercom to report to the manager's office. I had already seen the union steward enter the station well before this announcement was made so I knew that it was okay to go to the office. As I entered the office the same two management personnel were there along with the union steward.

Keeton did not wait for me to sit before she once again informed me that she was planning to transfer me to the GMF for creating a "hostile work environment." She went on to say that other employees had come to her complaining that I had been slowing down on my work and that they were tired of doing my job. She then gave me the date and time to report to the GMF.

I asked about the allegations. From the beginning, I wanted her to know that I was well aware of what she was trying to pull and that it was criminal, attempting to provoke me into some sort of aggressive reaction. What she was accusing me of was a flat out lie. The game that she was playing was dirty.

She said I should not worry about the other employees and that this was "between you and me." Nonsense! I then reminded her that her actions were premeditated, involving so many others to bear false witness. She had created the hostile work environment. She could not grasp that my rights were to face my accusers, and she repeated that it was between the two of us. So, I repeated my concerns. The results were the same.

I reminded her that I was the senior person whose job was abolished. Before she could remove me from the station, by agreement, there were three other employees at this station that were junior to me. Their jobs had also been abolished, so they should have been transferred before me.

The union steward reiterated my points and told the acting manager that she very well knew that this was a violation of management and the union's agreement. The steward informed her that she would be filing a grievance. Keeton responded by saying, "Do what you have to do." The union steward and I left the office after what I described as a witch hunt. I was never interviewed, much less, given the opportunity to tell my side, even though there was nothing to tell.

Prior to this meeting I had never been confronted by management with concerns about my productivity. She called me to her office to convey this. Yet disciplinary action was taken against me by removing me from my job, sending me to a completely different facility, changing my days off and my reporting time. This completely disrupted my life.

The union steward thought that maybe the tension would have been diffused had I not been present, knowing how Keeton felt about me. She made an attempt, after the meeting was over, to get together with management to find some sort of resolution instead of going to the extreme of sending me to the GMF.

She tried to convince Keeton that this was wrong, that I was the senior clerk accessed from the station, and that the postmaster's office and the APWU had an agreement that seniority would prevail when sending excess clerks back to the GMF. She would not budge. The union steward contacted the APWU president.

The APWU president was in disbelief after learning of Keeton's refusal to acknowledge the agreement. He contacted the postmaster's office in hopes of alleviating the problem. He discussed the issue with Dave Sims, the postmaster's assistant, who served in powerful roles including as the HR coordinator, the negotiator for this agreement and the primary person in charge of the entire realignment of the stations.

Sims was in agreement with the union's position that to remove me from the station and transfer me to the GMF would be a problem. The APWU president asked if he would call Keeton at the downtown station and fix the problem. He agreed. The president called the union steward and informed her that the HR coordinator agreed with the union's position and that the problem had been resolved.

Later that day, I was informed by my union steward that the problem had been resolved and to remain at the station. This sequence of events all took place on Thursday, April 30, 2009. The next day on May 1, 2009, I called the APWU president after receiving instructions from Keeton where nothing had changed. My detail assignment at the downtown station was still going to be terminated. I was to report to the GMF. He was shocked.

After reviewing the conversations with him from the previous day, he hung up and called Keeton. She then informed him that she and Sims had decided to terminate my detail assignment anyway and only keep window qualified clerks at the station on detail. There were three people that were junior to me who were qualified window clerks at the time. I was not.

The reason given for the termination of my detail assignment had changed. It was no longer for allegedly creating a hostile work environment. It was because I was not window qualified. The two had time to collaborate.

After the APWU president received this information from Keeton, he called the HR coordinator. This person had now changed his earlier position and went against his agreement with the union president and against his leadership as a spokesman for the postmaster's office.

The union and I had to conform to the operations of management. The president knew the story, but tried working with management, giving them the benefit of the doubt. If management used those clerks, who were junior to me on the window, then they would be grievance proof.

The next day window service began at 8 a.m. Those junior clerks, who remained at the station, reported to work at 4 a.m., performing those duties that I was terminated from doing. If they were for performing window duties, they would have been scheduled to report at 8 a.m.

I witnessed these junior employees reporting for work at 4 a.m., performing my day-old duties. The reason was that I had not yet left the downtown station. Through all of the confusion, management had instructed me to leave without giving me any sort of paperwork and the union, so far, had been telling me to remain at the station because everything had been resolved.

The union was to get back with me by the end of the day on Friday, April 30, 2009, but that communication never happened. Before I left for the day I went to Sharpe for instructions. Keeton had left for the weekend and I could not get in touch with the union. He was clueless and even more confused than I was, but he decided and instructed me to report at my regular time the next day to the station.

That was how I witnessed others doing my job at 4 a.m. I had to report somewhere or risk having an unauthorized absence (UA) which would have been an added feature as far as disciplinary action. The manager could have placed it into my personnel file, counting me AWOL.

I was under the instructions of my immediate supervisor where I could clock in and begin my tour working the flat case on that day. I felt very uncomfortable and extremely confused not knowing if I was doing the right thing by being there. In giving the instructions that he gave me, I knew he was clueless.

On Saturday, May 1, 2009, I immediately called the APWU president and informed him of what I saw. He called Keeton and informed her of the violation to that agreement and that the union would be filing a grievance. I was growing angrier by the minute, but stayed calm. I knew the traps. I admit that I was confused about where to report for work.

While I was working at the flat case my conscience got the best of me. I went to the supervisor's office and asked if he would call Keeton at home for instructions. The supervisor made the call and what I believed would happen, happened. She was outraged. Her voice pounded through the telephone. I heard every word. She wanted me to end my tour and leave the building.

I went home and waited to hear from my union representatives, which I did over the weekend. I received instructions from the APWU to proceed to the GMF that Sunday night and to report at 10 p.m. I reported to automation that night where management had no expectancy of my arrival. They didn't know my name, where I came from or why I was there. I explained the situation to the supervisor in charge that night. I gave her my name and previous station. I was then assigned to a crew on the automation machines where I worked for an entire week before any other supervisor knew I was in the building.

It was not until the end of the pay period when employee timesheets are processed through the system that the U.S. Postal Service realized they were missing an employee. I was lost in the system. My time was not being put in through the downtown station because I was no longer there. The GMF was not putting my time in because they never knew that I was even in the building, let alone working there.

The entire process was done illegally. The directions I received from management and the APWU were ambiguous. Keeton tried filing disciplinary action against me for not following instructions.

When I arrived for work on that Friday evening I was told by the supervisor to report to the manager's office. His first words were, "How did you get here?" and "Where's your paperwork?"

The entire sequence of events would not have transpired had the HR coordinator had just one ounce of integrity, just a smidgen of honesty, and a drop of decency. This coordinator was supposed to represent an agency that was supposed to be well-respected and possess quality standards and morals. The truth could be nasty and intense.

Unlike others, I believe I was fortunate that I could present true facts with true evidence. Each management personnel who had any sort of involvement or affiliation with this process was in violation of the rules within the agency and had broken several laws.

This scheme was not well thought out. It was a spontaneous move on her part that required a group of management personnel to meet her at a low level. The scheme would not have materialized without the contributions of her peers. Keeton's rage superseded any form of harassment and took it to another level. She got this far in her efforts because her behavior went unchallenged and not punished. It was the nucleus as to why she continued to violate the contract, ignoring rules and regulations. The violations speak for themselves.

57

THE BLUE LINE

The U.S. Postal Service relies on a recording device used for the purpose of attendance control. The ERMS (Employee Recorder Message System) received and monitored calls of unscheduled sick leave requests. When an employee called in requesting sick leave this device would activate. It recorded the information that identified and evaluated the status of the employee. If the caller was deemed to have abused his or her sick leave, they were placed on what was called "blue line" or flagging. These were terms used to identify a person on sick leave restriction.

The ERMS could be programmed to request the required documentation for that request. The Attendance Control system monitored sick leave usage of all employees and made the determination if an employee was abusing sick leave. The system then could make the recommendation for that employee to be placed on restriction.

This system had been used and abused for retaliation and intimidation. Managers had entered employees into the system without probable cause.

Before I knew it, Keeton had me illegally placed on this Blue Line list and on a sick leave restriction status. That meant that whenever I called in for sick leave, I was required to bring in documentation.

It was illegal and a violation of the national bargaining agreement where protocol was not followed and procedures were violated. When an employee was deemed to have abused his or her sick leave, the attendance control system notified the manager at the facility of the discrepancies. At that time, a manager from the attendance control unit would come to the station to meet with the employee to discuss the.

During the discussion, the discrepancies were laid out in detail for the employee to visually go over their excessive usage. The employee had due process or the right to be given an opportunity to correct the problem. If it was not rectified and the problem persisted, a letter of warning could then be issued. After that, sick leave restriction could be invoked.

I had not gone through one step of this procedure when on May 15, 2009, I was improperly placed on Blue Line. It left me flagged on the ERMS device that was put in place by her while I was at the GMF. I was illegally in the system and remained in that system for more than two and half months. While at the GMF, I filed a grievance for this illegal act that was taken against me by Keeton.

The manager at the GMF confirmed and expressed to me that it was not warranted and it was illegal. Eventually, I was removed from the restriction list. But I was astounded that Keeton's boss never challenged or reversed her illegal actions, when ultimately, she had the authority to do so.

Members of the APWU, the officials and I had discussed over the years what could possibly be done to get management off my back. Answers escaped us all. The best and only advice that the union could give was for me to watch myself.

Other employees were placed on sick leave restriction. Many in the station knew that Keeton had it out for me and feared that it could soon be them. The most frightening and intimidating aspect of it all was that most everyone knew I was being singled out. And as far as I was concerned it was accepted.

I challenged the illegal action and the violations that took place in April 2009 and on May 2 of that same year by going through the grievance process. The charges of those violations were rectified by either me being paid in full or given overtime make ups for the infraction. On April 30, 2009, a criminal action was taken to illegally remove me from the station. Keeton has falsified documents by providing names of people who never said the things that she reported. This issue was never settled because I was not given this job back and I was never compensated monetarily for working out of schedule in another job at the GMF.

There were two main reasons why this case was never settled. One of them was the APWU. The grievance was never heard because the union steward dropped the ball when they failed to process the grievance in a timely manner. It cost me thousands of dollars in out-of-schedule pay. A significant amount of damaging evidence was given to them, from memos and incident reports to statements.

The union had options and avenues to keep this case alive. If time was a factor, they could have easily requested an extension. The elements were there and available for the union to make the necessary preparations to present a strong and effective argument.

The EEO agency was the second reason and the most serious contributor to the unfair practices continuing in the United States Postal Service. The aggression and intimidation of managers at all levels would be at a minimum, if not eliminated, had this agency performed and defended the constitution of this government agency and maintained the practices of basic law.

The case went to an informal investigation. The same charges were presented with the same material of proof that was provided in the grievance process. In fact, the EEO agency had even more material than that of the grievance findings. Through those findings three of the four charges were found in my favor. The most serious one was that of the April 30, 2009 incident that presented a problem for both the APWU and EEO agency. It was the most serious charge that went against the law and gave the most incriminating evidence.

There were testimonies and statements of those that was involved or any sort of affiliation with what occurred on April 30, 2009. It included all documentation, official memos, etc. We did not, however, have the connection and conversation between Keeton and the HR coordinator between the time the HR coordinator conversed with the APWU and Keeton. It was during that time when he changed his position. So, what made him change?

Still, the EEO agency had all of the necessary documents to make a decisive and fair decision given the evidence. Filing this EEO gave clarity to a cover-up that was spearheaded by Keeton and her accomplice, the human resource coordinator.

The extent of lies and contradictions laid out a pattern by people who had done this before. Statements of testimonies were changed with a black magic pen marker. Paragraphs were altered with these markers that made sentences incomplete so that they could not be deciphered or understood. These actions made the documents unofficial.

The EEO investigators based their decision on statements that were inconsistent from week to week, and only from management personnel with no one else to confirm any of the allegations in the statements. My testimony and statements were never considered, not even that of the union steward or the statement of the APWU President. If they would have been considered their decision might have been completely different.

Her initial investigative statement reported that several employees had reported to her that they were tired of busting their butts doing their jobs, and that I wasn't helping. She said they were tired of my attitude and that they could see when I was upset about something because I would throw parcels of mail into gurneys provided for outgoing mail for the drivers as if they were rockets or missiles. I was allegedly creating a hostile work environment.

She went on to say the relay drivers stated that they would completely remove all the parcels and flats, which are larger envelopes of mail, from the flat cases that I worked. After their deliveries to carriers, which took about 90 minutes, she said that they would return for more mail only to find empty flat cases and letter cases. Her account was not true.

Keeton was asked why their complaints were not reported to upper management. She said because employees were afraid that I would retaliate against them if I knew who reported this to her. The investigative statement from the supervisor, who was in the meeting of April 30, 2009 to remove me from the downtown station, gave no sort of confirmation to these allegations. He was vague. These claims had not been investigated.

During the EEO investigation, Keeton could change her statement to address the fact that I was not qualified to work the window. It did not take a rocket scientist to realize that this investigation wasn't to find out the truth of what really happened on April 30, 2009. It was a cover up to activities unbecoming of a postal worker, which were grounds for termination up to imprisonment. Her actions were laced with criminal behavior.

It wasn't until two months later, on June 11, 2009, that the HR coordinator put this new version in a statement. Keeton did the same on the same date. The supervisor, who was also in the April 30, 2009 meeting, wrote his statement on Oct. 17, 2009 and including the same version. Sharpe, who had gotten involved by that point, confirmed both of their statements in a statement of his own on Oct. 29, 2009.

There should have been a thorough investigation conducted about the entire scheme and false allegations because: 1) this behavior that I was accused of was never reported to security or any one of authority, 2) I was never charged with behavior unbecoming of a postal worker, 3) there was never an investigation conducted as to the allegations, and 4) I was not notified by any management personnel of this behavior prior to being removed.

News traveled fast within the postal service that I had been removed from the downtown station. It astonished most everyone because they knew that I was senior to those employees that remained at the station.

One of those junior employees, who remained at the station happened to be a union steward. Self-preservation was his only concern, not the solidarity that the APWU officials preached to its members nor the integrity to stand up in defense for its members.

But there were also a few not afraid to voice their concerns. During my career, I had heard about and witnessed stressful situations that have caused people to commit suicide or go postal. On May 6, 2009 an employee, who worked at the Montclair postal facility, committed suicide. It was the same station that employed my brother, who had also committed suicide in January 1986.

58

THE PETITION?

One of my co-workers had faced many obstacles in the station and experienced more than her share of management's abusive tactics. I had worked with her for more than 20 years and she knew my struggles with management. On May 11, 2009, she took a stance where she typed up a form on my behalf. She asked every employee to read and sign at their discretion. It stated:

> "I have worked with and around 'Garland Lewis' and in my opinion, I have not had a problem in any way in which he performs his work assignments."

She gave this form to one of the relay drivers who was also a union steward for the letter carriers in the building. He knew me and had worked around me for more than 10 years. He was one of the first to sign the form and was more than happy to take the form around to each employee in the station to read.

There were more than 20 signatures on the form most of whom were relay drivers that came in contact with me every day. By this time, I was no longer at the station. I was at the GMF. I was amazed and flattered.

What was most intriguing and damaging to Keeton's initial statement was the list of names. They were the same people who had supposedly reported to her that I was not doing my job and creating a hostile work environment. She had listed them on the EEO affidavit.

In response to this letter circulating at her station, she expressed hostility and anger at a stand-up talk on June 26, 2009. As with any time that management gives a talk, most employees were in attendance. Afterward, a statement was written by the author of the letter, who was also at the meeting. This co-worker was the same person who gave the carriers union steward the letter for employees to sign about my performance. It stated:

> "On June 26, 2009 7:00 AM the acting manager had a standup talk with all employees she told everyone that she has had diabetes for the past 20 years and as a result she is having trouble with her vision so she is having surgery on her eye. That is why she will be leaving for a while and not because some idiot has a petition going around trying to get her removed from the station."

The fact that Keeton referred to the letter as a "petition" alarmed those who signed it. They were in a panic that she was putting them on notice. They were misled to believe that it was a petition to have her removed from the station. They were angry with me. I could not comprehend their logic. Didn't they read the letter before they signed it? The power of fear and intimidation derailed the importance of this form that would give proof and evidence that she lied.

Word got back to me at the GMF of their logic. They now believed I had tricked them into signing the form. I was bewildered.

In all honesty, they were just afraid of the system in the agency. They were in fear of retaliation, particularly from Keeton, who had already demonstrated juvenile behavior. The last thing that I would have wanted was for anyone to go through the punishment and torment of an "administrative scheme" that I knew all too well.

I knew that I would have to speak directly to each individual that signed the form to assure them that what they had signed was not a petition for the removal of Keeton, but a mere request to their opinion relating to my work habits. This would be difficult for me to do because I was not allowed to enter the downtown station, but faith had its way of making a way.

I was awarded a bid job back to the downtown station in June 2009. Many questioned this. Before bidding back to the downtown station I had bid a job at the GMF and was awarded the job. It consisted of driving around town from station to station collecting miss-sent priority and express mail, but I was not allowed to do the actual job. I was placed in a completely different operation, working the same job that I did at an entry-level when I first started with the U.S. Postal Service. That was sitting and placing mail in a case, which had late nights and bad days off.

I went to the APWU to file a grievance about management not allowing me to work the job that I bid on and was awarded. The union said that they could not do a thing about it because all bids read "or where needed." I was treated like a person with one year of service and not of the 29 years that I had. The job that I had bid for at the downtown station, and that I was awarded, had window qualifications.

Before I could be placed in the job I had to complete window training. I received instructions from the downtown station to report to the Sunnyside postal facility for training at the end of the month.

Upon my arrival to that station I was instructed to report to the manager's office. I knew the manager because at one time she was a supervisor at the downtown station. In fact, she was the same supervisor I reported the incident of April 6, 1995 to. Amos was now a manager after her many episodes of falsifying documents. She nor her staff had any idea why I was there. I told her. Her solution was to send me back to the downtown station.

I was instructed by the manager at the Sunnyside station to report to the downtown station on July 1, 2009. I reported on that day and they too had not the slightest idea of what was going on. Keeton was on sick leave. I was on the clock so I was given a temporary job at the station until they could sort out this entire mess. I knew that I wasn't going to be in the station long so the next day was the perfect opportunity to talk with those who felt victimized after hearing the acting manager speech in her standup talk.

I was under extreme fire and ridicule. I had to go about it delicately. It was difficult to connect with each one of them because of the different personalities. But, I could not let this opportunity slip away to reassure each person I saw on the list that in no way was it ever a petition to remove Keeton from her position. Her name nor her position was in the letter. I also informed them of my intentions to use it in my defense that could only help in proving of my innocence of the false allegations.

I gave each of those individuals who I had spoken with that day my word and asked if they would pass it on to others because I did not know how long I would be there. I gave them my word that I would not relinquish this form for any purpose other than for a grievance or an EEO complaint as part of my discovery. I also let them know that they could remove their name if they chose to do so.

The next day I was sent to another postal facility for window training.

On Tuesday, July 14, 2009, I completed my window training and reported back to the downtown station.

I made good on my promise by not releasing any information for any reason to anyone. I also brought the form into the station that day for those to read that were interested and if they had signed the form the opportunity was made available to remove your name if so desired. Not a single person removed their name. As a matter of fact, two others added their names.

The information that the EEO investigators had in their possession to make a fair and honest determination of what took place on April 30, 2009, included:

1. Written statements that my job was being done.
2. Over 20 signatures confirming that my job was getting done.
3. The two different stories Keeton gave as to why I was removed.
4. No witness statements to the allegations of not performing my job.
5. No investigative reports into the allegations.
6. Never was informed by any management personnel or disciplined for not performing my job.

Evidence showed management's blatant disregard for policies and procedures. Their cover-up revealed agreements breached, perjury and falsification of documents from management.

Those clerks that remained at the station were never used on the window because their starting times remained at 4 a.m. There was not at that time a United States Postal Service customer service window open in the state of Colorado at 4 a.m., yet those clerks who remained at the station were beginning their work at that time. The earliest that customer service windows would open was 8 a.m.

Between 4 a.m. and 8 a.m. the junior employees that remained were doing the job that I was illegally removed from. Their administrative scheme was in full effect.

There was a code of conduct that window clerks must display each day by portraying an atmosphere in the U.S. Postal Service that was pleasant and of tranquility. The clerks upfront were monitored by camera all day every day that are connected through the postmaster's office. The truth lies behind the wall.

There was no rhyme or reason as to why an agency of this global magnitude persisted to violate the fundamentals of equality and fairness. My life at the postal service had been plagued by a long history of grievances, EEO complaints, police, postal inspectors, the criminal justice system, removal, arbitration, suspensions, emergency placements, and even incarceration.

I was back in the station because of my principles along with perseverance and fortitude and "God Almighty." It was better for me to know my enemies in that station, than not, in another.

Two weeks had gone by since I had been back in the station and the atmosphere was pretty laid back. Word began going around that Keeton was on her way back to the station. I was very uncomfortable with her return, but it was principle that kept me strong and pushed me to complete the task at hand in finishing the course and retiring from the U.S. Postal Service.

I needed to keep my distance. I was intimidated to a degree but what frightened me most was the lack of professionalism and strong emphasis that was put on reprisal in this agency. Each one of us had a job to do that should have been priority, yet retaliation was priority to these managers and supervisors in this dysfunctional system that was behind many killings and suicides, unbeknownst to the public.

I wanted to be optimistic. I was very careful and aware of what could happen and what had happened in the past. I worked very hard each day not to attract her attention. I came to work on time, did my job. I followed the break schedule and I punched in and off of the clock at the precise time. I had no problems following orders or procedure hoping that this would be pleasing to her and that she would stay away from me. Unfortunately, it wasn't enough.

On Aug. 5, 2009, I was working at the customer service window when Keeton along with Johnson, who was under the EEO contract settlement agreement, approached me. Keeton was aware of the contract agreement that had been in place since Aug. 28, 2003 that stipulated that Johnson could not have any sort of contact or communication with me unless she and I both had a witness. I felt that this was intentional but I gave her the benefit of the doubt and politely asked her if she would not do that again.

Two days later, on Aug. 7, 2009, she repeated herself. Management had continued to violate this signed contract agreement since it was agreed upon six years ago through the redress system back in August 2003. The EEO office had condoned and encouraged the violation of this signed contract agreement.

Keeton was trying yet again to provoke me. I did not take the bait. She went back to bypassing me for over-time opportunities.

On Aug. 8, 2009, I called in for sick leave under FMLA that I had been approved of over five months earlier on March 20, 2009. Keeton refused to approve that request, which was not only a violation to the national bargaining agreement but, it was against the law. She claimed that the request for FMLA did not come across the ERMS as FMLA therefore she charged me with regular sick leave. I knew the intentions of management and had no desires to aid them to help destroy me.

Employees could abuse it and management could misuse it for personal reasons. I had always understood the importance of covering myself under sick leave usage and that provided me with a much needed edge for protection in the many years of abuse and harassment by management. It may sound like a game that both management and I were playing but for me it was nothing but survival.

Though Keeton refused to acknowledge the FMLA request, it was what I requested when I called in for sick leave on that day and what I wrote next to my signature on the 3971 form or notification of absence. Because she would not accept my request as FMLA I was not covered under the act's protection.

It was the beginning of a new episode so I made a request to hear the ERMS for myself to that day of my request but was denied with no reason. It was suspicious. I had not violated any terms or conditions of FMLA and it was covered by law. It was against the law for an employer to refuse FMLA approval.

She illegally flagged me once again on the ERMS, and I was required to provide documentation for any leave request. This was after the GMF deemed it to be improper and not warranted for me to be on this restriction. She knew her superiors would not challenge her.

On Aug. 21, 2009, I called in FMLA sick leave and was required to bring in documentation that I refused to provide for the simple fact that I was in my rights to use FMLA for my condition. It had already been determined that I met all of the requirements for FMLA approval. I was tired of being challenged and tested. It was an insult to me and to all combat war veterans to question the sacrifices we made that were reflected physically in our bodies and minds.

It had been about three weeks since her return to the station and once again I was working under those same hostile conditions.

The next day, Aug. 22, 2009, I did not return to work for the second day. Once again documentation was required. I gathered my composure from the day before and that made me realize by not providing documentation I was falling into management hands, though the request was illegal. It was producing a paper trail of not following directions. That would lead to disciplinary action so I had to do what was necessary to keep my head above water.

On the second day of my absence I visited my doctor's office. She provided me with the necessary documentation for that day. Upon my return to work I filed a grievance with the APWU for Aug. 21 and 22 for improper request of documentation. After going through the formalities, management agreed to pay for my mileage to the doctor's office for the improper request and any discipline removed from my files. Management's defense was that they had a right to mismanage. They loved their version of rights

It was a constant battle in the U.S. Postal Service, fighting a system that was determined to slip a criminal jacket on me.

My goal was to permanently be removed from this agency but on my terms, and I still had a long way to go. A lot of my time and effort was spent making sure that I made no mistakes filing grievances and EEO complaints. Ninety nine percent of the time the grievances were ruled in my favor. Management made it perfectly clear that by settling those grievances they were not confessing or admitting to doing anything wrong.

What ever happened to the zero-tolerance policy? When management continued to be found at fault in violation of one policy or another, what was most disturbing was that management referred to those violations as mistakes. It was appalling that those so-called mistakes continued to be against the same employee until either that employee resigned, or was terminated not to mention the unimaginable when lives were taken.

Though management settled every grievance that I filed monetarily for illegally having me on sick leave restriction by flagging me on the ERMS, it did not matter to them. Not one dime came out of their pockets. It was important to them to inconvenience me any time I called in for FMLA sick leave. I had to go to my doctor's office to obtain documentation because they made it a requirement. It was a vicious cycle that created tension and anxiety, most of all hatred and distrust for those responsible.

59

MY HEALTH

It had reached a point over several months that I was forced into filing a grievance once a week, sometimes every other week where management would abuse their authority. It was one of the reasons, among many, why the attack on me continued to intensify over the years. I could never release that kind of power to her or anyone else. Especially knowing how provocation was used in this agency to their advantage.

Tampering with my FMLA was a trigger point. Management was desperate to dirty my personnel file. Each time I was required to bring in documentation for my condition that was FMLA approved was against the law, but I would do it. Keeton could see that she wasn't getting anywhere but that did not stop her from trying.

My health condition was diagnosed as a lifelong condition. It was a chronic condition that required periodic visits for treatments by a healthcare provider. The employee rights and responsibilities under the Family and Medical Leave Act are clear, and reads, "FMLA makes it unlawful for any employer to interfere with restrain or deny the exercise of any right under FMLA discharge or discriminate against any person for opposing any practice made unlawful by FMLA or for involvement in any proceeding under or relating to FMLA."

Still I remained flagged on the ERMS. Oct. 24 and 31 of 2009, I was required to provide documentation for sick leave usage under FMLA.

Requesting documentation was management's way to deter employees from exercising their rights and to use their earned sick leave. I was put in for Leave Without Pay. Keeton claimed that the call was not FMLA so it was noted as regular sick leave and once again the ERMS recorder did not pick up the request that it was for FMLA. Once again through the grievance process I was paid for this illegal transaction of management but the on-going harassment and the violation of my rights was never addressed.

On Dec. 3, 2002, an article came in the National Association of Letter Carriers AFL-CIO about a class action where the parties agreed that the U.S. Postal Service may require employees' leave to be supported by an FMLA medical certification, unless waived by management for the absence to be protected. "When an employee uses leave due to a condition already supported by an FMLA certification the employee is not required to provide another certification for the absence to be FMLA protected."

What she was doing was illegal. The LWOP was illegal and because my call-in was not accepted as FMLA, Keeton recorded it as unscheduled absence. This got the attention of Attendance Control, so the supervisor of that unit was notified and subsequently visited the station to have an interview with me. My union steward was present during the interview as I tried explaining to the attendance supervisor that my actual request on Oct. 24 and 31, 2009 were FMLA.

I was so sure of what I had requested I went on to let the attendance supervisor know that I would gracefully accept any sort of punishment deemed fit, if my recording on the ERMS did not show that I requested FMLA. I then requested that my union steward and I be present for the review of this recording system.

The attendance control supervisor would not give me an answer to that request, but he went on to say that discipline was not up to him. It was up to my supervisor so I realized punishment was inevitable.

I was never given the opportunity to listen to the ERMS, yet I was disciplined with no proof of what management was claiming. I was given a letter of warning on management's word alone and charged with failure to be regular in attendance. She had an agenda with several reasons why she wanted the letter of warning placed into my personnel files. First and foremost, she wanted to trigger a violent response.

This letter of warning was supposed to address attendance only. She added two unrelated policies. The union referred to and argued this point during the proceedings. Here are the two items that were cited and her motive behind it.

1. *Discharge of duties= employees are expected to discharge their assigned duties conscientiously and effectively*
2. *Obedience to orders= employees must obey the instructions of their supervisor*

The two policies mentioned were a set-up for future harassment and discipline. It gave implications that I had violated these two policies before, along with attendance and had been warned. And this letter would set precedence for tougher disciplinary action up to removal. It was an illegal document. And management was notorious for using them. They should never be used or they should be exposed of after discipline has been served.

Through the grievance process I was compensated for the illegal requirement of documentation. The Letter of Warning worked its way through the system. I seriously wondered how far the agency would go to remove me. I had no protection under the law in this agency. Keeton's abuse of authority and obnoxious behavior for more than six years had gone unsupervised by upper management. The APWU knew. I felt that I was just spinning my wheels. It was like asking the police to police the police, which was in no way feasible. It was time to take it out of the U.S. Postal Service's hands, again.

On Dec. 15, 2009, I contacted the U.S. Labor Department to file a complaint.

PART TEN:

2010

60

FORCED TO TELL THE TRUTH

On Jan. 7, 2010, I received a letter from the U.S Labor Department notifying me that they had received my complaint and that they would be in touch in the near future. On Feb. 4, 2010, the complaint was reviewed and assigned to an investigator in that agency. On Feb.8, 2010 the records pertaining to the case were reviewed and several telephone calls were made to Keeton to get the U.S. Postal Service side of the complaint.

I was contacted by the labor agency the next day, Feb. 9, 2010, and was asked by the investigator to provide the necessary documentation, including my FMLA approved certification, the Letter of Warning, and both the 3971 leave request forms of FMLA sick leave for the days in question. The case was reviewed and conferred on Feb. 11, 2010 in association with the Baltimore, Maryland office.

On Feb. 12, 2010, I learned that there was no voice recorder only an electronic record of incoming calls that were scanned. When the acting manager was contacted she indicated that she could not respond to any further question from the Department of Labor until authorized by supervisors and attorneys and that she would call by Friday of that week.

The call never came in to the labor office. The investigators had made several attempts to reach the agency but to no avail. They did not receive a single call from the U.S. Postal Service that week. On that date, the case file was reviewed, and data entries were made and final conference reported. I was notified of the case results. The case files were reviewed and submitted for management viewing where the deposition of the U.S. Department of Labor followed.

The final conference was held and indicated that a miscommunication had occurred between the employee and management and that the allegations were remedied and the days in question now show as FMLA covered and will not have a negative impact on the employee.

After further review it was determined that there was no actual recording to be reviewed and evidence did show that I called and made a written request for FMLA sick leave through the 3971. A violation was charged and the employer agreed to remedy the situation by changing both days in question as being FMLA covered.

The performance of the U.S. Labor Department to assist me in my time of need was greatly appreciated. But for the agency and anyone that knew of the case or had any sort of affiliation with the case to use the term as a "miscommunication" between management and myself as to why the situation occurred was an injustice itself. That was not only an insult to my intelligence but a matter of politics.

The department expressed the decision that was made by the U.S. Postal Service was the "correct decision and the only decision considering the circumstances but mainly the facts." The facts showed evidence that did not discriminate against either party and to categorize this as a miscommunication where there was absolutely no foundation in making this determination was disturbing.

During the investigation, I was called by the labor investigator on several occasions to either provide information of some sort or answer some vital question. Requests were made to the U.S. Postal Service, but they would not return any of the calls that were made to them by the Labor Department. They had no justification or any sort of recording to substantiate the actions that were taken against me by the management personnel in the U.S. Postal Service. Mainly Keeton, yet it was labeled as a miscommunication.

The U.S. Labor Department's findings came out one week later on March 12, 2010 after the postal service settled the grievance at step two on March 5, 2010. They rescinded the letter of warning dated back on Nov. 12, 2009. The Labor Department had also ruled in my favor where evidence revealed that there never was a recording that the Postal Service ever produced. Had I not involved the Labor Department this information would have never been revealed.

This was not a voluntary act by the U.S. Postal Service to reveal this information. This was why an outside source was imperative to investigate any agency of misconduct and not leave it to that agency.

Those who were involved should not only lose their jobs, but should have served jail time. For three decades, I had been the victim of this brutality. Yet I was the only one that lost my job and had been put in jail. If there was any consolation, it was that I had been acquitted and not guilty to every criminal charge and disciplinary action that had been taken against me.

Though the Labor Department's presence made a difference in that instance for that moment on Dec. 23, 2009, management continued to illegally require documentation for approved FMLA sick leave request. I was compensated for the mileage to the doctor's office. Each time I was forced to provide documentation.

Management would always claim that it was legal to request documentation whenever they felt it necessary, even of a certified FMLA approved employee where a second document should not be requested. I would also ask that if such a request was legitimate and legal, why it was necessary to compensate me. I see it as nothing less than aggression and abuse of authority mainly on Keeton's part.

On Dec. 30, 2009, I received a letter of determination for my latest EEO complaint to the August 5 and 7, 2009 breach of agreement in the contract settlement. As in every conclusion of this EEO agency, the postal service was in favor of management. Once again, it was perfectly okay for management to disregard and ignore official documents. They concluded that it did not cause me any measurable harm as they had concluded before in response to the many times that this contract had been violated in the past.

On Jan. 19, 2010, I wrote to the EEO agency stating my disapproval of their conclusion to the breach of the contract settlement agreement in the December 2009 violation. I expressed my lack of trust and embarrassment for an institution that was only in *theory* for the protection and equal rights of the people. They continued to ignore and support the misconduct of an agency that had made a mockery out of the system.

How could an agency with a moral obligation to apply the law without prejudice and to enforce that law come to the same conclusion all the time? No one or nothing was 100 percent right but the supernatural, my God. I talked about how the agency looked for excuses instead of exploring the truth for solutions to rectify the many problems in the agency. Management had broken this contract agreement more than four different times.

The expenditure of energy that was used to cause any sort of adverse reactions from me was astonishing, especially after the results of the U.S. Labor Department investigation.

On Jan. 8, 2010, I received a letter from the FMLA coordinator suspending my FMLA certification after Keeton had reported that I had set a pattern for sick leave request, claiming that these requests were in conjunction with my days off and holidays.

She said that on Jan. 2, 2010 the request for FMLA sick leave occurred after New Year's Day in conjunction with a holiday and/or rest day. She said that failure to verify incapacitation on this date may result in the denial of FMLA protected leave as requested by the employee. In addition, my healthcare provider would need to explain the medical necessity for the need to be absent in conjunction with my scheduled days off and the holidays.

This was going on during the U.S. Department of Labor investigation. If she could not get me at one thing she tried another. Keeton was obsessed with the coverage that FMLA provided to employees because it limited her ability to deny and control when an employee could be sick and use their earned sick leave.

The suspension of my FMLA certification questioned if anyone inquired of the rules and regulations governing FMLA at the U.S. Postal Service. I wondered if it was business as usual for them to portray ignorance of these rules.

I took great pleasure explaining it to them.

Contractually an employee could not be disciplined for calling in sick in conjunction with their days off if those days are split days off. My days off were split, which were Sundays and Thursdays. I could not call in with a sick leave request without it being in conjunction with my days off. Here's why. Saturdays and Mondays were in conjunction with my day off on Sundays. Wednesdays and Fridays were in conjunction with my day off on Thursdays. The only day that was not in conjunction was Tuesdays. If I would have called in only on that day of Tuesday that would have been setting a pattern which held true for holidays, because most holidays are on Mondays.

On Jan. 14, 2010, I discussed this with the FMLA coordinator over the telephone and gave her my assessment of this unwarranted suspension by explaining those particulars. I believed this to be the sole reason why suspending my certification could not be done. She was intrigued, and asked why this information had not been brought to her attention. For management to arbitrarily suspend my certification without inquiring, or even to the point of ignoring the rules and procedures, led me to believe that it was done out of malice.

Her response suggested to me that she wanted me to believe that she was not familiar with those rules. I could never believe that but, what I did believe was that she thought I wasn't. It was so very important for employees to be familiar with and know the rules and regulations of their employment.

What was done was illegal and a violation of my FMLA certification, and the FMLA coordinator admitted so in a roundabout way when she asked, "Why was it not brought to her attention sooner?"

Still that did not change the outcome. I filed a grievance because of this action taken against me and because of what Keeton had reported to the FMLA office. I was reimbursed a total of $53.85 cents where $23.85

was for the mileage to the doctor's office and the other was $30 for the copayment. It took a couple of weeks before my FMLA certification was reinstated. Though it did not eliminate the harassment, knowing policies and being familiar with the rules and regulations neutralized and offset the potential danger of being ignorant to the management's tactics.

I knew that they would never let up and they knew that I would never give up. My guard remained. Each day I worked in the United States Postal Service was intense and very stressful and I had four years to go before I would complete my career with the agency. So, I knew it would get worse.

Now that this whole thing of being in violation by setting a pattern in conjunction with my days off no longer existed, I prepared for the next phase of attacks. It was not a long wait. The reinstatement of my FMLA certification lasted for about two weeks at most. On Feb. 5, 2010, I received another letter from the FMLA office declining my certification. It stated that the "absences for Jan. 2 and 6 of 2010 is/are not FMLA approved with no medical documentation submitted. Your FMLA approval has ended so your FMLA leave request is not approved."

It was one thing after another.

I was required to get re-evaluated for FMLA certification approval so once again I was in violation of failure to be regular in attendance. The U.S. Postal Service was asking the impossible for my doctor to determine a certain time when my condition would or would not flare-up. They wanted to establish a set schedule when I would visit my doctor in order for Keeton to dictate what days I would use when calling in for FMLA sick leave.

On Feb. 7, 2010, I contacted my doctor to make an appointment for this re-evaluation. Three days later on Feb. 10, 2010, the evaluation was completed. The doctor's report read: "The duration of my condition is life-long and that there is no scheduled treatment time." He added that it would be treated as needed and when the condition flared up I would be unable to work. He also increased the number of days off that it would take for me to recuperate. The evaluation was released to the FMLA office on that day for the reinstatement of my FMLA certification.

The FMLA coordinator was more concerned about why my doctor increased my number of days off from work more than anything. It bothered her to the point that in a telephone conversation with her she asked me why the increase for the number of days off. I politely responded by saying that it was a medical evaluation performed by a qualified physician and that question could best be answered by my doctor and that I would be happy to provide her with his telephone number. She refused my offer.

Again, this was the time and effort that was focused on me that fed an uncontrollable obsession by Keeton for my removal from the U.S. Postal Service. It was this unnecessary involvement of people that caused me a tremendous amount of tension and stress in my life. Though I was reimbursed for money out of my pocket, I was not compensated for the pain and suffering management employed to create intense and stressful situations in my life. They would not leave me alone.

I continued to be unjustifiably flagged and remained on sick leave restriction though it was against the law. I was required to bring in documentation anytime that I would use sick leave regardless of an FMLA certification. The APWU could do nothing about it.

On Feb. 23, 2010, just weeks after I was examined by my doctor for the evaluation and recertification for the third time, I was required to bring in documentation for an FMLA sick leave request. My patience had worn thin. I had many breaking points with this agency, but, each time through the grace of God, I dug deeper for strength to keep going.

Keeton was allowed to continue her assault on me and get away with what the zero tolerance policy specifically ruled against. It was exhausting working for an agency where individuals of authority would enforce what they believed while going against the rules and policies of the agency. I was a 30-year veteran at that point. I followed the written rules and went by the policies of the agency which was one of the biggest reasons among many others why management could not force me out.

61

HIRED HELP

I was not eligible for retirement as of yet, so to walk away from the dictatorship was not an option. But it would have been a delight for many to see me forced out, escorted out, or even carried out.

Keeton was highly artificial, articulate and manipulative. She was egocentric solely based on intimidation and abuse. A large percentage of the agency's problem was the inability to be fair and to stay in the balance of the law. The different entities of the agency could never seem to take control of the horrific misconduct, the constant harassment and injustice played out by those managers and supervisors in the agency.

The answer: You could never be the answer if you were the problem. People who had the authority but lacked the will or the integrity to make those changes were never able to grasp the concept that "enough is enough."

On Feb. 25, 2010, I hired a representative to handle my EEO complaints. Jerome Shain's background was in human resources, labor relations, contract negotiations, EEO and merit system protection. He was on the board for the U.S. Postal Service Dispute Resolutions and Complaint Appellants. The fee was $45 per hour with $500 down, payable upon signing a contract agreement. These were the extremes that I was forced into because I had no rights in the United States Postal Service. Those rights that I fought for in the military held no value because they were constantly being violated.

On March 12, 2010, my FMLA was finally amended that allowed me even more time off work than before. This was not pleasing to management. They were not happy about the representative that I selected to handle all of my EEOs. He was a former manager in the U.S. Postal Service that handled disputes. Yes, a former insider.

This was how I was forced to spend money I had earned working for the agency just to continue to work. I could rarely afford to go on vacations, to enjoy my life, or even the purchase of new things. That money was used for attorneys, representatives, and bail bondsman for the survival of me and my family.

The downtown station was one of the most chaotic facilities in the Colorado/Wyoming district. There were many other stations that were just as dysfunctional with the same or similar issues, but they too were the U.S. Postal Service. The station was a very troubled facility due to the lack of leadership and accountability that stemmed from law breakers mainly in upper positions. This allowed for an already cliquish atmosphere to grow stronger in numbers and intensity.

I learned how to fight in this agency because of them. I had never been a part of management's circle. It was one reason why I was never popular with managers and supervisors and those of my co-workers who were part of that circle.

Upper management knew in detail of the situation at the downtown station, not only from the information that was given to them by me through certified return receipt mail, but through a very few other employees. They, too, were harassed and made complaints through grievances and EEOs.

Through it all, upper management made no direct attempts to resolve any of the issues. Upper management would not directly get involved. They would only place memorandums on bulletin boards in postal facilities about the zero tolerance policy. In fact, on July 12, 2010, there was a memo placed on the bulletin board for all Colorado/ Wyoming cluster employees, which was signed by the district manager of customer service, sales, and the senior plant manager.

It covered a variety of directives that were in violation of the zero-tolerance policy. These were directives that management willfully committed. There was one directive in particular that went to the core of how management disguises its participation in the harassment of employees. The directive read:

> "We recognize that any intentional words, acts, or actions, meant to provoke another can escalate and result in injury if they are not immediately and appropriately addressed by management."

This was precisely what management had done to me for most of my time there in a quest to remove me from the United States Postal Service. They had gone precisely against what they enforced on others of their choosing. The memorandums served a purpose. It projected an image and created an illusion of concern for employee rights.

62

THE TARNISHING OF UNION STANDARDS

Of the many agencies set up in the U.S. Postal Service to protect employees, the APWU was the weakest of them all. This statement should not be taken out of context. It was the only entity that was not made up of management personnel.

The union had done some outstanding work over the years not only for me but for others. Personally speaking, they had been a friend to me, a safe haven of sorts, and a place I could go where 80 percent of the time justice would prevail.

I had taken a certain position on justice versus true justice. Justice would amend the wrong that was done where true justice eliminates the that created and initiated those wrongs. The APWU could not enforce the zero-tolerance policy, because it was so widely used and abused to the benefit of management personnel. This had created nothing but dissension among the workers, causing devastating effects where employees felt they had no other alternative and often turned to going postal.

Throughout my career I filed more than 40 different grievances and more than 30 EEO complaints. In these cases, the union could and did not provide the true justice. Most of the time I was compensated monetarily through the grievance process, but never through EEO. True justice did not prevail because those offenders who could continue their assault on me over many years of my career were never brought to justice.

The many union stewards and the five different APWU presidents throughout my career who knew that I was a target in this agency could not protect me from the onslaught of attacks from management personnel. They knew precisely who the perpetrators were and had proof to their misconduct. Over the years, I questioned the APWU's method of protecting the people.

The union had 33 years of my career to figure out how I could be protected and provided with a safe, hassle-free environment as promised by the United States Postal Service. Management's mentality was crystal clear. If an employee did not like where they were or the management, they could bid away from that place or resign from the U.S. Postal Service. I reached a point that I had no desire in doing either because I would have been a target no matter where I would have gone. A made-up reputation would have followed me and influenced even the new employees to judge. There was no escaping this agency. I had to stare it down by coming into work every day and fighting.

The APWU was truly the only agency where, for a period of time, I could go and be treated with some fairness. But times changed. As I got closer to the end of my career, the transition of new faces of presidents, directors, and stewards no longer carried the union pride and spirit of tranquility, solidarity, and brotherhood.

Over the years these negotiations turned into more of a cat and mouse game. A "scratch my back and I will scratch yours" mentality where negotiations would lead to employees receiving some sort of punishment for an infraction or a violation. These would be violations employees had been accused of, but were never committed or even proven. The words of managers and supervisors reigned supreme.

Many times, it was those managers and supervisors whose history showed to be controversial, who were always involved in some sort of dispute with an employee or in some sort of litigation within the justice system. They were management personnel who were not held accountable and were not under the jurisdiction of the zero-tolerance policy.

For three decades, I faced tremendous adversity. To make sense of it all was the least of my concerns while fighting to survive. History has shown that this management style has not changed since the beginning of my 33-year career. Knowing why management's aggression has always been rewarded in the United States Postal Service is something worth knowing, something I would like to know. However, I believe I absolutely knew why during my employment with the agency and was very much aware of the obstacles that were ahead of me for the remainder of my career. One of the obstacle ahead was in working with the APWU.

The unwelcome change in the APWU where the members seemed to no longer matter left me speechless at times. The union was cutting deals with management. Most disturbing where those employee grievances that were late being filed or never filed. Union stewards were lying to members and telephone calls were not being returned when a member was in trouble or in need of a steward. It was a different union that no longer held the tradition of solidarity.

Solidarity and brotherhood had structured our union but now was a thing of the past. It began to phase out and many began to void their membership. The officers who headed the union had lost the faith and trust of its members. Broken promises were imminent when managers and supervisors could and would violate the contract. For example, they regularly performed craftwork to make the station deadlines because they recognized and took advantage of the weak links in the APWU.

Many members were leaving the union while others threatened to go when much of this changed in the APWU. These were subjects that were relevant and were very important that would hopefully give meaningful structure to agency with serious problems.

For example, on Nov. 10, 2010, I experienced something with a union steward that was truly out of character with the APWU's mission. On that day, I approached one of the union stewards with a concern, an issue that pertained to the holiday sign-up sheet for volunteers to work on the holiday which happened to be Veterans Day.

The holiday list was not posted when it should have been and any time afterwards meant that it was not done in a timely manner. He responded by promising that he would check into the matter and get back with me. He never did. The issue was that on Nov. 7-9, of 2010, I was out of the office on vacation and had no way of signing the holiday list.

This list, by contract of the national bargaining agreement, was required to be posted one week before the actual holiday. It should have been posted on Nov. 6, 2010, one day before I was scheduled to leave the office. Had the list been posted it in a timely manner on that day I would have had access to sign the list and there never would have been an issue.

On Nov. 8, 2010 while I was out I called the station by telephone and spoke with the supervisor on duty, Susan Lamas. I explained my situation to her by informing her that the holiday list was not posted on the day before I left so therefore I was unable to sign the volunteer sign-up sheet. She said that she would look into it and call me back.

I gave her my telephone number so that there would be no problems, but never received that callback. After three to four hours had passed once again I called the station and spoke with her. She then informed me that she could not find the holiday sign-up list and that it was still not posted on the bulletin board.

She also said that she had no idea if my supervisor, J.C. Jones, had scheduled me to work on that day because he was not there at that time. Later that day I received a telephone call from Jones. He informed me that he did schedule me to work on the holiday of Nov. 11, 2010.

The day after on Nov. 12, 2010, I caught up with the union steward on the workroom floor, who seemed to be avoiding me much of the day. I just wanted to bring to his attention that in fact the holiday list was not posted, which was confirmed by the carrier supervisor who I had spoken to on Nov. 8, 2010. The list was not posted and nowhere in sight. I also wanted to know if there was any clear reason why he did not get back with me. He replied by saying that the list was posted on the 10th of November, one day before the actual holiday, which supported and backed-up what I was inquiring about.

There were two other employees who were unable to sign the list because it was not posted, but I gave the benefit of the doubt to the union steward. The list was posted the same day that I had confronted him about the list not being posted.

Why did he not tell me this in our conversation instead of promising that he would get back with me? Because it was a "lie" and for whatever reason he continued to look for excuses to cover management. In fact, he began to give me several reasons why the list was not posted in a timely manner, including saying that the list was posted at one time but that I just did not see it. I was offended.

My immediate thought was that he was weak and was a sellout. Then I informed him that being a union steward he should know the contract of the national bargaining agreement, which states that the holiday list was required to be posted a week before the actual holiday.

I went on to express my disapproval by letting him know that I thought he was a liar, who was covering up for management. I let him know that it was very offensive to me, not because he was protecting management, but because he was lying to do so and betraying union members. I admit that his disloyalty made me angry but I believe that I kept my composure especially after watching his performance on the workroom floor.

He aggressively stepped towards me and got approximately four inches from my face, and in a loud and rambunctious voice said, "fuck you!" at the top of his lungs. At the time, we were standing in the middle of the workroom floor and his voice carried throughout the building, getting the attention of other workers and Keeton, who was in an office at least 30 to 40 feet away.

She came out of the supervisor's office and immediately addressed me by giving me a command to walk away. She said not one word to him when it was his obnoxious behavior and erratic outbursts that drew her attention. I knew the most important thing for me to do at that moment was for me to keep my composure and follow that command knowing what had just happened was threatening. I was the one who was under attack but perceived as the perpetrator. I walked away.

I spoke the truth to him. He responded with aggression, which could have triggered a spontaneous reaction from me leaving him face-down on the floor. I knew the next step was up to me. I chose to use my willpower. This was a situation that was very intense and got ugly quickly, especially when the manager arrived and the odds turned even greater against me.

As I walked away Keeton took the union steward aside and engaged in a conversation with him. Not once did she contact me to hear anything that I had to say about what happened.

There were plenty of witnesses who heard the altercation, so I immediately began asking around in hopes that they would be honest and not afraid to tell what they had heard. Only one person wrote out a statement as to what she heard and what she said in her statement was exactly what was said and by whom. I do not want to speculate or make assumptions as to why other statements were not obtained, but I never lost sight of the fact that I was in an environment of people who feared the retaliation of management.

A week had gone by and still not a word of the disturbance had been mentioned. This was very unusual, especially when it involved me. I confronted my supervisor about why I had not been contacted or even informed of what, if any action, would be taken because of last week's altercation. He said he had nothing and had not heard of any probable action being taken, but he would advise me of any changes, which never happened.

There was a lot wrong with this entire scope of things. An altercation had taken place on the workroom floor that disrupted day-to-day operations and violated the zero-tolerance policy. I knew I did nothing wrong and that I had not violated any policies or provoked the misconduct of the union steward. I was only responsible for my behavior as he was for his own behavior. I was fully under control where he was disruptive.

Postal rules and regulations stated any incident that occurs on postal grounds was required to have an investigation conducted. I personally wanted the incident to be investigated and was the reason I continued to inquire about it. Not only was it the responsibility of the manager to have investigated, it was her duty. But there was no investigation and I wanted to know why.

It bothered me more than ever that the union steward's behavior had gone unpunished. It was a prime example of how I was treated differently from all other employees. It did not matter if I was attacked by others where their behavior was acceptable by the management staff as long as it was directed against me because management's goal was to get rid of me. I protected myself.

On Nov. 16, 2010, I wrote a letter to the APWU president, John Ancona, expressing the concerns that I had about the union steward's behavior. I explained the situation in detail as to what took place between the steward and me on that day. I made no qualms and had no interests in talking about the position that management took and the role the manager played. My concern was of the union steward behavior. He was a person that I had known for more than 25 years. He had represented me over several decades in some of the most trying cases.

He was someone who knew of the adversities, the lies, and constant attacks of me by management. It was reprehensible for him to have turned his back on me in such an abrupt manner to try to provoke me into a situation that he knew I would lose.

I expressed my concern of his erratic behavior that I felt should not go unpunished but mainly his disloyalty to all union members that he should have been an example of union pride. I made a respectful request to the APWU president and its officials for the demand of the union steward's resignation.

I felt that he not only compromised himself but the principles and values of the organization that at one time had prided itself on solidarity, brotherhood and a place of tranquility. The president contacted me by telephone and conveyed his apology for the behavior of his union steward. He also informed me the steward admitted that he lost control because I made him mad.

The contact was by telephone to ensure that there would be no record of the steward's confession that the president conveyed to me. It was his word against mine had I tried to take it any further. He flat out refused to demand his resignation. I had been a faithful member of the organization for 33 years and had witnessed a union that had been weakened due to people of this caliber whose main interests was of personal gain and not of the honor and integrity of a once organized APWU unit.

Many deals were now being cut and made with management by union officials at the expense of its members where communication with the members was no longer a priority. Respecting members was now a burden to union personnel that had to put a sincere effort into protecting the members.

On Dec. 4, 2010, I contacted the postmaster's office by telephone and spoke with Sims, the postmaster's assistant. I explained the situation bringing him up to speed about the altercation. He informed me that he knew of the altercation and that Keeton had expressed her assessment of the situation and found me to be the aggressor.

I replied simply by saying that if this was true why was I not charged with a violation, for starters, disrupting day-to-day operations or creating a hostile work environment. Why not? I have been falsely accused and charged with that previously. I told him that if you truly had something that was positively incriminating that would give proof to me being at fault there is no way that you or Keeton would not take disciplinary action against me. So, I asked, "Tell me what would make this violation so different?"

Disciplinary action would have been taken, undoubtedly removal. As usual, policy enforcement was at the discretion of management. The union steward was never disciplined for his actions because the manager's obsession for getting rid of me was a lot stronger than doing her job.

This was just one example of Keeton's manipulation, along with her negligence to assess the situation without bias and in a professional manner. She should have investigated so that both sides of the story could be told. Though I was not disciplined, I was not treated fairly or protected by the zero-tolerance policy.

PART ELEVEN:

2011

63

13 BELOW ZERO

On Feb. 1, 2011, I was emergency placed at 5:35 a.m. by Lamas, the 204-B carrier supervisor, also recognized as the acting supervisor. Around 5:05 a.m., she instructed another employee to open the locked doors that led to the dock area and retrieve the mail that had been sitting on the dock. It was the station's first dispatch from the main plant for the day. It was also one of his assigned job duties that he was required to perform each day. This day was different from most other days with some most unusual weather conditions. The temperature outside was a frigid 13-below zero and the dock was just as cold.

It was a normal day as far as operations was concerned. Workers were at their assigned duty stations performing their daily jobs as I was. I heard the acting supervisor give the employee instructions to open the dock doors and retrieve the mail that was there on the dock, but after five or so minutes the doors were still closed. Not long after Lamas came over to my work area and instructed me to perform his daily assigned duties in opening those doors. This employee, who she instructed from the beginning to perform his assigned duties and failed to do so, was someone that she went to lunch with every day.

For the past 15 years it had been the duty of the Zone 2 parcel clerk, who was the very first employee in the building at 4 a.m. to perform the duties of opening all dock doors. It was required to be done immediately after punching in on the clock. It was standard practice to open the dock doors and retrieving the mail, which was always on the dock from the main plant at 3 a.m. Dispatch to the station each day was to be performed without being instructed or reminded to do so.

I had performed the same job for four and a half years. I knew my responsibilities and I carried them out without being instructed or reminded to do so. Minutes later I was approached by her and instructed to do his job. It bothered me that she was giving me those orders. I asked her why she would not make this employee do his job and if she was afraid to demand that he carry out his assigned job duties. She walked away from me in an abrasive manner. She responded by snapping, "you just open the dock doors and get the mail."

My hands were full of mail that I was working at the time. I had to take the mail back to their respective work stations each day to avoid any sort of misplacement. I would have taken no longer than a minute or two. As I was walking toward the dock area to carry out her instructions, a voice came over the intercom. It was her screaming at the top of her lungs in a very obnoxious tone. She instructed me to get to the dock and get that mail inside.

This was provoking and only added fuel to a fire that she had already ignited. By sheer reaction my response was spontaneously louder than normal. In fact, it was just as loud and abrasive as hers when I shouted that I was half way to the dock area and to stop screaming my name over the intercom throughout the building and to stop harassing me.

This took her over the edge. She responded by screaming, "I'm calling the police. I am sick of this shit." I asked her why was she calling the police. She then repeated what she had first said and called the police. I continued my way to the dock area to open the doors where another co-worker joined in helping me. It was not the co-worker who was ultimately responsible for this task. He never came to help.

After my co-worker and I completed the job, I went back and began performing my original duties. Minutes later the police arrived. Upon their arrival, the two Denver police officers went into the supervisor's office. After about five minutes the officers came out of the office and approached me asking what had happened. I explained what had gone on and what part I played in it. The two of them thought it was hilarious.

I told the officers that if the supervisor would like for me to leave, I would do that to diffuse the situation. It was then that they asked me to go back to work.

I went back to work and the police exited the building. About 15 to 20 minutes later the security guard approached me informing me that the acting supervisor would like for me to leave. I informed the security guard that if I was being emergency placed that she would need to follow protocol and provide me with the necessary paperwork and I would do just that.

Thirty minutes later I was given the paperwork by the acting supervisor. I gathered my belongings and left the building. The paperwork covered me so there would be no mistake as to why I left the building. Secondly, it gave her very little time to concoct a story by changing what really happened to a degree which suggested and led to me being the perpetrator.

She had to implement some sort of disciplinary action now because she had committed herself by calling the police from the beginning and implied what was going on in the building was threatening and serious. It would have been a grave mistake for me to allow management any sort of time to embellish those lies that would undoubtedly be told to justify why the emergency placement was necessary.

I had known Lamas more than 20 years. She was conniving and dishonest. Anyone that knew her, if they were truthful and not afraid to let their feelings show, would agree.

Her original position was as a mail carrier, but for the last eight years she had been a 204-B, a noncertified supervisor. It was well known that she aspired of becoming a certified supervisor and those individuals were the most dangerous people in the U.S. Postal Service. They were trying to make a name for themselves and they would do most anything to impress their superiors. Being a hard-ass supervisor in this agency had always been praised and rewarded. Having me permanently removed from the agency would have catapulted her to a higher position.

I was very careful how I talked to anyone in management, not to use any profanity or make any derogatory statements, or comments that would even touch the surface of even suggesting that a threat was being made or belligerent. I had developed this self-awareness and control over the years. It was an intricate part of my defense to survive in this agency.

After many years of legal battles with this agency I was now very well-educated and had lots of experience in the ways that management conducted itself. In her statement that she presented in the emergency placement form accusing me of being out-of-control she reported that I used the phrase "fucking!"

She finished her statement in trying to vilify me by saying that I proceeded to get in her path as she was trying to walk away from me restricting her movement. She implied that I was violent and a threat to justify her actions in removing me from the station. This was never reported to the police or even heard of until she was required to give reason to her actions for the emergency placement.

This was the main reason why I did not leave the station until I was given the proper paperwork because these accusations were never in the emergency placement form. She was aware of past history that it was standard procedure in the station to call the police on me. Most times it would result in me receiving a ticket, a summons to appear in court, or being handcuffed and taken to jail, which was her full intention of having me arrested on that morning.

She was there in the station the last time the police were called where I was escorted from the building in handcuffs, then taken and falsely jailed, fired from my job and removed from the U.S. Postal Service for three years.

For this latest incident, I filed a grievance on that day in February, and on the seventh of the month I filed an EEO complaint. The statements and documents that I had provided for the grievance process were the same information given in the EEO complaint. There was a total of seven different statements and four of the statements were from people who witnessed what had taken place on the morning of Feb. 1, 2011.

The remaining three were from those who had prior confrontations with this acting supervisor. Three out of four of the statements did confirm that I raised my voice responding to the acting supervisor to stop her from yelling my name over the intercom and to quit harassing me. I owned it. No one said that I used any sort of profanity or if I ever threatened or was threatening to this acting supervisor. In fact, her statement was the only one that claimed this had happened.

The other three statements were of those employees who had experienced several confrontations with this acting supervisor and had written statements exclusively for the EEO investigation to present factual evidence that I was treated differently from other employees by her calling the police and emergency placing me from the building. The statements were direct and to the point that revealed some of the most damaging and incriminating information that not only showed that I was treated different but also showed that I was discriminated against.

The three statements were part of the discovery in the EEO complaint:

> A. That this acting supervisor has had verbal confrontation with several other employees before including myself. But she has never called the police.
> B. I had a confrontation with the acting supervisor as she proceeded to ride me all morning even though I did every duty and job task she asked me to do. Yet she accused me of bothering co-workers if I needed medication out of my bag that was near a co-worker and asked if I could go get it. We had a heated exchange of words. She kept yelling for me to go back to work. I had to tell her to get off my back because I was working. After that incident, we rarely talked much. She never took any action against me that I know of.
> C. I had several issues with the 204-B acting supervisor and had a few good heated exchanges between us. She had never removed or had me removed from the work room floor. This could be because she had elevated

these sometimes or just because we had agreed to disagree. But for whatever reason it had never gone to the point of her having me leave. The acting supervisor did at times overstep her authority and took things to a higher level than it needed to be.

For whatever reason, she carried herself to this degree of superiority to impress her superiors for validation, or she just had a nasty disposition, it was all so common among management. There were very few words that were exchanged between the two of us, none of which were provocative that came from my mouth. I used no profanity.

Not only was I improperly emergency place out of the building, but the police were called to further complicate things. The three other employees who had heated confrontations with this acting supervisor faced no emergency placement, no police officers, and no disciplinary action for unbecoming behavior. This underscored my role as a target of this agency even more.

It could have easily been construed as discrimination after receiving and reading those statements of the three employees who were victims themselves of her aggression. Now she had to make it appear as though she was intimidated and afraid of my presence. She banked on the police removing me from the building. But she had to do it.

It would not be out of the question to say her actions were racially motivated. This acting supervisor was a Hispanic female. The three employees, who made statements, included one Hispanic female, one Caucasian female, and one Caucasian male. I was the only African-American and the only one subject to this type of treatment where the police were called.

I was the only one emergency placed and given a letter for failure to follow instructions. Those allegations that were made in her statement were never proven to be true.

I subsequently learned that she supposedly felt threatened by my presence after the security guard brought it to my attention and after the police had gone, but she never expressed those feelings to the police. Although I said very little to her, this was nothing more than a façade to make everything that she was claiming believable and to cover her aggression. In fact, I was the one that was in immediate danger because of the police presence. Many would argue that portraying the image of an intimidating aggressive black man to authorities was the same as threatening my life.

What comforted me and gave me a sense of calm was that I knew how to handle myself after being in so many of these abusive situations with management. The key was not to take the bait, not to allow anger to rise, and my IQ to slip.

The grievance that I had filed was substantiated in my favor that LWOP for each day that I was out. The emergency placement was changed to paid leave and the emergency placement letter was removed from my files. The decision went no further than step one where it was agreed upon by both union and management that the acting supervisor had no grounds or any sort of proof in support of the action that was taken against me.

She was a liability to the agency because of the rage that she would display and her abuse of authority that continued to lead to confrontations with employees. The revenue continued to come from the U.S. Postal Service payout of unwarranted and unnecessary complaints. They continued to allow this behavior of management to go unpunished with no accountability which gave reason to why she continued on her rampage for years.

On Sept. 17, 2011, word was going around the station that an altercation had taken place over the weekend on Saturday, Sept. 15 between this same 204-B supervisor and a vim driver at the station. On that Monday morning, a few co-workers informed me of the altercation with the understanding that it had gotten heated, and disrupted the day-to-day operation. Others voiced their opinion as to how I was treated when the police were called in and the acting supervisor emergency placed me and how I received a letter of discipline.

One co-worker informed me that she had been talking with one of the other vim drivers who informed her of what happened that day, telling her that he was present when it all took place. He told her that he had a hard time calming the driver because he was so upset by the altercation.

He and the acting supervisor were face-to-face, nose-to-nose screaming at one another.

The altercation occurred outside of the doors on the dock and had something to do with the driver's equipment being moved and dispatched out of the building. I was sure the exchange was not the least bit intimidating to her. He was not being hunted, he was not a target. I could not definitely say my treatment by her was because of my race, but I know it adds another dimension when you call authorities on a black man.

I asked the driver who had witnessed the altercation if he would write a statement as to exactly what he witnessed. He graciously declined and said that he would rather not because the guy who was involved was a friend of his and that he did not want to get him into any sort of trouble. These were the hard-core challenges put before me to survive the torture of an agency that had me in the line of fire.

The stress alone kept me on the edge each day knowing that I would be under fire each time I set foot into that building with no one there to protect me. It was a daunting and lonely feeling. I realized those services of the different entities in the United States Postal Service that claimed to be for the protection of the employees' rights was there for no one -- only for the rights of management.

The only agency that was truly there in the early part of my career that protected those rights was the APWU. Toward the end of my career those values had changed. New faces, different agendas, and principles could no longer be used as strength for brotherhood and solidarity.

The EEO had always been an extension of management. Through each complaint that I had filed, the EEO had the same discovery and just as much information if not more than the grievance process. Still they could never come to a fair and honest determination in the 33 years of my postal career.

This was one of the reasons that I felt compelled to hire a personal representative. And because of the disparity of treatment in the Feb. 1, 2011 incident where the 204-B acting supervisor singled me out and treated me differently from other employees.

My representative and I felt that this EEO complaint held a lot of weight. It was one of my strongest complaints where the grievance was sustained and completely in my favor. Step One found management's actions to be unwarranted and not justified. My advocate could now give his undivided attention to this case and to those future complaints that undoubtedly would come. I was inspired by his charismatic demeanor as he worked diligently with U.S. Postal Service attorneys throughout the discrimination process of the complaint.

We were required to make several personal visits to the U.S. attorney's office for "settlement hearings." I don't know why they were called that. The postal service never attempted to make a settlement. This went on for months, and during that time, the EEO contacted me more than six times to compromise a settlement agreement.

The first few calls the agency tried talking me out of moving forward with the complaint, informing me that less than one percent of EEO complaints were won by the complainant. They offered me $250 to withdraw the complaint. I declined. The case was new and I wasn't driven by money. My motivation was principle to right a wrong. I was seeking justice.

Three or four days later I received another call from the EEO agency with an offer of $500 to withdraw my complaint. I declined. I received two more calls from the agency. It was always the same person. I was then offered $850 to withdraw the complaint and the next time I was offered $1,000. I declined both times.

After the thousand-dollar offer, I knew there would not be any more attempts by the agency to make a settlement agreement. I was perfectly content with that, but what I also knew was that my complaint was in serious jeopardy of being dismissed. Two weeks later the complaint was denied. It happened exactly the way I thought it would, as if I had written the outcome myself knowing this agency. Their conclusion was that there was never any type of discrimination and that I was not treated any differently than other employees at the postal service.

The conclusion stated: "After a review of the records in its entirety, including consideration of all statements submitted on appeal, is the decision of the equal opportunity commission to affirm the agency's final decision because the preponderance of the evidence of record does not establish that discrimination occurred."

The defining word in this assessment was "preponderance." According to Webster's, the word means "a superiority in weight, power, importance or strength." This decision was very difficult to even relate to, let alone understand.

My understanding of discrimination: to make distinctions in treatment by showing partiality or prejudice. I believe that was shown between my treatment and the other three employees who provided statements.

What the EEO did in this case was relied solely on the acting supervisor's word as if they witnessed exactly what she reported. The grievance process viewed the case completely different. A case of uncertainty could go as many as four steps and even to the point of arbitration before a decision was rendered. This case went no further than Step One and was substantiated in my favor that I produced the designating evidence that established a fact, "prima facie."

It was the same evidence provided to the EEO which was the reason the emergency placement was changed to paid leave and all disciplinary letters were expunged from my personnel file.

On April 10, 2012, I appealed the decision after years of paperwork and numerous visits with my advocate, looking over discovery and putting together additional evidence. At this point the process had cost me more than $5,000.

This EEO complaint was filed on Feb. 7, 2011. I received five to six different telephone calls from the agency about what they referred to as settlement offerings. I visited the U.S. attorney's office four to five times. I was required to be on an enormous number of conference calls between my advocate and postal attorneys.

It ultimately took the EEO agency three years and eight months to conclude and to render a decision on a complaint that had less than a one percent chance of receiving a fair and honest decision with a 100 percent thorough investigation. I was never compensated for this EEO complaint or have been compensated for any other complaint through this agency.

64

THE STICKY GLUE

This EEO agency was the glue that held the United States Postal Service together through my 33 years in the agency. It had supported and covered up 100 percent of the illegal activity and those actions that had been taken against me in this agency. It had defended the dishonesty of those managers who disregarded contracts that governed the agency. This EEO had guided a path for law breakers in this agency to continue breaking the law.

65

A WALK IN THE PARK

On Feb. 8, 2011, I was one out of two other employees who were bypassed for overtime on that day where management did the work themselves. It prevented the payout of overtime and the work got done. This was a violation of the national bargaining agreement. By contract, they are not allowed to work the mail.

Intimidation and retaliation prevented many employees from filing grievances against a manager or supervisor in violation of the national bargaining agreement.

For me to file a grievance was just a walk in the park because I was retaliated against daily. Of course, I filed a grievance for being bypassed on this day and management settled it by agreeing to a lump sum payment of $250. It was divided among those few employees who were bypassed.

Two weeks later, retaliation followed the filing of that grievance. On Feb 22, 2011, management allowed a non-volunteer employee to work overtime before me. I was next in position as the senior clerk to work that overtime. Again, this was another violation of the contract and again management had to settle where I received a payment of $78. Again, this may seem tedious. Looking at the numbers, you could argue that it is only $78. To leave it unchallenged, the $78 would add up to $234 weekly, then $936 monthly. It was also the principle regarding unfair practices.

I have yet to comprehend the strategy, if there was ever one. I could only see and identify a breakdown in the system of this agency where the defiance and arrogance of managers was encouraged and rewarded instead of discouraged and disciplined. The technicalities that were involved in meeting the criterion of what the EEO determined as a legitimate complaint was disturbing and was the reason why complaints had less than a one percent chance that favored the complainant.

Rejected and dismissed, even with loads of proof.

This had happened in each of the complaints I had filed with the EEO office. I did not have anything to hide and I did not want anything to be hidden. It was important and imperative that everyone knew how management and the agency as a whole had made things personal.

On Feb. 9, 2011, I wrote a letter to the postmaster of Denver, Colorado. He was not the postmaster that was summoned to appear in those earlier court trials, but had been in the position for quite a few years and had visited the station on many occasions. He was aware of the situation and the station's history.

This ongoing situation was ridiculously out of control and spiraling into a regrettable outcome, perhaps for me. I felt like a punching bag. If one supervisor did not succeed in knocking me out, the next one would take their best shot. It felt as though the entire world was against me. No one in the agency would lift a finger to help me. It's one thing to settle a situation. It's another to stop the situation from happening at all.

The biggest challenge throughout the decades of despair and frustration was to continue controlling my emotions. I had to keep my composure in check and follow protocol by going through the chain of command seeking help from those in management. Yes, this would be the same individuals who were out to destroy me and feed into my greatest fear of homicidal and suicidal thoughts.

It was ironic that those in the agency who kept this fight going with me never actually realized or understood how potentially each one of us could have possibly become a statistic. This was not the answer nor was it a legacy that I would have wanted to leave or be remembered for.

In my letter to the postmaster I gave him a brief history of myself and respectfully asked for help by his office. I wanted an independent investigation into the ongoing harassment and discrimination of me by the management staff at the downtown station. I meticulously described the all-out assault I experienced over my time with the postal service. I provided him with some history of past arbitrators, rulings and decisions especially that one where I was removed from the agency for close to three years, before my job was awarded back to me.

I gave him a summary of the latest incident at the downtown station that on Feb. 1, 2011 where management tried once again to use the services of the Denver Police Department in support of the 204-B supervisor's temper tantrum.

I ended the letter by reminding him of the telephone call I made to his office on Jan. 4, 2011. During that call, I discussed a similar matter with his aide that took place in the station on Nov. 12, 2010. At that time, I was promised by his office that there would be an investigation. I informed him that it never happened and that I would greatly appreciate a response to my letter and a follow-up regarding my concerns.

The letter was delivered by certified return receipt mail and signed for by his office on Feb. 19, 2011. Three months passed. No word from his office. If this matter was meant to be trivialized, it would be an injustice itself, but to be completely ignored and dismissed altogether was unacceptable. I had no intentions of allowing this to go unanswered.

My resiliency catapulted and had my military-trained mind racing 1,000 miles per $1/10^{th}$ of a second understanding that much more was needed to be done to put this agency on notice. That would give clear and precise evidence of a system that was tarnished and an agency that was broken. The arrogance of these nonprofessional people in this agency was becoming even clearer. They showed no embarrassment in their incompetency.

After not hearing a single word from the postmaster or anyone from his office, I went a step above him.

On May 18, 2011, I wrote to the district manager, Selwyn Epperson. His office received the letter by certified return receipt mail on the next day May 19, 2011. The letter was identical, much of the same as the letter that I had sent to the postmaster giving him a summary and my affiliation with the U.S. Postal Service. I brought him up to speed on my reasons for writing to him. My concerns addressed the postal service's zero tolerance policy. I even noted that the station manager had recently passed out handouts to each employee about the policy and made it the subject matter of stand-up talks. It essentially placed employees on notice.

But who had the authority to place management on notice? Who was the gatekeeper? I included names of employees and management personnel who were in constant violation of this policy. I also identified the different agencies within the U.S. Postal Service that had been notified and made aware that a serious problem existed in the downtown station.

Those agencies included the APWU, EAP, Labor Relations, EEO agency, and the postmaster's office. The postmaster was given a personal invitation, as a respectful request, to investigate the situation there at the downtown station on Feb. 9, 2011. My request was ignored. I reminded him that I did have rights as an employee of this agency to perform my assignments and duties in an atmosphere free of threats, harassment, assaults and any other acts of workplace violence that continued to be compromised by management.

For this policy to be enforced at the discretion of management against a select few was discriminatory, particularly when management, along with certain others are not governed by the same policy. As far as I was concerned, passing out these handouts by her at this standup talk was dishonest and pure propaganda.

I ended the letter by saying that I would greatly appreciate a response to my letter and a follow-up regarding my concerns. I was most grateful and very pleased to say that I did receive a response to my letter from his office dated June 3, 2011 and I truly respected the district manager responding to the letter.

What I did not respect was that he came up with all sorts of reasons not to investigate. He noted that I did not give any specific reference to an incident that could be investigated.

He made contradictory statements when he informed me of those different agencies that I did contact. He found that the labor relations representative was working with the EEO representative and offered to personally go to the downtown station at my suggestion. He also conveyed his understanding that I declined for an equal number of craft employees and management employees to be interviewed about any issues at the station.

By him stating that the labor relations and EEO representative worked together and offered to come in the station to do an investigation I believe should have given him reason to inquire as to what was truly going on. He needed to have launched an investigation of his own as to why there was even an investigation needed in the station.

Had he done so and been committed to that investigation by asking the necessary questions, instead of banking on a one-sided story that I supposedly had declined their investigation, he would have obtained the real reason as to why the investigation by those agencies did not take place at that time.

He would have had the truth and a complete analysis of why the investigation from those two agencies never was conducted. The supposed investigation was nothing more than a proposition for me to withdraw my EEO complaints before an investigation could be conducted.

Ending his correspondence, he gave a generic response by saying that all employees, whether management or craft, are covered by the district zero tolerance policy. He added "that specific incidents that you believe violate this policy should be addressed through your chain of command."

Word obviously got back to those managers and supervisors at the station of my contact with their bosses because the screws began to tighten. Their eyes followed me like a laser, looking for reasons to push any button they thought would create havoc.

On June 20, 2011, around 10 a.m. I was in the box section area distributing out-going mail for box holding customers. At that time the manager approached me, gave me instructions to relieve a clerk at the customer service window for a break. My hands were full of mail when these instructions were given to me. I completed what was in my hands and proceeded to carry out those instructions.

Postal uniforms were required for full-time window clerks when on the window serving the public. I was not a full-time window clerk and was only required to wear part of the uniform, which was the U.S. Postal Service shirt, any time I was on the window. So, wearing civilian clothes was perfectly acceptable.

I had no locker, not because I was not ever issued one, but because I would never accept a locker. I was very careful not to be placed in a compromising position by making myself accessible to contraband being placed in my locker. I kept my postal shirts in my vehicle where I had easy access to and that management was fully aware of for the past three and a half years since I became a window clerk.

The time it took me to complete the remaining mail and get my uniform was too long for Keeton. She made it an issue where she claimed that she was timing me which was unusual and unnecessary pressure. As far as I could recall I had never heard of or known anyone to be timed from one station to the next, but I did know exactly why this was taking place.

On June 27, 2011, I was put in for disciplinary action where I received a letter of warning for failure to follow instructions. Though I followed the instructions that were given to me she determined that I did not attempt to carry out those instructions in a timely manner. The microscope was burning into me, but it was just another day for me at the postal service.

I filed both a grievance and an EEO complaint on July 8, 2011 for this latest disciplinary action taken against me. Of course, the EEO complaint went in the same direction as did all complaints in the past 29 years that it was okay to treat me different from all other employees. This was something that I could and no longer would get upset about. It provided me the necessary documentation to prove an unfair and incompetent environment existed in the U.S. Postal Service.

66

TRADEMARK EXCUSES

I took this latest incident as an opportunity to follow the instructions of the district manager in his correspondence where he suggested that I follow the chain of command for any specific incidents that I believed violated the zero-tolerance policy.

I contacted Manager of Customer Service Operations Andrea Dallas, who served as Keeton's boss. I requested a meeting that would include the manager of the station to be present. I requested this meeting to comply with the district manager's suggestion and to remove any of those trademark excuses that management did not know or has never been made aware of an existing problem in the station.

On July 13, 2011, a meeting was set with the station manager along with her boss to hear my concerns that were scheduled to take place at 11 a.m. that morning. My concerns were straight forward. The meeting started off very explosive. There was no mistake that there was an enormous amount of tension that had generated at just that precise moment of contact with one another. The evidence was clear in black and white that the animosity in the room was heavy. Our negative opinions of one another showed in the introductions.

I had no intentions of being intimidated. Neither did Dallas. To say that the meeting was a complete failure was an understatement. I had no doubts that the station manager and rumors of me had a lot to do with it. As far as I was concerned, the meeting validated my feelings of distrust and the lack of collaboration to resolve issues. It kept me on the alert with my guard remaining stationary.

I had no respect for either of them. I was perfectly aware of what these meetings entailed and though it was held at my request, it was for putting management on notice to cover myself. There had been many meetings that I had approached with optimism, hoping that management would do what was right. I was mostly disappointed. Management would lie for each other, even if it meant the loss of an employee's job. I did not have a witness in the meeting with me, but I did inform two of my co-workers of the meeting.

There were several times that the conversation rose to a boiling point, where voices got extremely high which seemed to give Keeton an enormous amount of pleasure and satisfaction. I had become so intense at times that I no longer wanted to participate in the meeting. I was very close to excusing myself from their presence. I had my fair share in creating and keeping the intensity level at a high rate.

I realized that it was just a waste of time to go on with the meeting after the manager of customer service operations mentioned that she was once in the Marine Corps, which was irrelevant. That had nothing to do with why we were there. I looked at it as more of a challenge than anything. It was more important for me to let her know how I had been harshly treated and abused by this station manager, who was supposed to be a person of trust in a leadership position.

I let her know that this manager attacked me at will. Then she would cite postal rules and regulations that she herself constantly violated in taking disciplinary action against me. It defied logic.

A week had gone by and that meeting still troubled me. I also thought about how important it was to document the meeting and the conversation.

On July 22, 2011, I wrote a letter to Dallas and sent it by certified return receipt mail to show that the meeting had taken place. The other reason for the letter was that she could not say that she was not aware of the situation at the station between the manager and me. Also, it was documentation for the district manager that I not only followed the chain of command, but I made an extreme effort to rectify this problem not only by bringing these problems to her personally, but in correspondences as well.

Enclosed in the letter to her was a list of documents such as my complaints to the EEO agency, grievances and personal statements of coworkers who had witnessed the aggression and the harassment.

I wrote that I was looking forward to any questions, concerns, or comments that she might have and for her to please feel free to contact me. I never heard a word from her. I sincerely wanted to keep my lines of communication open to upper management now that I had at least a response and the attention of one of them through the district manager, which was very hard to come by. Retaliation was inevitable.

Regret never entered my mind when exposing the abusive type managerial style that I was victim to over the last three decades while working at the postal service. I did not stand or act in fear.

I followed up with a letter to the district manager's correspondence dated June 3, 2011. I expressed my disappointment with the contents in his letter, but mainly to clarify the immoralities that he referred to as his reasoning for not doing his job.

I began my letter informing him that I would like to address two statements that were made in his correspondence where he claimed that I made no specific reference to any incident that could be investigated. I reminded him of the information that was enclosed in a letter that I had written to the postmaster regarding those specifics where each incident was described in black and white.

Therefore, inquiries to any specifics that he claims kept him from doing his job I believe should have gone through his colleague the postmaster which would have been a start of him doing his job and working towards an investigation.

He could have given the situation the slightest consideration, and looked into the situation. This would have eliminated the process of him defending actions where he had no knowledge. I also informed him that I took his advice by following the chain of command when on July 13, 2011, I met with the station manager and her boss, the manager of customer service operations. I informed him that it was a "total disaster, to say the least."

I enclosed a list of documents that were provided to the manager of customer service operations. They included:

1. The letter dated July 22, 2011 to the manager of customer service operations.
2. The warning letter.
3. The settlement agreement.
4. A list of the EEO complaints and grievances since March 2009.
5. The district manager's correspondence letter.

I thanked him for his cooperation and that I would greatly appreciate a response to my letter and a follow-up regarding my concerns. It was important that I kept the attention of those that were higher up in management, making and keeping them aware of the entire situation, keeping the ball in their court.

67

MY BROTHER

Targeting was dangerous and illegal in any shape or form and just downright wrong to provoke and antagonize situations that could produce violent results. To refrain from this ever happening was difficult. But what was even more difficult was not to react to these types of situations in a violent or a negative manner.

Much of this, the public did not hear about. For example, it was not publicized when my 38-year-old blood brother put a bullet in his brain. He was employed by the U.S. Postal Service at the time, and I knew for a fact that he had succumbed to atrocities that I and a lot of postal workers faced. Very few knew anything about his death, not even the local news reported it.

The downtown station was not the only facility that was troubled. There were and still are many postal facilities where employees have gone as far as to take their own life and the lives of others.

Much of these situations had to do with people in power that should not have been there. I could not stress enough how the U.S. Postal Service loses hundreds of thousands of dollars a year because of contract violations that ignored the national bargaining agreement. I have worked in many facilities throughout the agency where the criteria were the same and the attitudes were identical.

From Sept. 6, 2011 to March 2012, a six-month time span, management committed more than 38 violations working the mail. Twenty-seven complaints were written up against them by several employees including myself. The complaints were given to the APWU, but not one single complaint was ever processed that management ever had to answer to because of a weakened union.

I had known many of those union stewards for years on a personal level. They sold me and other union members out. Lavinea Vargas, a union steward who worked with the downtown station, received statements from more than four different employees with times, dates and names of managers and supervisors that continued to violate the contract by working the mail. The statements were in detail from the time they would start working the mail until they would no longer work it and the location in the station where they would work. The union steward did not file one of these reports that she had in her possession.

The union president, John Ancona, was made aware of this by those who filed the complaints against management. The union steward had no other choice but to admit that she was reckless in not filing those complaints. The president made no efforts to rectify the situation or to comfort those who lost their grievances.

I did not get a response from the customer service manager of operations or the postmaster. The district manager did respond to my first letter and in my second letter to him I provided the material he claimed was needed for him to perform an investigation of those concerns, including proof that I followed the chain of command. I didn't hear a word from him again.

I waited months to hear from those upper managers to at least acknowledge that it was nothing more than a cry out for help. It never came. I knew that I had to do something more than just wait for those managers to respond to what they had known and had been aware, with the most recent altercation for the last eight months— since Feb. 9, 2011.

On Sept. 14, 2011, I went further up the chain of command and wrote to Sylvester Black, the vice president of the Western Area Office by certified return receipt mail. Once again as in all letters to upper management I introduced myself and apologized for this contact under these unfortunate circumstances, but it was necessary. I began the letter by saying "I am respectfully writing to you with unbelievable concerns. One is why I cannot be treated as a citizen of the United States of America in the U.S. Postal Service where I am treated less than a human being." I explained the last three decades of torture I endured at the hands of management. I reported that there were five different EEO complaints filed. I explained that at the current time they were in the formal stages in Washington D.C. against this manager and another one was also in the formal stage in Phoenix, Arizona against one of her supervisors.

I enclosed a list of people and those different entities within the agency that I had contacted either by telephone, in person, or by certified return receipt mail. They included: APWU, EAP, EEO representative, manager of customer service operation, postmaster's assistant, postmaster, and the district manager, but to no avail.

In closing I expressed my sincere belief that there had been crimes committed in this facility by management and those who had made false accusations against me. I explained that management was aware, yet they had done absolutely nothing in deterrence of those responsible for such heinous acts. I said that a full investigation was warranted.

"This sort of engagement goes far beyond the zero tolerance policy and should be taken seriously. By following the chain of command, I am desperately asking for your help and would greatly appreciate having a personal meeting with you to further discuss this outrageous behavior and aggression of this management in the downtown station."

I provided him with 12 different documents in support of my concerns. I was truly desperate this time, reflecting on the leadership of those I had contacted who did absolutely nothing but ignore me. But as a veteran of the postal services, I had little hope of anything being done.

I continued to write to those whose job it was to protect me instead of putting me in harm's way. My fortitude and persistence allowed me to continue writing management and to keep all necessary records that were essential for my survival in the United States Postal Service. On that same day that I wrote the vice president of the Western Area office, I wrote the president of the APWU. If I could have let the entire world know what was going on with me in this downtown postal facility I would have.

The letter that I sent to the APWU questioned their ability to represent and protect its members. I questioned the resources that were in place and available to the APWU when employees were confronted and subjected to confrontational and irrational management personnel – time and time again.

I informed the APWU of his acknowledgement and awareness that a serious problem had existed with the manager, her staff, and me at the downtown station for many years. I reminded him that many of the union stewards had represented me in countless grievances, many that found management to be in violation of the zero-tolerance policy.

I informed him that I had on many occasions contacted numerous members of upper management to the unsuitable conditions for me at the downtown station, only to be ignored. Their unconcerned attitude gave confirmation that this was an agency where this abusive managerial style was condoned, taught, expected, praised and rewarded.

In closing, I provided 13 different documents in support of the letter that I sent to the APWU. I respectfully encouraged the president to carefully examine all material provided in hope that he would reach an assessment that could possibly give him a touch of integrity and desperately needed courage in finding a way to effectively represent me and other members. Also, to present a case that would ultimately relieve me from so much humiliation and stress of this agency and the torture that I had endured the last 29 years of my career.

The management staff at the downtown station was very much aware that I continued to inform upper management of the isolated treatment of me by each of them. They were also aware that nothing was being done because of those letters to upper management so there was no threat or deterrent to discontinue their abuse of me.

During this time in September 2011, where I continued to inform those in higher positions of my circumstances, ironically, I received a letter from the postmaster on the 13th of the month. This was eight months from the time that I had brought much of everything that was going on in the downtown station to his attention by certified return receipt mail on Feb. 9, 2011 that he ignored.

This letter was about the Aug. 19, 2011 letter that I had sent to the district manager, which was the second letter that he had received from me. He informed me that the district manager had referred this letter to his attention. I honestly wondered what happened to the first letter that I sent to the district manager dated May 18, 2011. Why was that letter not referred to him? If it was, why did he not act on it as he has done with this one?

The letter he sent was a repeat of the district manager's correspondence where a few words were changed with now the postmaster's signature. Excuses gave management permission to violate contract agreements and to break the rules and regulations. The postmaster's response and solution, stated:

> *"In July 2011, a fact-finding team was sent to the Denver downtown station. This team interviewed seven different carriers and seven clerks to try and establish the climate of the downtown station. These interviews provided us no evidence of a hostile work environment. In fact, of those interviewed the station seems to be well-managed and the overall response from the craft is that management treats them fairly."*

He went on to say:

> *"You again have provided no specific incidents whereby anyone at the downtown station has violated the provisions of the zero-tolerance policy. It is impossible to investigate a violation of the zero-tolerance policy without a specific incident. Specific incidents that you believe violate this policy should be addressed through your chain of command please contact me directly with any future issues."*

I was stunned, but quickly recovered and collected my thoughts remembering the career-long battle with management where justifying all and any action taken against me by those in authority was always defended at any cost. Each time they were within their rights.

This correspondence from the postmaster was a perfect example of postal leadership that for decades had forced employees into the ultimate sacrifice by taking matters into their own hands.

This letter depicted me as a disgruntled and troubled employee, whose reality was distorted mainly through the imaginary images of conflicts in the agency. Thus, his reference to the fact-finding team.

This team was of the same caliber as the EEO that consisted of management personnel and given a title as fact-finders by management themselves. Their purpose and only purpose was to justify those actions of those managers in the station as the EEO had done since I had been employed at the postal service.

I was not shocked at their findings, considering the craft employees who were interviewed. Many were new to the station and others did not work directly in the station for an eight-hour day. They did not interview those employees who had filed complaints against management at one time or another. They did not interview those employees who provided written statements on my behalf, where confirmation to their statements was provided to several upper managers such as the postmaster by certified return receipt mail.

The people they interviewed were those employees who had not witnessed the aggression, the stalking, and the harassment of me almost every day by the management staff at the downtown station. Not even one of those employees who knew of the abuse was interviewed. They knew who not to interview.

68

WRITING

The true fact-finding was that the postmaster did not do his job on Feb. 9, 2011. That required leadership. After he had received the vital information of a serious problem in the downtown station he chose to ignore it. After eight months of silence he was forced to get involved since the district manager put this issue on his desk and referred all matters to him. This issue for so many years was now beginning to get some sort of traction.

I believed undoubtedly that a lot had to do with my relentless pursuit of writing to his colleagues and those above him. I thought maybe those that I had now involved would realize that I was not going to fall into traps of management nor was I going to go away.

The dialogue in the postmaster's correspondence gave me a clear indication that he knew nothing of this issue. What the district manager put before him was now an obligation for him to get involved. Writing to me was merely formality, realizing that he was now on the hot seat and had no other choice but to respond knowing that his colleagues were aware of the situation and who also knew that these issues at the downtown station were put before him a while back when he had the opportunity to get involved and investigate.

I truly believed that he thought I would just go away after his report and analysis. Had there been an independent investigation through an impartial agency I would have been more inclined to believe that an honest and true assessment to an investigation had been performed. Due to his self-righteousness, and that of the agency, it was impossible that a true and unbiased investigation was ever performed because of the dictatorship, their arrogance, and the disloyalty to the employees in the agency.

It was ludicrous that he or any other member of management believed that I would give into this self-organized investigation that entailed postal managers and supervisors. This ideology goes beyond comprehension. His letter was intrusive, insulting, and questioned my intelligence.

This so-called investigation did not even touch the surface of concerns or complaints that I had written or met with anyone in management about over the years. What the postmaster claimed that this fact-finding team found through an investigation of their own was irrelevant. It was not the subject or the issue as to how those employees were treated at the downtown station.

Had he been diligent and gotten involved in this matter from the beginning, and had he not piggybacked off of the district manager's correspondence to write such a ridiculous letter to me about his fact-finding team, he would have realized that this matter was not about those employees in the station. It was about me and how I was treated by management and their harassment of me.

I never wrote to anyone in upper management about how the police were being called at random on other employees at the station or how they were being stalked by the manager and supervisors just to be written up and disciplined every other week. Nor did I write about how they were being emergency placed and on a consistent basis, having to answer to false allegations of making threats and intimidating co-workers.

I never talked about these sorts of things happening to the employees in the downtown station because they were not happening to them. Those employees were being treated fairly by management. It was his lack of leadership and failure to act, along with his ignorance, that brought us to this point of a so-called investigation. It was nothing more than a smokescreen to avoid the real issue.

I received the letter dated Sept 13, 2011 on Sept. 16, 2011, two days after I had written the Vice President of Western Area Offices on Sep. 14, 2011. I was shocked that the Postmaster responded to my letter. I believed that anyone would have felt the same after eight months had gone by and heard nothing. I could also not help but to wonder if it would take those same eight months to hear from the vice president. After all he was also management, and although I continued to write upper management, I had absolutely no faith or trust in the system. Writing to them was for my protection.

To be perfectly honest, I highly anticipated hearing from the vice president. I am sure it was because I wanted to believe that there were some good people out there that were managers in the U.S postal service.

The week had gone by quickly. I guess it felt as though it did because I was fully occupied walking on eggshells after contacting the vice president of the Western Area office and receiving the correspondence of the postmaster. Retaliation was still in full effect. It was near the end of the second week since I had written the vice president and not a word. At that time, I viewed it as management in the U.S Postal Service.

On Sept. 27, 2011, I received a second letter from the postmaster. This was very unusual and out of character for anyone in management to give this kind of attention to craft employees. I was completely taken off guard by this letter and what immediately came to mind was that he was informing me of new charges that were being taken and filed against me for whatever reason management gave. I also remember how he ignored my cry for help until the district manager forced him to pay attention.

The postmaster's letter caught me off guard. He proposed a meeting for Oct. 4, 2011 at 11:30 a.m. to be held in the administrative building. Participants would include the downtown station manager, labor relations manager, human resource manager, MSCO manager, APWU president with two union stewards and myself.

Receiving this second letter from him wasn't because he had found religion and wanted to do what was right, it was because once again he was called out onto the carpet by the vice president of Western area offices on Sept. 14, 2011. So why would he schedule a meeting for Oct. 4, 2011 when a determination had been made and finalized through his office of no existing problem in the downtown facility?

I had much admiration and a great deal of gratitude for the follow-up and the attention that the vice president of Western area offices gave to my letter. I knew this meeting would have never been scheduled had I not continued writing upper management and had the vice president not taken a leadership role. His was the voice of persuasion.

69

THE MEETING

On Oct. 4, 2011, I reported to the administration building at 11:20 a.m. Gaining access into the building was difficult because of the security. One of the union stewards, who was at the meeting, had to come to the front entrance of the building to allow me access. This caused a five to 10-minute delay to the start of the meeting.

All eyes were fixated on the union steward and me as we entered the conference room where there were six other people sitting at tables. We sat at the table where the APWU president and another union steward sat across from management personnel. Each person in the room introduced themselves and the meeting began. This meeting was no different from any other meeting with management. There was an enormous amount of tension in the room. The atmosphere was very uncomfortable. It was the same feeling that I had felt throughout most of my career.

I was given the floor by the postmaster and the union president. I felt it was appropriate. I was very much prepared. I had statements provided by other employees, documents, certified return receipts of those letters that I had written to the different people in management as proof that they were received by them. Conveniently, none had in their possession at the meeting.

I exposed and revisited the trials and tribulations of my life in this agency that most who were sitting at the table knew about and for how long these negative issues had been going on. I called out both Char Ehrenshaft, labor relations manager, and Mark Talbott, the postmaster. I talked about several meetings that this labor manager and I had pertaining to these issues. Specifically, I pointed out Keeton's aggression and her constant harassment of me.

I then directed my attention to the postmaster, where I not only talked about his awareness of the meetings that I have had with some of his colleagues, but of this dysfunctional facility that he had full knowledge of but chose to ignore. I then distributed to each person at the table copies of the examples that were provided to the postmaster describing the atmosphere in the downtown station including the many emergency placements, EEO complaints, grievances and of the police activity that was always directed towards me.

I wasn't feeling very liked at that moment but that was the story of my career.

All of the attention was now on Sharon Keeton, the station manager. She was now in the spotlight and had the floor. The lies began to flow from her mouth with ease. It was all about defending her position to justify the cruelty and the illegal action that had been taken against me over the course of many years.

One matter that she brought up was about the illegal action that was taken by her where she removed me from the downtown station to the General Mail Facility. It was a violation of this agreement between management and the APWU of those employees whose job were taken in the realignment of the station. Each employee was to be removed individually from the station by seniority. She chose to ignore and to violate that agreement by removing me before those employee's junior to me.

There were two people in the meeting, one of the union stewards and the MSCO (Manager Customer Service Operation.) Both were new to their positions, and seemed to be pretty interested to hear her reasoning.

In her version, she talked about how I was not a customer service window clerk but those who remained at the station were junior to me and window qualified, and that was her reason for allowing them to remain at the station.

I sat waiting patiently for some time while I listened to her lies. I had come prepared to present my case and to prove that those actions that were taken against me by this manager were not only wrong and against the zero-tolerance policy, but were illegal and against the law.

The entire meeting had taken the course to address management's only concern – defending their actions. Those upper management personnel at the table were adamant in defending the station manager. The APWU representative sat there silent. I felt as if I was there alone without representation. I was feeling this way 10 minutes into the meeting and in that time, I had wished that I would have been there alone. The meeting was just formality. But, it never would have taken place had the vice president not gotten involved.

At times, it came to a boiling point and got real heated where timeouts were needed to restore order. But I was there in my defense. I was there to stand up for my rights and to provide the necessary documentation in proof of those actions taken against me by management that violated those rights. I would not be intimidated.

Keeton stuck with the reason that she and the HR coordinator removed me from the downtown station and that I was not customer service window clerk qualified. That was a mistake on her part. After this bold statement of hers, I reached for the documents and statements that I had brought along with me hoping that I would get this sort of opportunity to expose her.

I provided each person sitting at the table a copy of the union steward's report.

Her notes read that the station manager "informed Garland Lewis that he was being removed from the downtown station because he was not doing his job which had created and caused a hostile working environment."

Everyone was also provided certain pages of documentation from her affidavit that was part of my EEO complaint. It stated, I was "removed from the downtown station because she had received many complaints from co-workers at the station that I was not doing my job and they were tired of doing my job that it was causing a hostile work environment."

The room was silent for a good while as I waited patiently for everyone to finish reading these documents. No one said a word even after most had finished reading. These were documents and statements that had been sent to the postmaster months before this meeting and if he had read them at that time or had not ignored them he could have saved time for everyone because he knew exactly what management was up against.

I believed that he was familiar with the documents because he said nothing more after reading what was provided to everyone only to say, "What is next?"

I talked earlier about how management throughout this meeting selected the issues they choose to defend or ignore and this subject was one they chose to ignore. But it was one that I chose to talk about openly and was definitely one that needed to be answered so I asked a question of Mark Talbott, but in actuality it was really a statement.

I recall saying, "Mr. Postmaster, in knowing what you have learned by reading those notes of the union steward that was in the meeting on the day in question as to the dialogue of that meeting and reading the statement of the station managers in the EEO complaint, where does her credibility lie with you as of now? You know as well as everyone in this meeting that I was illegally removed from the downtown station and this manager sat before each one of us and has lied to everyone about the real reason behind her unlawful actions on that particular day."

I continued: "What else had she lied about? So, given the lies and her dishonesty I believe that any credibility that she may have had at one time has been destroyed and in all fairness this meeting should be over where she should be reprimanded up to removal."

This seemed to have irritated the entire management staff and in all honesty, I believe what I had said did not go over well with the APWU president, who seemed to be irritated as well. Through most of the meeting he was silent, then suddenly at this moment he made a comment that ended with a question to me that I felt to be a very inappropriate.

He said, "okay we have been talking of the same subject for over three hours" and asked of me "what were we going to do about this?" I answered him by saying that this was not a question for me, this was a question that should be addressed to the postmaster and because you are here to please him I will do your job by asking him, and so I did.

The meeting ended by the postmaster saying that he would be in touch with me. A week later I heard from his secretary. I was offered what the postal service referred to as a settlement proposal for me to retire using the rest of my earned annual and sick leave, and they would give me three free days total. That together would come to two extra months of service that would be added to my retirement benefits.

This communication of the proposal was delivered over the telephone. I believe that the postmaster felt that he was doing me a favor and at the end of our conversation the secretary informed me that it was take it or leave it and that there would be no negotiations. I thought it was a bold statement and an offer that I could refuse, so I did. There was never anything put in writing.

Though the postmaster knew of Keeton's wrong doing and of the violations that had occurred he did what he had always done whenever it involves a manager or supervisor. He ignored it and covered it up. She remained the manager of the station and continued her assault on me.

Those times when managers and supervisors were exposed to a degree of any sort of misconduct they were moved from one facility to the next. I guessed that this was what they consider a reprimand. This was bad for the agency. It suggested superiority was for those who were in management. It created a slavery mentality among the workers that for some caused anger and hostility. Others, who accepted that management was superior, put them on pedestals.

Again, this was victory for all of management though I continued to go to those in positions of trust. They continued to turn their backs on me. But again, the effort that I made served its purpose. I still had my job, I stayed out of jail, and again management was put on notice. I was in control of my life and I refused to allow them to dictate who I was and to be in control of my actions and of my destination. Everything that was done to me by this management crew at the downtown station was done out of malice to invoke confrontation.

Keeton had gotten away with whatever she chose to do to me. Anything she believed that would make my life miserable was sufficient and worth trying. She would target and make it her focal point. Overtime opportunities, with most managers, was used as a tool for the purpose of favoritism, rewards and retaliation.

Writing upper managers during those pressured times took its toll on me. I was weary. I was tired. So much so that all I wanted and could think about was to get away from the facility, but especially this station manager.

70

ON VACATION

I had some vacation time scheduled while all this was going on during the scheduling of different meetings between different managers. I took it. While I was on vacation I could not help but think of all the chaos and confusion in the station and the one person, the station manager, which made my time there miserable. I also remembered that the 4th quarter "overtime desired" list was not posted before I had gone on vacation. Sound familiar? It kept confusion brewing in the station and I knew that an issue would be made out of this by the station manager if I was allowed to sign the list on my return back from vacation.

I called the APWU and spoke with my union steward informing her of the situation and asking if it was possible for her to contact one of the supervisors on duty to bring them up to speed as to what was going on. I desired to sign the list for the new quarter, but at the present time I was on vacation and was not available to do so.

The union steward made the call that same day and talked with that supervisor. The supervisor assured her that I would be able to sign the list upon my return back to work on Oct. 5, 2011. When I did return to work, the supervisor kept her word by allowing me to sign the overtime list. Hours later she approached me and informed me that the station manager had ordered her to remove me from the overtime list and that I should have signed it before I went out on vacation. I immediately called and talked with my union steward over the telephone and she appeared at the station the very next day on Oct. 6, 2011 and talked with the station manager.

The union steward provided the manager with a copy of the language of the CBA collective bargaining agreement that states if an employee was on bid annual/vacation they must be allowed to sign the overtime desired list upon return to work. It was only then that she permitted me to remain on the overtime list. Again, this was a trivial action that was taken by this manager and unnecessary, but an effort to provoke me.

These were tribulations that few faced in the station where I was constantly challenged and harassed. Fighting the many adversities were no more than triggers to provoke me into confrontations with management that could lead up to my removal.

71

MOTIVE

An Oct. 23, 2011 article in The Federal Times stated:

> *"Besides paying tens of billions of dollars each year in compensation, operations and overhead costs the financially struggling U.S. Postal Service has another huge annual expense, hundreds of millions of dollars in settlements to disgruntled employees and former employees. The article gives many figures on postal payout of contracts violation, grievances, and lawsuits it talks a lot about huge class-action lawsuits where the U.S. Postal Service disputes much of what is said."*

But of course, the U.S. Postal Service would every time dispute those negatives that revealed the truth about the agency, mainly when it came to them breaking laws. I have given examples of those negatives, those real situations that I faced in the agency.

Many laws were broken in an effort to cause my demise. Not only by the agency, but of those in the agency that participated and joined in management's quest not only to have me removed from the USPS, but to create lifelong effects on me and my family.

The most intriguing assessment about the postal service in the Federal Times article was made in the comment section by a reader that said:

> "Good to see someone reporting on this management failure to follow the contract is costing the post office a lot of money. For the life of me I can't understand why supervisors, managers, and postmasters are not held accountable for their most of the time total disregard of the contract. You can tell it's not their money that goes to settle contract violations they should be held accountable. But in the postal world they are actually promoted I have seen it happen countless times (good reporting)."

This comment was one voice that hundreds of thousands of people could relate to in this agency. Many could add to what was said and agree that it represented a place of dictatorship that oppresses its people, that breaks those rules they enforce on certain employees, and for those who do not meet their criteria to bow down and accept being treated less than an animal.

This was a surprising comment, but a welcome one made by the reader. People were afraid and intimidated to tell the truth, to expose a government agency like the United States Postal Service. I respected the reader and truly thanked that person for having a voice, but mainly for having the courage to express and expose the truth.

This was impressive for the Federal Times to report these violations and disregard for policy that had dominated the U.S Postal Service for decades. It was courageous to expose the fact that management was given promotions after breaking rules and regulations rather than being held accountable for their actions. They did not face disciplinary action such as demotions, suspension, or even removals. I had never known an employee to receive such benefits after committing any sort of violation or breaking the rules.

Not much time passed before I read another news report that captured my attention. And I couldn't help but analyze the situation every time. But there was one particular shooting in December 2011 that happened at a post office in Montgomery, Alabama and kept my attention through the sentencing of the suspect in 2013.

On Dec. 2, 2011, Montgomery, Alabama news outlets, among many other news sources including the Associated Press, reported that 29-year-old Arthur Lee Darby Jr. was arrested after a post office shooting. The police investigated the shooting and discovered that Darby, the alleged shooter, was an employee of the post office.

The reports described him as a part-time mail handler at the main post office on Winton Blount Boulevard. He allegedly went to work around 6:30 p.m. on Dec. 1, 2011 and opened fire on two postal employees, though no one was hit by any bullets. I couldn't find where the police publicly identified a motive for his actions. But, news reports did hint at his military background and PTSD diagnosis. Veterans work in all areas of the economy, and they don't go off because of their service to their country. A military background shouldn't always be the default answer for adverse reactions in the workplace.

There were even reports about him maybe being upset because a family member had died. Family members pass. It happens. But those left behind usually don't go to work and start shooting. Why did violence need to become an option?

I would not condone violence, but understood that for every action there was a reaction. There was no doubt in my mind that this employee reacted to something that was there.

Sentencing was handed down in 2013, nearly two years to the day of the incident. He pleaded guilty to attempted assault, discharging a firearm in furtherance of the attempted assault, and possession of a firearm in a federal facility. He was sentenced to 10 years and one day in federal prison.

In following the story, it appeared to me that the police department, the U.S. postal inspector's agency and the US attorney office gave each other a pat on the back for a job well done. They were proud that their efforts made a difference in closing an incident without loss of life. They probably did save lives. But, where was the pro-active accountability and responsibility in a joint effort to make the agency a safe place.

72

THE "F" WORD

The Federal Times came out with an article on Dec. 5, 2011 on its website where it talked about three myths of the EEO process. It read the misconceptions abound about federal equal employment opportunities EEO process and employees who file complaints. The "F" word "frivolous" was frequently used to describe EEO complaints.

Co-workers and supervisors often view complainants as whiners and poor performers at the same time discrimination complaints are increasing and the resources to process and adjudicate them are under fire.

1. Discrimination is found in less than 2 percent of EEO complaints
2. Complaints are increasing because more employees are harassed at work
3. Agencies devote too many resources to processing frivolous discrimination complaints.

I could attest to those findings. The same held true for the U.S. Postal Service where, after the more than 38 EEO complaints that I had filed over the course of my career, this EEO agency never determined that discrimination took place. It was incomprehensible. The evidence that was provided in 95 percent of those complaints was precise and damaging. It was proof that validated each one that gave me the confidence in knowing discrimination was found but was never determined in a single case.

The percentage in the agency was less than one percent of EEO complaints that are substantiated in the complainant's favor, just five percent of the complaints that I filed ended with settlement agreements and those were breached by management every time. The remaining 95 percent was either adjudicated or dismissed because each one was determined that either I did not give sufficient proof or there was something that I failed to include to determine if discrimination or harassment had ever occurred and though each EEO complaint was different the determination read the same.

The article reported how most complaints are filed when co-workers and management officials make racial slurs or ethnic jokes or engage in negative stereotyping. None of the complaints that I filed was in the spectrum of this sort of misconduct. My complaints were of retribution that resulted from the harassment of management and fictitious allegations of co-workers that lead to management acting against me that developed into physical consequences.

The last report of the article talked about frivolous discrimination complaints where employees do not cooperate in the EEO process by refusing to provide affidavits during the investigation phase and disobeying other judge's orders to provide information or attend status conferences.

The subjects in this report do not comprise what had taken place with me or the actions taken by me to the many offences of the U.S postal service. I followed the guidelines of those rules and regulations of the agency when in disputes or disagreements with management.

I knew that without a doubt I had provided some of the most incriminating evidence in proof of my complaints, including affidavits. I went beyond that by providing court transcripts, documents, statements, the outcome and decisions of grievances and settlement agreement to past EEO complaints.

I attended all EEO hearings that I was made aware of and allowed to attend. I was also present along with my representatives and attorneys at the many conferences and hearings of the judges and administrative personnel where I was required to be in attendance. I had given an all-out and sincere effort in exercising and preserving my rights as a human being.

I made a commitment to do just that to fight through the assaults, harassment, and the persecution of me in this agency and those courts of the land that also push me to the limit due to their erroneous excuses that led to poor decision-making.

PART TWELVE:

2012

73

98 PERCENT

It was now 2012. The heat was just as hot as it was in 1983. Even after losing 98 percent of the grievances that I had filed against them over the last 30 years, and being engulfed in paperwork by the many EEO complaints that they constantly had to answer to, the U.S. Postal Service would not let up. Management was determined and continued to be true to their obsession of removing me from the agency.

Nevertheless, I was not surprised or had any real expectations of management ever leaving me alone. They were relentless. By any means necessary – by resignation, termination, or death – they wanted me out.

Throughout the year of 2012 I spent much of my time filing grievances and EEO complaints that had taught me much about expectations. They were merely fantasies and unrealistic wishes.

In that year I was forced to file several EEO complaints between February and May, none of which was frivolous but of formality. My many EEO complaints were either rejected or dismissed. Formality kept me honest. It provided me with proof and gave me records to the disorder of an agency where change was not foreseeable in the future.

My intentions were never to be the answer to the U.S. Postal Service's problems. I just wanted to be left alone. I had one choice in what I did and that was to defend myself. To be walked on was not a choice. As evidenced by the many letters I wrote and people I contacted for assistance, I was not silent about my outrage with what was happening to me.

I tapped into every resource I could think of to help me in my pursuit of the American dream. I was astounded by all the resources that I needed to make it through all that was happening to me. In hindsight, I needed a civil attorney, a team of criminal attorneys, a bail bondsman, an employment specialist, the support of the union, marriage counseling, group therapy, Alcoholics Anonymous and my buddies at the gym just to keep my job and not lose my mind while there.

Everything was starting to converge for me. I had to ask myself, "Is this what a black man needs to survive in this country?"

On Sept. 19, 2012, I contacted the inspector general's office by certified return receipt mail. It was the end of the road for me. I could no longer stand the abuse of being targeted each day not knowing if I was going to jail on that day or having a job the next. It had even gotten to the point that I feared for my life knowing the ramifications of when police officers responded to calls on black men. The senseless death of 17-year-old Trayvon Benjamin Martin earlier that year (Feb. 26, 2012) in Florida also haunted me and my mortality.

I retired effective Jan. 31, 2013. I received 70 percent retirement benefit, more than most retiring from the postal service. The maximum was 80 percent.

But before I left, I wrote one more letter to USPS authorities, specifically to the inspector general. It was pretty much the same as with all management personnel. I introduced myself and shared some of my background as a disabled Vietnam combat veteran who served during the evacuation of Saigon.

I am respectfully writing to this agency in desperation of your immediate attention to an ongoing problem since March 2009. I have been attacked and unjustly accused by the station manager and her staff of a multitude of alleged infractions where I feared the Denver Police Department would be called on me is and was also encouraged by others and those of authority. I assure you that I have gone through the proper procedure in following the chain of command for the past 33 years of my service to the U.S postal service in hopes of rectifying and eliminating these unfortunate occurrences before I made any contact with this agency.

I have contacted many of the different entities within the agency one being human resources where that office assigned a violence assessment team and what the postmaster referred to as a "fact finding team" to visit the station who did absolutely nothing but hand-pick those to conduct their interview. Many were new to the station and others were those who had close ties with the manager and supervisors. No one who has ever written a statement on my behalf or had been a witness in any hearing against management was ever interviewed. I have made management as well as upper management aware of the hostile conditions and the continuous assaults on me and have given them the opportunities to rectify the situation but more so to eliminate these attacks of me by filing an overwhelming amount of grievances and EEO complaints yet I remain with a price on my head to be singled out and targeted.

I strongly emphasized this point that after more than 38 different EEO complaints not a single one had yet to be ruled in my favor, which I felt substantiated my claim of an agency that was nothing more than an extension of management. The obvious had been proven time and time again. These constant attacks on me and the criminal behavior of management for more than 30 years had been proven not to have anything to do with the zero tolerance policy but everything to do with criminal activity.

I showed my sincerity in good faith by providing the inspector general's office with 16 different documents in support of my serious situation in hopes that it would encourage his office to commit to and perform a criminal investigation of the Denver downtown station and the agency as a whole.

I included all contact information including my address, telephone number, and my place of business and its telephone number and asked to please not hesitate to contact me concerning any questions about the correspondence. The post card response that I received from the inspector general's office, stated:

> *Thank you for contacting the United States Postal Service office of Inspector General's hotline. We have received your correspondence and*

your concern will be documented in our database. If additional information is necessary someone will be contacting you.

Sincerely:
The Hotline United States Postal Service Office of Inspector General

--THE END-

POSTSCRIPT

Q&A WITH THE AUTHOR

Q: Why did you write that final letter?
A: My final letter to the U.S. Postal Service was one of the steps suggested by an article published in *The Federal Times* on Sept. 3, 2012, entitled, "How to Manage a Difficult Supervisor."

Q: What struck you as important about the article?
A: It talks about difficult supervisors. It talks about ways an employee can handle these types of situations that identify when or if a difficult supervisor is really a problem, if the supervisor's just tough and demanding, or is the supervisor abusive, retaliatory or discriminatory. Sometimes a supervisor's demands could be reasonable but harsh. There are many variations on the theme of the difficult supervisor. There are a few others that the report suggests could be reasons or question as to why a supervisor could be difficult.

The report addresses what employees can do about it. It suggests assessing whether you are the only one that believes you have a difficult supervisor. Is it a systematic problem or are you the victim of discrimination? Next, assess higher-level manager's support of your supervisor. Do they want your office cleaned up or do they seem unaware of the abusive environment? It gives remedies that are available to deal with these issues, including filing a grievance, considering an equal opportunity complaint and contacting the inspector general.

Q: Were you surprised at the honesty in the article?
A: Yes. After filing this sort of complaint, the article reports that the difficulty with EEO is that in the long run you have to prove discrimination based on a category such as race, gender or ethnicity. The act of proving is difficult. The article goes on to say that the third thing you can do is file a complaint with the inspector general's office.

Q: What do you think about insubordination?
A: The article points out that one bad strategy that is likely to never work is to be insubordinate or disrespectful to the difficult supervisor. It says not to take on the supervisor yourself. This would just allow the supervisor to overcome your legitimate complaints by saying to his or her higher-ups that you are a problem.

Q: What do you see as missing when you cross reference your actions with the steps proposed in the article?
A: This article was not published until 2012, so for more than 29 years I had done everything the article had suggested. Unfortunately, the article did not give me a single clue or any suggestions on how to manage a cliquish and dysfunctional agency.

The article does gives encouragement. It captures one's faith and heightens your hope and belief in a system that works. I respected the article for two reasons. One, it informs employees about things you can do in hopes of managing a difficult supervisor which is promising and it all looks good on paper. My second reason is the honesty that is expressed when it says that the strategies are no guarantee. This is a very true statement because I initiated and pursued everything that this article talked about.

Q: Would you suggest employees who feel victimized visit the EEO?
A: There is no guarantee that filing an EEO would rectify any problems as the article mentioned and talked about was extremely true. Nearly 40

different times I had done just that. Each and every time it just brought animosity, retaliation and hatred that enhanced conflicts. This is why accountability is a necessity. It is essential for an agency to take control and make those responsible for the use in abusing the authority given to them for the purpose of personal vendettas and retaliation, in the comfort of building their own self-esteem.

Q: Is there ever a time when insubordination is appropriate?
A: There is one other topic that this article speaks of that I would like to talk about and that I must challenge. It talks about the one bad strategy that is likely to never work is to be insubordinate or disrespectful to a difficult supervisor.

I challenge this because when an employee exercises his or her rights by following protocol as to utilize the chain of command to procedurally file grievances and EEO complaints this is construed as taking on your manager or supervisor as to challenge or to question their authority. Those actions alone taken by an employee will always open the door to that person being judged and labeled as a troublemaker along with other unfavorable and demeaning titles such as being disgruntled, unapproachable, intimidating, and threatening.

Q: When was your last day?
A: I retired on Jan. 31, 2013.

Q: Did you keep tabs on the station after your retirement?
A: Six months after my retirement the entire management staff was removed from the downtown station with the exception of one supervisor. For whatever reason, he was allowed to remain at the station. One bad apple can spoil the bunch. Through him, I figure the new management learned to carry on the tradition of unaccountability.

Q: Why did you choose to include the term "going postal" in your title?
A: Over the years I have talked to people outside of the agency who had no true understanding about why there had been so many killings in the United States Postal Service. Many would repeat what had been told to

them by family members, friends, or just someone who worked or had some sort of affiliation with the agency at one time or another. But not everyone believes or will say that the agency is a terrible place to work for which I would not argue with because it is true for some. Everyone is not treated the same. The important fact to take into the utmost consideration is that there is a reason for disgruntled postal workers and why the term "going postal" had become and will forever be a trademark of the U.S. Postal Service.

Q: When did you knowingly start writing this book?
A: During my last year or two at the U.S. Postal Service. In reality, I started writing this book at the beginning of my career with the agency.

Q: Why do you say the beginning of your career?
A: There was never a moment that I actually felt completely comfortable at the postal service. There were just too many times that I did not agree with the way employees were being treated. Something just wasn't right. At times, I took it with a grain of salt and looked at it as optimistically as possible for the sake of keeping a job. That was the case until management turned their undivided attention toward me. It was then that I began to document everything I possibly could that pertained primarily to me, but also details about others. I knew the only way possible for me to survive was to take good notes, including legal documentation, in access of more than 12,400 pages.

Q: As you read through this manuscript right before publishing, do you think it captures your experience.
A: This book highlights the torture that plagued me for most of my 33-year career in the U.S. Postal Service. It gives the reader a strong idea about why someone would want to pull the trigger?

Q: How hard would it have been to get your hands on a gun?
A: Not hard at all.

Q: Looking back, what do you think brought you to this point?
A: Knowing the truth, along with my faith in God, is the reason that I was able to survive an agency that manipulated laws, broke the law and provided me the first-hand experiences necessary to tell my story. I did not want to bring the postal service into my home, so I only shared a little bit with my wife when things were actually happening. But having her by my side was invaluable. I tried my best to shelter her from the stress.

Q: Do you believe the United States Postal Service is unique?
A: I do not believe that the agency is unique in regard to the cruel and insensitive ways management can treat their employees. I can't say for sure how employees are treated in other corporations and businesses or the work sector in general. What I can say is what I experienced.

After it had been shown through court trials and many different legal proceedings that management representatives lied under oath, falsified documents, and gave false information to a law enforcement officers, no one went to jail or lost their job—except me. Time after time, I was declared guilty until proven innocent. In the end I was acquitted or exonerated on all charges.

Q: Do you believe you received this treatment because you are an African American man?
A: In a costly and peculiar sense, my experiences at the U.S. Postal Service educated, but saddened me because it was reminiscent of American history that strongly identified with discrimination. It provided proof that discrimination in the country has not gotten better with time. The majority of people that I saw being treated like me were minorities.

Q: As a disabled Vietnam veteran, what troubles you the most when you think back on the lack of support you received in the American workforce and from government agencies?
A: As a Vietnam veteran, I was already carrying a lot of weight, too heavy for the average person to handle alone. Yet, I was truly surprised at how

many government agencies left me flying solo, with little to no back up in sight. It was disheartening. To fight for my country and then come home to closed doors is still unfathomable to me. I experienced it time and time again. It was like coming home and having my mother slam the door in my face for no reason. I know it happened, but I don't want to believe it. I can't believe it. To do so would shatter the American dream. My faith and that dream kept me going. It's probably one of the main reasons I documented so much. I couldn't believe it.

Q: Did you have a retirement party?
A: After I had already retired, I heard management held a party to celebrate my retirement.

Q: Do you feel that you won?
A: Yes and No. Yes, because they didn't get what they wanted. My records are clean. I'm not in prison. I am not a former postal worker who is disgruntled or seeking any sort of revenge on the U.S. Postal Service. But I realize that after leaving the postal service on my own two feet – not in a body bag or facing a prison sentence – that I do have a story to tell.

No, because I believe we lost the court case after the summary judgment was awarded to the detective. There were many legal motions chipping away at my case, but the summary judgment practically knocked it out. A lot of what is written in this book was not allowed at the trial. At the time, I truly did not understand it. Today, I have come to the conclusion that the detective was awarded summary judgment because of qualified immunity, which protects a government official from being sued for civil damages as long as he does not violate constitutional or legal rights that are clearly established. I clearly felt that my basic human rights were violated, but in my case the legal system made it practically impossible to prevail.

Q: There are a lot of layers to this book. What is one take away for the reader?
A: In writing this book, I especially hope that it brings comfort and some sort of closure to those who have lost loved ones in this agency not knowing why or how the shootings happened.

Q: Do you recall your final day?

A: Yes. I only worked a partial shift. It was 8:15 a.m. I just walked over and punched the clock. I told a few people, shook some hands. I gathered my belongings and walked out of there like it was another working day. As I was walking to my car one of my co-workers came up to me. He shook my hand and said, "That was stand up. You walked out of there with dignity." That was a good feeling.

TIPS TO PROTECT YOURSELF ON THE JOB

Here are some steps you might want to consider in an effort to be vigilant in protecting yourself if you find yourself in a dangerous work environment:

1.) Documentation = keep and take good notes (times, dates, etc.)
2.) Know your union
3.) Familiarize yourself to the rules and regulations
4.) Do your job
5.) Follow instructions
6.) Be prompt and on time
7.) Be regular in attendance
8.) Refrain from gossip
9.) Be careful of the people you select as friends
10.) Notify the proper authority to any trouble (Document)
11.) Be cautious when selecting your words in any conversation
12.) Secure witnesses to any sort of trouble
13.) Do not react to provocation

IN MEMORIAM

…Anthony Deculit, Betty Ann Jarred, Beverly Graham, Bruce Clark, Carol Ott, Charles Jenning, Charles McGee, Charles T. Barbagallo, Charlotte Colton, Cornelius Kasten, Christopher Carlisle, Dexter Shannon, Donald Mc Naught, Elizabeth Taylor, Frances Hilbun, Gary Montes, Genevieve Paez, Grant Gallaher, Guadalupe Swartz, Jackie Lawrence Scurles, James Brooks, James Whooper III, Jesus Antonio Tamayo, Jerry Ralph Pyle, John Merlin Taylor, Jonna Gragert Hamilton, Joseph VanderPaauw, Judy Stephens Denney, Keith Ciszewski, Kenneth W. Morey, Kevin Tartt, Lawrence Jasion, Leroy Orrin Phillips, Lori Hayes-Kotter, Maleka Higgins, Mary Benincasa, Nicola Grant, Oscar Johnson, Patti Lou Welch, Patricia Ann Chambers, Patricia A. Gabbard, Patty Jean Husband, Paul Michael Rockne, Perry Smith, Richard Berni, Richard C. Esser Jr., Ron Williams, Rose Marie Proos, Roy Barnes, Russell Smith, Steven Brownlee, Thomas Wade Shader Jr., William F. Miller, Ze Fairchild…